Praise for *The F... ....* *Guide to Lean*

'Andy's book explores a holistic approach to Lean transformation balancing the strategic "hoshin" business case for change with respect for people and a practical "how to" illustration of the core Lean practices; in addition it covers a generically proven Lean road map and management system for cultural transformation that is required for sustained continuous improvement.'

Matthew E. May, Toyota innovation advisor and author of *The Laws of Subtraction* and *The Elegant Solution*

'Andy Brophy has done a good job explaining a challenging and vital subject in a simple yet comprehensive manner. He explains the central role of Little's Law as the foundation of Lean, a fact often missed by other expositions of Lean. This insight allows the application of Lean beyond repetitive manufacturing, to service, product development and indeed to any business process.'

Michael L. George, author of *Lean Six Sigma* and former CEO of the George Group

'This is a very good overview of Lean basics, from tools, to problem solving, people, and leadership. Filled with diagrams and practical tips, this guide should help any organisation off to a great start on the Lean journey.'

Jeffrey K. Liker, Professor, University of Michigan and Author, *The Toyota Way*

'Andy does a great job taking you through "Lean" from A to Z including the steps to implement but what really stands out is that he highlights the need and process to maximise the employee experience, which is what so many companies miss.'

Pete Gritton, Former Vice President of HR, Toyota Motor Manufacturing of North America

'Andy's book will prove a valuable reference for newcomers to Lean. Experienced Lean practitioners will also be able to pick up useful insights – particularly from the chapters on Lean Culture and Idea Management. The book includes wide coverage of Lean, with the right balance between breadth and depth for an easy read. I would think the book would be very useful for managers outside of actual operations but who nevertheless require an insight into what Lean success really requires across an organisation. The book provides a step-by-step guide that would be applicable to many aspiring Lean organisations.'

John Bicheno, author of *The Lean Toolbox*, and *The Service Systems Toolbox*

'If you're going ahead with a Lean programme, this is a good place to start. Andy's engaging book is clear and well written and does a great job of presenting both the Lean tools and the wider management system – and, in particular, the fact that Lean is all about people. I would definitely have every one in the organisation read this guide as a common base to explore the Lean journey.'

Michael Ballé, Shingo Prize co-author of *The Gold Mine*, and *The Lean Manager*, and co-founder of the Institut Lean France

'This book will help readers gain a much better understanding of Lean management, and it will inspire them to move forward and do great things for customers and other key stakeholders.'

Bob Emiliani Author of *Better Thinking, Better Results* and Professor, Connecticut State University

'Andy Brophy's crystal clear prose and deep subject knowledge make this book a must-read for anyone involved in or contemplating a Lean journey.'

Charles Kenney, author of *Transforming Health Care: Virginia Mason Medical Center's Pursuit of the Perfect Patient Experience*, and co-author with Maureen Bisognano of *Pursuing the Triple Aim: Seven Innovators Show the Way to Better Care, Better Health, and Lower Costs*

'If I were asked by a newcomer to Lean, "What is the one book that will get me through my first year as a Lean champion?" I would do well to recommend Andy Brophy's book, *The Financial Times Guide to Lean*. While he offers a greater set of tools than most Lean introductions, they are firmly set in the framework of the strategic purposes of employing Lean, and recognition of how people learn and grow into Lean thinkers. It's an informal, readable blueprint for a launch of Lean in any type of organisation.'

Karen Wilhelm, blogger at *Lean Reflections*

'Andy does and excellent job of tackling a large subject by including all the relevant Lean concepts, not the least of which is that Lean is about people and is not just a set of tools. He also makes the critical point that, "Lean is not a bolt on; to work it needs to umbrella all the functions that are performed in the organisaton." And that means any organisation.'

Don Dinero, TWI Institute Conductor at The TWI Learning Partnership, and author of *Training Within Industry: The Foundation of Lean*

'Andy Brophy has written a clear and comprehensive guide to Lean. All the major concepts are explained in detail, and as a system, with the insight that only extensive implementation experience can provide.'

Alan G. Robinson, PhD, Professor, Isenberg School of Management at the University of Massachusetts and author of Ideas Are Free: *How the Idea Revolution Is Liberating People and Transforming Organizations*

'Andy Brophy has ambitiously summarised Lean principles, systems and tools in just over 300 pages! His work is accessible and value-added for both the neophyte and experienced practitioner.'

Mark R. Hamel, Shingo-award winning author of the *Kaizen Event Fieldbook* and founder of *Gemba Tales* blog.

The Financial Times
Guide to Lean

The Financial
Times Guide
to Lean

How to streamline your organisation, engage employees and create a competitive edge

Andy Brophy

Harlow, England • London • New York • Boston • San Francisco • Toronto • Sydney • Auckland • Singapore • Hong Kong
Tokyo • Seoul • Taipei • New Delhi • Cape Town • São Paulo • Mexico City • Madrid • Amsterdam • Munich • Paris • Milan

PEARSON EDUCATION LIMITED

Edinburgh Gate
Harlow CM20 2JE
Tel: +44 (0)1279 623623
Fax: +44 (0)1279 431059
Web: www.pearson.com/uk

First published 2013 (print and electronic)

© Andy Brophy 2013 (print and electronic)

The right of Andy Brophy to be identified as author of this work has been asserted by him in accordance with the Copyright, Designs and Patents Act 1988.

Pearson Education is not responsible for the content of third-party internet sites.

ISBN: 978-0-273-77050-3 (print)
      978-0-273-77230-9 (PDF)
      978-0-273-77231-6 (ePub)

British Library Cataloguing-in-Publication Data
A catalogue record for the print edition is available from the British Library

Library of Congress Cataloging-in-Publication Data
A catalog record for the print edition is available from the Library of Congress

10 9 8 7 6 5 4 3 2
16 15 14

Print edition typeset in 10pt Stone Serif by 30
Printed by Ashford Colour Press Ltd., Gosport

NOTE THAT ANY PAGE CROSS REFERENCES REFER TO THE PRINT EDITION

Contents

Acknowledgements

My passion for Lean began almost 15 years ago. I am continuously deepening my knowledge every day on the power of Lean when deployed as a people centric management system. Learning never ends; this book reflects my current knowledge and experience of the Lean philosophy – errors and mistakes are all mine. I feel privileged to make a living studying something I love and coaching a diverse spectrum of organisations on their improvement journeys. I thank all my clients for having the courage to take the leap of faith into the rewarding but challenging journey towards operational excellence. I owe a sincere debt of gratitude to the network of Lean professionals throughout the world whose members have directly or indirectly contributed to my knowledge of Lean. Too numerous to mention, your collective intelligence is echoed throughout this book. I genuinely stand on the shoulders of giants in my endeavours to condense the 60 plus years of formal Lean evolution into this book.

My enthusiasm for Lean grew through completion of the MSc in Lean Operations at Cardiff University. It was here I was fortunate to be mentored by John Bicheno, the Director of the Lean Enterprise Research Centre. Our book together, *Innovative Lean: A Guide to Releasing the Untapped Gold in Your Organisation to Engage Employees, Drive Out Waste, and Create Prosperity*, laid an important foundation for this book. Special thanks to Frank Devine of Accelerated Improvement Ltd for sharing the Cathedral model he created. This proven model for accelerated Lean cultural change and mass employee engagement is illustrated in Chapter 10. I would also like to sincerely thank Chris Cudmore, Editor in Chief at Pearson Education, for his continuous support and guidance throughout the challenging, yet thoroughly rewarding, process of creating this book.

To my parents; Eileen, words do not capture the wholesome person you are; Mick, you are missed every day, and I can't believe you're gone from this world, but the memories and your great work live on – you are close in spirit. I could never even begin to repay all that you both have given me, both personally and by way of education throughout my life.

Finally, I'd like to thank my wonderful family, Aideen and our dazzling little son Cian who entered the world during the creation of this book, making the last few months a little busy! Thanks Aideen for your hard work, continuous support and encouragement, you both mean the world to me. This book is dedicated to you both.

Publisher's acknowledgements

We are grateful to the following for permission to reproduce copyright material:

Figure 7.7 pitstop photo courtesy of Getty Images; Figure 13.2 Kano model courtesy of the Asian Productivity Organisation; Table 10.1 courtesy of Accelerated Improvement Ltd; Figure 10.2 Behavioural Standards example courtesy of DePuy, Cork, Ireland.

In some instances we have been unable to trace the owners of copyright material and would appreciate any information that would enable us to do so.

Introduction

Lean has evolved in the past decade or so from beyond being principally applied in the manufacturing sector to gaining widespread acceptance in almost all industries. It is a deep and profound management system for the attainment of balanced performance excellence.

The current demanding global economic conditions have created an environment where being Lean and fit is now an operational imperative. Lean is no longer a 'nice to do' activity that you will get around to when you get on top of the pressing day-to-day issues. Lean offers an alternative from cutting your way to improving your way through challenging business conditions. This book aims to be your consultative guide to getting started on the Lean journey, to provide guidance on the core Lean transformation practices, and finally to articulate the leadership skills and behaviours required to both navigate the journey and sustain the gains.

Book overview

Part 1 – Getting started: Lean orientation and diagnostic phase

Chapter 1 describes the five guiding principles of Lean that guide the transition towards excellence and the two equally important pillars of continuous improvement and respect for people. A brief history of the evolution of Lean is charted. The business case for Lean is outlined in generic terms to build tension for change for readers. The Lean trilogy of muda, muri and mura is introduced to outline a powerful catalyst for change.

Chapter 2 details how to both align Lean with the overall business strategy and accelerate the delivery of the agreed strategic objectives. The process for the accomplishment of this dual aim is known as *hoshin kanri* strategy deployment.

Chapter 3 illustrates a case study in value stream mapping from a hospital setting. Value stream mapping is a powerful diagnostic methodology for identifying obstacles to the end-to-end flow of value in your organisation. The process moves through three phases; namely, identifying the existing state, designing perfection and finally the creation of a realistic future state map with a plan to arrive there.

Part 2 – Lean transformation practices

Chapters 4 through 9 present the core Lean practices that collectively are designed to bring abnormal conditions and problems to the surface rapidly. The design of the Lean system creates tension to solve these problems when they are still small and relatively easy to crack. The effect is an organic system of living improvement through everyday problem solving.

Part 3 – Leading the Lean transformation

Chapter 10 tackles the hard–soft side of Lean transformation. The development of the culture for Lean to thrive takes deliberate nurturing. Frank Devine's Cathedral model for accelerated cultural change cultivates the behavioural changes required for performance excellence.

Chapters 11 and 12 take a deep dive into the technical and people dimensions of sustaining and producing a continuous stream of improvement activity. This requires a blend of both management and leadership: leadership to produce change and management to lock in the progress towards the ideal state identified in the diagnostic phase of Lean deployment.

Finally Chapter 13 knits the book together through the development of a generic roadmap for transformation that will serve as your guide and barometer along the various stages of Lean maturity. No two Lean journeys will look the same but there are guiding sequences of milestones along the journey that will help you stay the course.

How to read this book

The book is split into three discrete parts:

- Part 1 – Getting started: Lean orientation and diagnostic phase
- Part 2 – Lean transformation practices
- Part 3 – Leading the Lean transformation

I recommend that you read the book in the following order:

1 Read Part 1, Chapters 1 to 3 to familiarise yourself with the Lean philosophy and diagnostic methods that deeply uncover the current state of your organisation and provide a baseline for improvement. This part also (in Chapter 2) frames Lean in a strategic context to ensure that Lean management is not viewed simply as a set of tools that you can bolt onto your existing management system.

2 Armed with your current performance baseline and gap analysis from Part 1 you can then acquaint yourself with the core Lean methods and tools in Part 2. Need should drive change, therefore the methods selected here should be deployed to address problems identified in the diagnosis phase in Part 1. For example, if your organisation is struggling to meet customer demand you might select quick changeover and total productive maintenance (Chapter 7) to increase the capacity of current equipment. You could then deploy a kaizen event (Chapter 6) to compress the time for the impact of these Lean methods to hit the bottom line.

3 Part 3 mainly covers the leadership and human side of transformation. Technical elements for sustaining the gains are discussed in Chapter 11. Chapter 13 covers the Lean roadmap and is really useful for providing context of where you are and what you need to do next (again dependent on need). I recommend you read this chapter before sustaining the gains (Chapters 11 and 12), but these will soon be required! Chapter 10 covers the cultural enrichment aspects that are required for sustained Lean transformation. Cultural change is profoundly influenced by management actions. It would be helpful to have a grasp of this chapter when tending to the 'soft' side of improvement work so keep this chapter to hand when you are building consensus among your senior leadership team that Lean is the strategic weapon that the organisation is committing towards, to drive long-term operational excellence.

Getting started:

Lean orientation and diagnostic phase

Part 1 provides the knowledge necessary to get started on your journey to excellence. Chapter 1 introduces the Lean philosophy and provides a foundational overview of the Lean Management system. Chapter 2 aligns and merges Lean with the strategic objectives of your organisation. Chapter 3 details the diagnostic process of discovery that illustrates the dramatic increases in performance that are achievable for your organisation.

1

Lean management

What is Lean?

Lean is a way of collective thinking to methodically stamp out waste whilst simultaneously maximising value. It requires that employees transition from a singular focus on doing their daily work to a *dual focus of doing their work **and** being motivated to performing their work even better, every day*. This means that all employees need to think deeply about their work in order to understand the shortfalls and develop improved methods.

Why Lean?

Lean delivers a vast competitive edge over competitors who don't use it at all or use it ineffectively. On the cost saving side (just one target of Lean), every £1 saved drops directly to the bottom line. The smaller your profit margins are, the greater the value of cost reduction. For example, if your organisation is operating in a market with a 3% profit margin, saving £150,000 would contribute to the bottom line the equivalent of bringing in an extra £5 million in revenue. That is assuming the extra revenue was produced 100% defect free first time! So, should Lean occupy a central position in your organisation's boardroom and beyond? Lean improvement should be cost positive – no cost, low cost solutions – spend employee ideas and ingenuity not pounds!

Lean is so much more than cost reduction (we discuss True North metrics later in this chapter), it is a business strategy. Lean is also a culture change programme that progressively changes the thinking process of all your employees (hence it is known in Toyota as the thinking production system). This enables people to proactively improve their processes and products/services every day. Lean takes a balanced look at both the process and the people involved in the process, simultaneously bringing both bottom line impact and human growth.

There is widespread misunderstanding that Lean is just another round of traditional cost cutting with 'headcount' reduction as the primary target. However, this would violate the Lean pillar of 'respect for people' (discussed later in this chapter) and destroy lasting true Lean business transformation. The great majority of traditional cost-cutting exercises fail to categorise between the two forms of cost outlined below (value and waste). This is why cost cutting often ends up causing more harm than good in the long term. Traditional cost cutting is in effect cutting activity as opposed to improving the system and generally leads to an awful, destructive cycle in the long term.

Every organisation incurs two types of cost (both private and public):

1 Costs that provide value to your customers. These costs are good and are to be encouraged if they bring competitive advantage and enhanced service. They result in value that people will pay for. An example of value that a customer buying a mobile phone would be willing to pay for is assembling the keypad into the plastic cover.

2 Costs that are incurred, but don't end up providing value to your customers. These costs are waste. Lean is about abolishing this waste to improve the ratio of good cost to bad. Most pre-Lean processes have a bad to good cost ratio of approximately 19:1. This means that for a process that, say, takes 20 minutes to perform, for every 1 minute we are providing value that the customer is willing to pay for, we are also delivering 19 minutes of non-value-added, or waste, that the customer is not willing to pay for. An example of waste that a customer buying a mobile

phone would not be willing to pay for is searching for the keypad to attach it into the plastic cover.

Can you think about both categories of cost that are incurred in your organisation? What opportunities for improvement immediately spring to mind?

Lean strongly makes this distinction between waste and value. Eliminating waste would appear to be a no brainer, but much of the waste in our organisations is invisible. Value, on the other hand, is often much misunderstood and can also be non-obvious and unspoken. You need to ensure that your products/services are of value to the customer as a first step before striving to perform better.

> *'There is nothing so useless as doing efficiently, that which should not be done at all.'*
>
> Peter Drucker (management writer and consultant)

This is where we need to merge Lean with an intimate appreciation of what our customers perceive as value.

Lean makes workplaces visible (anyone can quickly grasp how the area is performing in real time) so that abnormal conditions and problems are revealed as soon as they occur. A problem is any deviation between the target standard and the current actual situation. The Lean system is designed and supported so that these problems are countermeasured immediately and pursued until the root cause(s) has been dissolved. Lean frames problems as opportunities for improvement and for engaging the creative talents of your frontline people working their processes. Problems are opportunities because they identify thresholds in our current workplace knowledge. Traditionally, problems are viewed negatively and solved by 'specialists', or they are worked around. Worse still, problems are often concealed or brushed under the carpet. There are infinite problems, and opportunities to improve in all your processes; hence no problem is viewed in Lean as the biggest problem! How does your organisation currently view its problems?

> *'No one has more trouble, than the person who claims to have no trouble.'* (Having no problems is the biggest problem of all.)
>
> Taiichi Ohno[1]

The primary method for developing new improvement practices is the scientific method or PDSA (plan, do, study, act) cycle. Dr W. Deming finalised the PDSA cycle in 1993.[2] Sustained application of PDSA embeds new cognitive patterns in employees and helps to build the Lean culture through its ingrained philosophy of:

- truly questioning every process – bringing problems to the surface and carefully defining them, not just at the level of their symptoms
- understanding the root cause(s) – there is often more than one root cause; causes can interact and stack up
- developing countermeasures that are viewed as interim until tested under a wide range of conditions and over a defined period of time
- planning the test of change on a small scale (or larger scale if the degree of belief is very strong that the change will be successful and that people affected are receptive to the proposed change)
- closely monitoring and studying what is going on in the test
- learning from what happened and turning the learning into the next PDSA cycle.

Brief history of Lean

The term 'Lean' was coined by John Krafcik, a MIT graduate, in an article published in 1988.[3] *The Machine that Changed the World*[4] was published in 1991 highlighting the great accomplishments of Toyota at NUMMI (a joint venture between Toyota and GM from 1984 to 2010) and the huge gap between Japanese quality and productivity and car manufacturers in the West.

The term gained widespread popularity when James Womack and Daniel Jones wrote the book *Lean Thinking*[5] in 1996. However Lean history goes much further back; it is decades of accumulated wisdom. Lean uses many established tools and concepts along with some newer ones to help organisations remove waste from their processes.

Lean history can be traced back to the late 1700s when possibly one of the oldest concepts of Lean was developed. Eli Whitney developed the principle of standardised parts to mass produce guns.[6] In the late 1800s Frederick Taylor's[7] work on scientific management investigated workplace efficiencies and Frank Gilbreth looked at time and motion studies in the early 1900s.[8] Both of these works influenced the design of the ground breaking assembly line by Henry Ford in 1910 when he started mass producing Ford Model T cars.

Frank G. Woollard (1883–1957) made major contributions to progressive manufacturing management practices in the British automotive industry of the 1920s, and was also the first to develop automatic transfer machines while working at Morris Motors Ltd., Engines Branch, in Coventry, U.K. His work is highly relevant to contemporary Lean management, in that he understood the idea and practice of continuous improvement in a flow environment. Woollard also recognised that flow production will not work properly if used by management in a zero-sum (winner and loser) manner, and this shows he understood the importance of the 'respect for people' pillar in Lean management.

In 1941 the US Department of War introduced the 'Training Within Industry' programmes of job instruction, job methods, job relations, and programme development as ways to teach millions of workers in the wartime industries.

After World War II, Toyota started building cars in Japan. Company leaders Eiji Toyoda and Taiichi Ohno visited Ford to gain a deeper understanding of how Ford was managed in the US. Both were also inspired by Henry Ford's book, *Today and Tomorrow*,[9] first published in 1926, in which the basic ideas of Lean manufacturing are presented. Toyota was also heavily influenced by the visits of Dr W. Edwards Deming who ran quality and productivity seminars in Japan after World War II and encouraged the Japanese to adopt systematic problem solving.

In the 1960s Shigeo Shingo (Toyota's external consultant) developed the method of SMED and poka yoke (mistake proofing) and

Professor Ishikawa at the University of Tokyo formulated the concept of quality circles which give employees far more involvement in the day-to-day running of their local workplaces.

The Toyota Production System (TPS) was developed between 1945 and 1970 and it is still being enhanced today. The growing gap in performance between Toyota and other Japanese companies in the 1970s attracted the interest of others and TPS began spreading rapidly within Japan.

In April 2001, Toyota Motor Corporation produced a document for internal use called 'The Toyota Way 2001'.[10] This 13-page document describes the distinctive aspects of Toyota's culture which contributed to its success. The document was produced to help ensure a consistent understanding of the Toyota Way among all associates across the rapidly growing and increasingly global Toyota Motor Corporation.

Lean today

Lean has traditionally been called Lean Manufacturing. In the past 10 years the 'Manufacturing' has been widely omitted. Lean is now being adopted across all industries such as manufacturing, healthcare, government, financial services, construction, software, transactional processes, tourism, logistics, customer service, hotels and insurance. Since all work is a process, and all value is delivered as a result of a process, the application of Lean is applicable to all industries. The common denominator is people undertaking work.

Recent Toyota recall crisis

In 2010 Toyota recalled 5 million cars for suspected unintended acceleration. This has since transpired to be a defect in the use of the cars rather than in the vehicles themselves. A 2011 NASA report concluded that the unintended acceleration incidents were the result of floor mats being improperly installed on top of other floor mats, or driver error, and that there were no electronic flaws in the cars that would cause unintended acceleration.

That said, Toyota has reflected on the company's strategic direction. Chief executive officer (CEO) Akio Toyoda testified in 2010 to the United States Congress that the company had erred by pursuing growth that exceeded 'the speed at which we were able to develop our people and our organisation', and Toyota would reinvigorate its traditional focus on 'quality over quantity'.[11] The company has come back stronger and sharper than ever before despite a dramatic downturn in sales in the global car industry due to the worldwide recession and the closer-to-home supplier and production disruption caused by the catastrophic Japanese tsunami in 2011.

True North Lean

'True North' refers to what we should do, not what we can do. It is a term used in the Lean lexicon to describe the ideal or state of perfection that your business should be continually striving towards. Lean is a journey without an absolute destination point, we will never achieve perfection. Opportunities for improvement never end, and it is only when we take the next step that we in fact see possible future steps. However, like a sailor we must be guided towards our shoreline. We look to True North metrics to guide us while knowing that we can never arrive at the True North; it is a concept not a goal. It is the persistent practice of daily improvement by all your employees to advance to True North that makes organisations first class.

True North metrics you can use in your business to achieve a balanced blend of success are:

1. People growth

- Safety (zero physical and psychological incidences)
- Job security (zero layoffs due to improvements, revenue growth)
- Challenge and engagement (number of problems solved)
- Coaching (one-to-one development sessions)

2. Quality

- Zero defects (end customer, internal rework, number of mistake proofing devices/process)

3. Delivery

▪ One piece flow on demand (cycle time, OEE (overall equipment effectiveness), changeover metrics, EPEI (every product every interval) – see later chapters

4. Cost

▪ 100% value-added steps (zero waste)

The five principles[12]

Lean is based on five principles (see Table 1.1 below). The principles are supported by two pillars called continuous improvement and respect for people. These pillars are discussed later in this chapter.

Table 1.1 The Lean principles

Principle	Description
1. Purpose	The purpose of all Lean activity is to enable an organisation to prosper. Organisations need to clearly define expectations of what they are trying to accomplish. This of course means different things at different levels in the organisation and these aims must be made explicit. It calls for a deep understanding and appreciation of our customers' spoken and unspoken needs. Customers buy benefits not product features or services. What benefits do our products or services deliver? Step into the shoes of your customers. As John Bicheno[13] states, 'are we selling cosmetics or hope?' Think about the purpose of your product/service range.
2. System	A system can be broadly defined as a set of integrated and dependent elements that accomplishes a defined purpose. Organisations are systems, much like people, organic plants and the car you drive. They are more than the sum of their parts; they are complex, constantly changing over time and interacting. Improvement means change

Principle	Description
2. System (cont)	and hence making changes without an appreciation of the organisation as a system can have unintended consequences. Lean focuses on total system improvement rather than on isolated 'islands of excellence'.
3. Flow	Pre-Lean processes generally contain greater than 95% of steps that do not add value from the customer's perspective. Hence the incredible potential for improvement in business performance across all sectors using Lean to analyse existing processes and reorganising for flow. Tackling the 3Ms: muda (waste), mura (variation), and muri (overburden) provide huge improvement leverage to build smooth work flow.
4. Perfection	Lean is never fully implemented; it is truly a journey without an end point as the possibilities for improvement are endless. Perfection is the concept that we are striving for. It is the proactive advancement towards this ideal state that makes Lean organisations exceptional. There *are* always opportunities for improvement. Lean is like peeling an onion: as each layer of waste is exposed and dissolved at the root cause level, the next layer becomes visible.
5. People	People are the true engine of Lean. The most successful Lean organisations thrive because they have intrinsically motivated people nurtured by the 'respect for people' pillar of Lean (discussed later in this chapter). They are actively engaged in daily problem solving to remove the sources of waste as made visible through the design of Lean systems.

Best-in-class Lean organisations are meeting and exceeding their customers' expectations using half of everything in comparison with traditionally managed organisations. That is half labour hours, half facility space, half capital investment, half on-hand inventory, half defects and half the number of adverse safety incidents. These results are not achieved overnight; they require a long-term commitment to improvement. If you work in an organisation with strong leadership you should be well on your way to gains of this magnitude within two to four years. Harnessing the 'respect for people' principle this impressive maximisation of resources can be achieved with greatly enhanced levels of employee inclusion and engagement than at the start of the Lean journey.

The Lean operating system

A Lean operating system (see Figure 1.1 below) is based on continuous improvement, respect for people and elimination of waste. The operating system integrates six elements:

1 principles to drive aligned thinking and behaviour
2 systems thinking to understand the interconnected areas and dependencies of the business
3 Lean methods to make abnormal conditions stand out
4 metrics to tell us how we are doing
5 respect for people to keep the continuous improvement element balanced
6 a foundation of constructive dissatisfaction with the current performance level, leadership engagement with the people doing the work, and a strong teamwork ethic.

First pillar: Continuous improvement

'We are what we repeatedly do. Excellence, then, is not an act, but habit.'

Aristotle

Continuous improvement is a way of life for Lean organisations. It is closely aligned with the principle of perfection – the recognition that there are always opportunities to improve your business. The word 'continuous' means just that, it is a commitment to everyday improvement, not a one-off burst of change activity. Entropy is at play in every workplace; this is the level of randomness in systems or the drift toward disintegration. This means that if we are not continuously improving every day we are in fact sliding backwards due to the deterioration effect of entropy. Everything essentially degrades over time. Hence this would suggest that Lean is not a nice to do (or when we get time), it is mandatory for long-term survival.

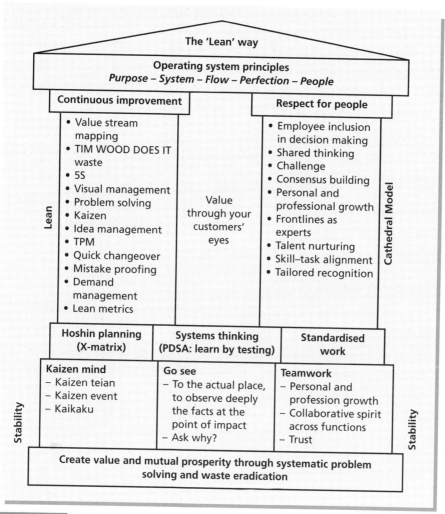

The 'Lean' way

Operating system principles
Purpose – System – Flow – Perfection – People

Continuous improvement

- Value stream mapping
- TIM WOOD DOES IT waste
- 5S
- Visual management
- Problem solving
- Kaizen
- Idea management
- TPM
- Quick changeover
- Mistake proofing
- Demand management
- Lean metrics

Value through your customers' eyes

Respect for people

- Employee inclusion in decision making
- Shared thinking
- Challenge
- Consensus building
- Personal and professional growth
- Frontlines as experts
- Talent nurturing
- Skill–task alignment
- Tailored recognition

Lean

Cathedral Model

Hoshin planning (X-matrix)

Systems thinking (PDSA: learn by testing)

Standardised work

Kaizen mind
- Kaizen teian
- Kaizen event
- Kaikaku

Go see
- To the actual place, to observe deeply the facts at the point of impact
- Ask why?

Teamwork
- Personal and profession growth
- Collaborative spirit across functions
- Trust

Stability

Stability

Create value and mutual prosperity through systematic problem solving and waste eradication

Figure 1.1 Lean operating system

One of the under-appreciated aspects of Lean is the immense compounding impact that small incremental improvements have over time. If everyone just improved their job 0.1% every day that adds up to a 25% improvement per person year on year. That equates to a colossal advantage in the fullness of time. You should think about how you can challenge and support your staff to improve their own work by even 0.5% every week, to achieve remarkable gains.

Lean systems are designed to make normally invisible small problems and non-conformances visible. Waste is made evident every day and there is pressure from the process – by way of design, tightly linked processes highlight problems – for people to fix problems in relative real time. The core purpose of all of the Lean methods discussed in Chapters 4 to 9 is to surface problems and opportunities for improvement.

The popular parable of the woodcutter captures well the intent of continuous improvement:

The woodcutter

A young man approached the foreman of a logging crew and asked for a job. 'That depends,' replied the foreman. 'Let's see you chop down this tree.' The young man stepped forward and skilfully chopped down a great tree. Impressed, the foreman exclaimed, 'You can start on Monday.' Monday, Tuesday, Wednesday, Thursday rolled by – and Thursday afternoon the foreman approached the young man and said, 'You can pick up your pay check on the way out today.' Startled, the young man replied, 'I thought you paid on Friday.' 'Normally we do,' said the foreman. 'But we're letting you go today because you've fallen behind. Our daily felling charts show that you've dropped from first place on Monday to last place today.' 'But I'm a hard worker,' the young man objected. 'I arrive first, leave last and even have worked through my coffee breaks!' The foreman, sensing the young man's integrity, thought for a minute and then asked, 'Have you been sharpening your saw?' The young man replied, 'No sir, I've been working too hard to take time for that!'

Are there examples in your organisation where there is no time to 'sharpen the saw'?

Second pillar: Respect for people

'Respect a man, he will do the more.'

James Howell (historian, 1594–1666)

Lean is a voyage to developing outstanding and aligned people through involvement in continuous improvement. The focus is on eliminating waste, not making people redundant. It goes without saying that people are not waste, they are in fact the only organisational asset (properly led) that appreciates and becomes more valuable over time. To grow people who will continuously improve your organisation you need to engage their collective intelligence. The expert is the person nearest the actual job. This means that we must respect and nurture people's talent and brainpower. It is management's responsibility to champion excellence in thinking and to challenge people to do great things. A challenge generally brings out the best in people and inspires them to achieve greater levels of personal and professional performance.

Respect for people is not a motherhood and apple pie concept. It brings value and prosperity to a business. We respect people because we want employee engagement and their discretionary endeavours. The best methods and tools are worthless if people won't engage with and practise them! Engaged employees are involved team players who strive to improve. They look for ways to implement and share ideas. All of the Lean methods, when deployed properly, exemplify respect for people. This is because seasoned Lean practitioners frame the methods and tools to both improve the process under study and develop the people using them. For example, standard work allows time for improvement and people development as there is less time spent fire fighting (wasteful work is disrespectful), which in turn leads to more engaged people. When engagement levels are high, turnover is low, which leads to higher productivity as there is less time spent training people to become competent in their job roles. A true virtuous cycle transpires.

Respect for people is not one dimensional; it must extend to all stakeholders, namely shareholders, employees, customers, suppliers and the community within which we work.

All the categories of operational waste are known as muda (Japanese for waste) in Lean and they violate the pillar of 'respect for people'. For example if you were to waste people's time through making them wait for a meeting, it conveys the subtle message that your time is more valuable than theirs. Similarly, making defective products is disrespectful; it is a waste of physical and human resources and erodes an organisation's competitiveness. Overburdening (muri) people and unevenness (mura) also violate this pillar. Examples of this that you see in many businesses are price promotions. They cause employees to work like crazy one week to meet an artificially created demand. But the next week they have little work to do because real end user demand generally stays relatively constant.

A waste walk, also referred to as a gemba walk (the actual place where the work is performed), is one of the Lean practices that demonstrates a strong sense of respect by management for the people adding value on the frontlines. Management walk the frontlines regularly to stay in touch with reality. To lead improvement they must be humble and spend more time at the frontlines where the real customer value-added work takes place. There is no substitute for seeing the actual facts (richer than data from the office) at the source. It sends the clear message to people that their work is important.

Respect for people also means:

- Clear roles and responsibilities are communicated and there is regular constructive feedback on performance (respect means that people know what is expected of them).
- The correct equipment is provided to perform the work (respect means that people have the resources to perform their jobs well).
- Individual strengths and talents of employees are known and utilised daily, tasks are aligned to people's skill-sets (respect means that people get the opportunity to work on what they are qualified to do).
- Tailored recognition is given to people in a timely manner to nurture excellent performance (respect means that people are appreciated).
- Development opportunities are encouraged through participation in improvement teams and cross training (respect means that people are given the opportunity to grow and develop as individuals).
- There is a strong sense that the welfare of the organisation's people matters through management's actions (respect means that management's actions are people centric).
- Ideas for improvement are expected as a normal part of the job and support is provided to put these into practice (respect means that people have input into improving their own work areas).

▪ The purpose of the organisation and its wider benefit to society are clearly articulated (respect means that people are led by purpose rather than being assigned tasks).

▪ The opportunity to perform high-quality work in a safe environment is provided (respect means that people can perform their work to a high standard without fear of danger).

▪ Regular opportunities are provided for people to interact socially both internally and at externally organised events (respect means that management recognises the social aspect of work and that loyalty between employees promotes teamwork).

Respect for people encourages employees to be self-reliant; to act as if they owned the business themselves. Instead of waiting to improve things, people are empowered to test changes and implement successful experiments. There is mutual trust that people will do the right thing for the business at all levels.

Problem solving is at the heart of Lean organisations and is one of the uppermost demonstrations of respect for people. The message to employees is that management can't solve all the problems single-handedly.

Managers often get the wrong idea about the 'respect for people' pillar because they think it is fuzzy and not businesslike. In my experience the root cause of most Lean transformation failures can be traced back to not practising this pillar. Hence for Lean to succeed, the 'respect for people' pillar is mandatory.

> *'He who wants a rose must respect the thorn.'*
>
> *Anon*

Hidden waste is robbing our profits

> *'If the nut has 15 threads on it, it cannot be tightened unless it is turned 15 times. In reality, though, it is that last turn that tightens the bolt and the first one that loosens it. The remaining 14 turns are waste (motion).'*
>
> *Shigeo Shingo (industrial engineer and thought leader)*

The elimination of waste is integral to Lean, and there are three broad types of waste: muda, muri and mura. You need to hunt down all three of this triad to realise the full benefits of Lean.

Muda

The actual time spent adding value (often referred to as core touch time) to a product or service is tiny in comparison with the overall delivery lead time. The value-adding core touch time is often less than 5% of the overall lead time before the application of Lean. The travesty is that it is all too common in many organisations to have all their technical expertise focused on maximising these value-adding steps, for example making a machine cycle faster. The greater opportunity is to tackle operational waste. The remaining steps fall into value-added enabling (approximately 35% of pre-Lean process steps) and non-value-added (approximately 60% of pre-Lean process steps).

Value-added

For a step to be classified in this category it should satisfy *all three* of the following questions:

1 Would the customer be willing to pay for this activity if they knew we were doing it?
2 Does this step progress the product or service towards completion?
3 Is it done right the first time?

Value-added enabling

These steps do not pass all three of the value-added questions above but are necessary to operate the business. However, the customer is unwilling to pay for them as they do not add direct value to your product or service (e.g. inspection, budget tracking).

Questions to determine if a process step is value-added enabling include:

▨ Is this step required by law or regulation?

▨ Does this step reduce the financial risk for the shareholders?

▨ Does this step support financial reporting obligations?

▨ Would the process fail if this step were removed?

It is important to recognise that these activities are really non-value-adding but you currently need to perform them. You need to strive to eliminate or at least reduce their cost.

Non-value-added

Lastly the pure waste category of process steps falls into one or other of the 13 waste types detailed in Table 1.2 below. Waste is not confined to the stuff that we throw in the bin! The acronym of TIM WOOD DOES IT is useful to help to commit these waste categories to memory and to build a culture where the shared way of employee thinking is to view their work through this common lens of waste identification. This is an extremely powerful lens to view your workplace processes through; the magnitude of the improvement potential becomes clear. It is important to state that the actual waste types are symptoms of deeper problems which must be rooted out. For example the waste of searching (motion waste) for something is perhaps a symptom of poor workplace organisation. Over-processing is generally considered one of the worst of all the waste categories as its occurrence generates many of the other wastes. Think about over-cooking your dinner and the waste that generates: defects (burnt food), inventory (wasted ingredients), motion (extra stubborn washing-up), energy (oven), waiting (call pizza delivery!), overhead (light on in kitchen), safety (smoke alarm), etc.

In reality all waste cannot be removed; it is a goal to aspire to. A world-class process would be considered as having a 25–30% value-added ratio (value-added time divided by overall lead time). Think about all the money and employee aggravation that these waste categories are draining from your organisation.

Table 1.2 Waste categories for the manufacturing and hospital domains

Waste category	Manufacturing examples	Healthcare examples
1. **T**ransport (excessive movement of product, people, information, poor layout)	Product travelling over 2 kilometres in the factory due to poor arrangement of processing machines and tools not at point of use	Walking for linen in remote storeroom, patients in the emergency department walking from the first to fifth floor for imaging scan
2. **I**nventory (excessive raw material/supplies, large batches, finished goods, stock-outs, obsolescence)	Three years' supply of one stock part in raw material store, dispatch area overflowing with unsold finished goods, line stopped due to missing part resulting in 50 people idle for 2 hours, running machines without orders to keep workers busy	Overstuffed supplies racking, expired baby foods on paediatrics ward, some medications out of stock
3. **M**otion (excessive employee or customer walking, poor ergonomics, searching for items)	Tool missing from workstation, conveyor is too high leading to repetitive strain injury risk, poor access to machine during changeover clean-down	One copier between three clinics, 'treasure hunts' searching for supplies/who has the keys?, nurses walking several kilometres per shift due to poor ward layout
4. **W**aiting (waiting for equipment, material and/or information, queuing, watching – automated equipment run)	Waiting for the schedule to be published delays the shift start-up, moulded parts wait in queue for three weeks before final assembly uses them	Patients waiting for procedures for hours as everyone scheduled to arrive at the same time, staff waiting 30 minutes at shift handover for their relevant 2 minutes of information

Waste category	Manufacturing examples	Healthcare examples
5. **O**ver-processing (general inefficiency due to machine condition, etc., duplication, doing more than is necessary, completely unnecessary services, excessive legacy testing)	Extra inspection steps added in stamping after quality escalation rather than dissolving the root cause at source, excessive packaging on incoming material, unnecessary meetings	Redundant checks, duplicate questions, unnecessary diagnostic tests and procedures, over-medicating patients
6. **O**ver production (producing before needed or in greater quantities than required)	Making 3 months' supply of part A as the changeover time is 6 hours, making extra parts to keep the employee utilisation metric on target	Getting patients ready significantly before the next stage is ready for them, pulling patients' medical record charts a day ahead of clinics and 20% of patients do not arrive
7. **D**efects (errors and rework, customer returns/complaints)	Paint defects touched up in the dispatch yard, defect discovered in final assembly from an upstream process and 3 weeks' inventory to rework, customer returns	Procedure cancellations due to poor scheduling, family not included in care plan development
8. **D**esign (equipment not designed to support ease of use etc.)	8 bolts with 12 threads to be removed manually to change out a die, product is not designed to enable ease of final assembly, poor facility layout	Medication cart supplies not organised in alphabetical order to reduce search time, sink not fitted with anti-scald device, equipment not mistake proofed

Waste category	Manufacturing examples	Healthcare examples
9. **O**verhead (larger facility or equipment and resources than necessary, idle rooms or machines)	Inventory taking up 50% of facility floor space, 100T press used where 25T press would be sufficient, higher spec equipment than required, employees worked overtime last week to meet food 'Buy One, Get One Free' offer, orders 50% lower than normal this week, same number of staff on shift now idle	Large centralised scanner versus right-sized, lower-spec local scanner for low-acuity cases, low equipment utilisation despite community access issues, emergency department closed from 12 am to 7 am due to budget constraints
10. **E**nergy (wastage of electricity, air, light and heating, poorly performing equipment)	Air leaks on compressor main line, motion sensor lights not used in warehouse, air conditioning excessively cold	Excess heat so windows left open, lights left on all night in day case units, air leaks on equipment
11. **S**afety (adverse incidents, near misses, not reporting concerns, injuries, psychological fear of speaking out in case of retribution)	Non-compliance to safety standards, spills, leaks, wet floors, material and loose strapping on floor which could cause a fall, non-compliance to safety glasses or steel toe boots in designated areas	Medication errors, patient falling, pressure sores, nurse interrupted during patient admission, non-compliance with hand sanitation standards

Waste category	Manufacturing examples	Healthcare examples
12. Ideas and talent (customer and employee ideas not captured on a continuous basis, not sharing best practice, not engaging or listening to your employees)	Ideas posted on ideas board for the past 3 months and no progress is evident	Surgeon waiting for the operating room is a waste of talent, staff not given the time and resources to implement ideas to save time
13. Technology (IT issues, scanner problems, excessive manual systems, training needs not addressed to use IT systems)	Material requirements planning (MRP) driven schedule is causing over-production waste, handwriting data and then transferring to computer a second time, no system to page supervisors when they are needed to react to a problem	Barcode scanners not working, old and slow computer at nurses' station, no colour printer in the area, new scan machine idle as staff not trained in its use

Muri

Muri is the excessive overburden of work inflicted on employees and equipment because of poor planning, organisation and badly designed work processes. It is pushing an employee or piece of equipment beyond the accepted limits. Unreasonable work is almost always a cause of variation, shortcuts and quality concerns.

One example of muri includes people working crazy long hours due to being overwhelmed with work. Removing muda or waste in this situation will help but may not be sufficient. Matching capacity to demand is one of the tactics to countermeasure the overburdening of people and equipment. Other examples of muri include:

▪ bending or awkward movements to perform the work

▪ heavy lifting

▪ repetitive, tiring work.

Mura

Mura is the variation in the operation of a process and in the demand that is placed on your organisation. It is the unevenness and unbalanced exertion placed on people and machines. Variation is the enemy of Lean and creates many categories of the waste listed in Table 1.2. Not conforming to or absence of standardised work is a widespread cause of mura. Artificially created demand driven by organisational policies, etc. is also a major cause of mura. Other examples include:

- not following software development coding standards
- multiple physician surgery tray preferences
- food promotions causing demand spikes
- month end hockey stick effect – shipping everything on the last day of the month to make the financial numbers.

Review

The instinctive gut reaction that people get when they hear the word 'Lean' in organisations is fear about ruthless cost cutting and head count reduction. The term Lean can have a negative connotation and infer that the philosophy is a totally reductionist strategy. I have been involved in successful Lean journeys where the word 'Lean' was substituted by 'operational excellence' or the organisation's own version (e.g. 'The "X" production system') where the 'X' refers to the organisation's name. Continuous improvement merged with the 'respect for people' pillar is not about cutting value-added costs or people layoffs. It is about engaging the hands, hearts and minds of all employees to improve their workplace. It is about growing your business, securing jobs, saving taxpayers' money in the public sector and saving thousands of preventable deaths in our hospitals through delivering better quality care at lower cost.

2

Hoshin kanri strategy deployment

Introduction

'If you always do what you've always done, you'll always get what you've always got.'

Einstein

Hoshin drives the tempo of improvement during your Lean transformation. It puts operational improvement on the same stage as making the numbers or doing the normal day-to-day routine work. In my view it can be the potent advantage that sets your organisation ahead of the competition.

Hoshin kanri is often formally conducted after Lean has been piloted for a short period in an organisation. The reason for this is to prove the concept of Lean first and to build confidence through a demonstrated success story.

The Japanese term hoshin means compass, or pointing direction, kanri means management or control.[1] Hoshin kanri is a systematic method of expressing the strategic aims for the next 3–5 year time horizon and to lock in the critical few breakthroughs that the organisation will pursue for the forthcoming year. A breakthrough is defined as an objective that will close the gap between True North and our current reality. Accountability is assigned and execution is monitored on a periodic basis. At a high level, hoshin is a large application of the PDSA cycle introduced in Chapter 1, and multiple PDSA cycles are effected to develop and implement the individual objectives. PDSA ensures that we have solid but flexible plans in place that are executed and that their effectiveness is confirmed.

Hoshin cascades top management intentions throughout the organisation into actionable deliverables at each level. Hence actions at all levels are aligned towards delivering the strategic aims. Without hoshin each department could be working on its own processes in a piecemeal fashion. This lack of joined up thinking often makes overall performance worse, despite people's best intended efforts.

The hoshin kanri process

Members of the senior leadership team come together over a number of workshops (the number is dependent on the size and Lean maturity of the organisation) to work through the following steps:

1 Reflection on the previous year's performance
2 Review of the organisation's vision, mission and values
3 Objectives for the forthcoming year
4 Alignment building and action plans
5 X-matrix development
6 Implementation
7 Monthly evaluation
8 Annual evaluation.

1. Reflection on the previous year's performance

Reflection is a common practice in Lean organisations. It means to analyse past performance to look specifically at:

▪ What went well last year?
▪ What could we improve on this year?
▪ What insights were learned?

This process looks at what we achieved last year against what we set out to do. It's very important to understand what is already working and to do more of what works. Reflection is also consistent with the 'continuous improvement' pillar of Lean; we are constantly looking at better ways of performing and learning in a constructive way from past problems. It is surprisingly uncommon for organisations to review past performance in this way, especially if things are deemed to be going acceptably well. Lean organisations foster a healthy attitude of constructive discontent.

2. Review of the organisation's mission, vision and values

Mission, vision and values should assimilate the True North ideals of Lean in terms of people growth, quality, delivery and cost.

The mission statement describes the *purpose* (Lean principle 1) of an organisation: what it does and for whom and why.

The vision describes the organisation's ideal future (think True North!). For example, it is good practice for you to conduct a review session of both the mission and vision and ask questions such as:

▪ Is it articulated?

▪ Is it still relevant to our business today and into the future?

▪ Are people at all levels in the organisation able to tell a visitor what our vision is?

▪ Does it inspire action?

Values help to guide daily behaviour, which in turn helps to shape the culture of your organisation, which ultimately determines habits and hence performance. The list of values below can be used to contrast against your current values if the latter are already specified. If not the list can be used as a trigger to see which values speak to the organisation's preferred ideals. It is common to have between five and seven core values and these are then crafted into the organisation's personal context (see 'Behavioural Standards' in Chapter 10) to make them real.

> **Examples of core values** |
>
> respect, continuous improvement, drive, competency, fairness, integrity, service, responsibility, perseverance, diversity, fun, loyalty, creativity, teamwork, excellence, accountability, self-reliance, quality, collaboration, empathy, courage, challenge, learning, kindness, discipline, generosity, optimism, dependability, flexibility, pride, camaraderie, humility

Taken as a group the mission, vision and values unite an organisation to follow a common, refined path. Hence they greatly enable the hoshin alignment process.

3. Objectives for the forthcoming year

The Lean assessment (see the appendix) and value stream mapping should be done just before hoshin by senior management with frontline personnel and a Lean coach (either an externally appointed Lean expert or an internal expert). The assessment and mapping workshops provide essential input to the process of framing objectives. Value stream mapping is discussed in Chapter 3.

The process of deciding the breakthrough objectives depends on an intensive period of gathering data and facts. In my view it is helpful if this work is completed prior to the teams meeting as a group and should include numerous hours understanding reality at the gemba. (The gemba is a Japanese term that means to go to the actual place where the work is being performed and to observe the process deeply with your own eyes.) The selection of your breakthrough objectives can come from the collective business knowledge both inside and outside the meeting.

Utilisation of more formal tools such as the classic SWOT (strengths, weaknesses, opportunities and threats) matrix,[2] for example, can also be deployed. Another method often used at this stage is a strategy map.[3] This is a form of environmental scanning and assesses internal factors (e.g. financials, productivity and growth strategies, customer offerings and branding, employee learning and development, and innovation processes) as well as external competitor offerings in the marketplace. To identify breakthroughs, organisations should have a deep understanding of what their customers truly value (see Figure 13.2, the Kano model).

The use of 'what-if' can also be deployed to mould breakthrough objectives. For example: what if it is three to five years in the future. We are incredibly thriving. What does this look like, and what breakthroughs got us here?

It is common for a greater number of breakthroughs to be proposed than the 'vital few' that can be realistically resourced. You need to prioritise based on benefit–effort ratings and/or other business needs. It is important to ensure that a balanced approach to the breakthrough objectives is taken. That is, there should be at least one breakthrough from all four areas of True North, namely people growth, quality, delivery and cost. Improving any one in isolation will eventually limit the systemic improvements that are possible. Some items that you deem to be important (but at a lower level than the hoshin objectives) can be delegated to the normal, routine, daily management process to be progressed. A 'discontinue doing' list is also helpful at this stage to park existing low-priority projects and make time for more value-added breakthroughs. Critical projects in progress but not yet complete from last year can also make up a breakthrough objective.

4. Alignment building and action plans

The process of building alignment and consensus throughout the organisation is known as catchball. This quite literally means passing the ball up and down, back and forth, and across the organisational silos. Consensus does not mean that everyone agrees: it does mean however that everyone has had input into the process and their voice is heard and truly listened to.

Consensus building is the big differentiator from traditional command and control strategy development. This is where all stakeholders have the opportunity to enrich the plans that are being developed in a collaborative manner. It also builds ownership. Management gets the opportunity to obtain reaction on their beliefs of current actuality. This is very much in keeping with the Lean gemba principle of going to the actual source of the action. Goals are made more area specific as they are cascaded throughout the organisation.

When the team finally decides on the vital few breakthroughs (to close the gap from current and future state) for the coming year, detailed plans are developed and further catchball takes place.

The extent to which catchball is played out depends on the maturity of Lean in the organisation and people's capability with Lean and in the leadership of their teams. Organisations just embarking on their Lean journey would typically not use the concept of catchball directly on the frontlines. As problem solving skills grow and the credibility of Lean deepens (by actual results), catchball can be carried out throughout the organisation.

A detailed action plan (see Figure 2.1) is developed for each breakthrough. Activities are outlined that will deliver the objective. Timelines for delivery are planned and metrics to assess the progress of the line items are tracked. Colour coding facilitates the tracking process: for example, items that are planned but not yet begun are grey, items that are complete are green, items that are slipping are yellow, and items that were not done are red. Red items are assigned a 'back to green' plan.

Some individual activities that require more detailed planning may merit another lower level plan. These become known as a child plan and feed into the main or mother plan. Seasoned Lean veterans always take the time to plan well and recognise that a good plan is half the work done.

Bowling charts (see Figure 2.2) are used to track monthly progress against the planned gains. Each one of your breakthrough plans can use a bowling chart. They are reviewed monthly to drive accountability. The delicate point and great value of these charts is that they force us to slice the improvements down into smaller increments and to learn and adjust (PDSA) every month. They help us track the pathway to the next destination – the achievement of the breakthrough.

The plans are typically displayed in a visual management centre (VMC – see Figure 2.3). The VMC is an area where performance data is visually displayed and kept up to date. The purpose of the VMC is so that anyone in the workplace, even those who are unfamiliar with the detail of the processes, can rapidly see what is going on, and distinguish what is under control and what isn't. The VMC craftily increases the level of accountability (through increased transparency) and urgency for delivering the plans. I often use a sporting analogy – 'If we are not keeping score, we are just practising!' – to diminish resistance to increased levels of performance transparency.

A word on metrics

Typically, most organisations track results oriented measures. Yet measures focused solely on results represent after the fact data: the horse has already bolted. Process metrics are also needed to measure and track the performance of a process, and provide real-time feedback that can be acted on swiftly. If we get the process right the results *will* always follow. Effective measurement systems should alloy a blend of both result and process measures (four times the number of process metrics in general).

A car's dashboard provides a good analogy. The mileage clock tracks results – how far your car has travelled in a trip. However, without process metrics such as the fuel or oil gauge, we cannot be sure or predict that we will arrive at our destination. And so it is with organisations: we need to track both the results and the means that deliver those results.

A third type of metric encouraged by Associates in Process Improvement[4] is called a balancing measure. This metric helps to prevent an improvement accomplished in some measures degrading performance in others. When making changes to results and process measures we need to ensure that any related measures are maintained or improved. This will help safeguard against any unintended consequences of your improvement activities.

Table 2.1 Metric categories

Result measures	Process measures	Balancing measures
Units produced	OEE[5]	Employee engagement ratio
Inventory £ on-hand	Changeover time	Number of stock-outs
% defectives	Number of processes mistake proofed	Process capability (Cpk)[6]

True North Metric: Cost

Department: Final Assembly
Sponsor: Department Head
Lead: Area Supervisor

Activity	High Level Actions Required
Reduce Operational Waste (hidden profit pillers)	1. Run waste awareness simulation game with all Final Assembly (FA) staff and implement action plans from these workshops 2. Implement a cascaded plant wide waste walk program in FA 3. Implement visual management in FA 4. Roll out systematic problem solving across FA
Inventory Reduction	1. Improved final assembly machine uptime (see Delivery Hoshin Breakthrough plan) 2. Reduce finished good inventory by 5 days 3. Reduce changeover time in final assembly by 50%
Supply Chain Improvement	1. Work collaboratively with suppliers to reduce system overall costs and reduce cost of supplies by 3% 2. Introduce returnable packaging system with top 5 suppliers 3. Eliminate incoming inspection on top 20% of suppliers by implementing the supplier development plan (see Quality Hoshin Breakthrough plan)
Improve Overall Equipment Effectiveness (OEE)	1. Collect equipment history and performance analysis at FA pacemaker 2. Calculate baseline OEE 3. Assess six big losses and set priorities and corrective actions
Productivity Improvement	1. Improve FA productivity by 5% using a focused 5 day kaizen event 2. Implement 5S Workplace Organisation 3. Conduct a detailed ergonomic assessment on manual assembly operations 4. Implement cellular layout on manual assembly stations (30% of labour)
Energy Reduction Program	1. Implement FA start-up and shut down procedures 2. Repair all air leaks in the area 3. Install motion sensor low energy rating lights in the area and all meeting rooms 4. Install slide doors on all open shipping bays 5. Replace air activated pistons on all machines with low energy servo motor mechanisms

Figure 2.1 Action plan sample (details are not significant)

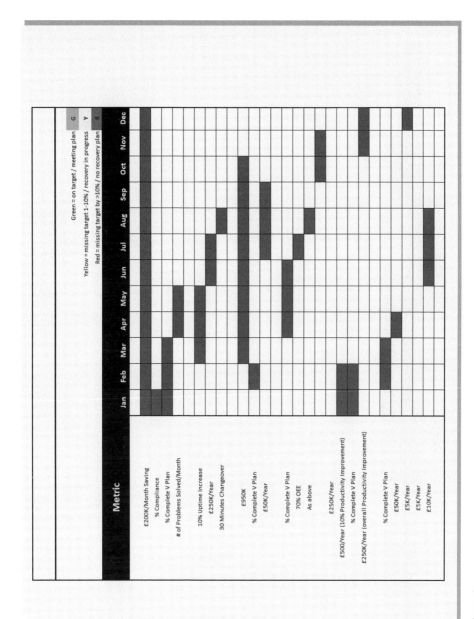

Figure 2.1 Continued

Resource:

No.	Strategy: Double Conversion Rate	2012	Jan	Feb	Mar	Apr	May	Jun	Jul	Aug	Sep	Oct	Nov	Dec	Deliverable
1		Plan													
		Actual													
2		Plan													
		Actual													
3		Plan													
		Actual													
4		Plan													
		Actual													
5		Plan													
		Actual													
6		Plan													
		Actual													
7		Plan													
		Actual													

Figure 2.2 Blank bowling chart example

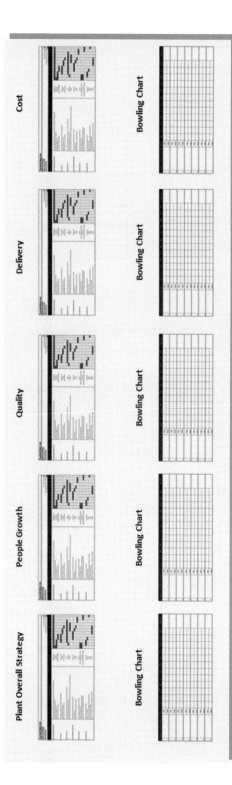

Figure 2.3 Visual management centre hoshin kanri section

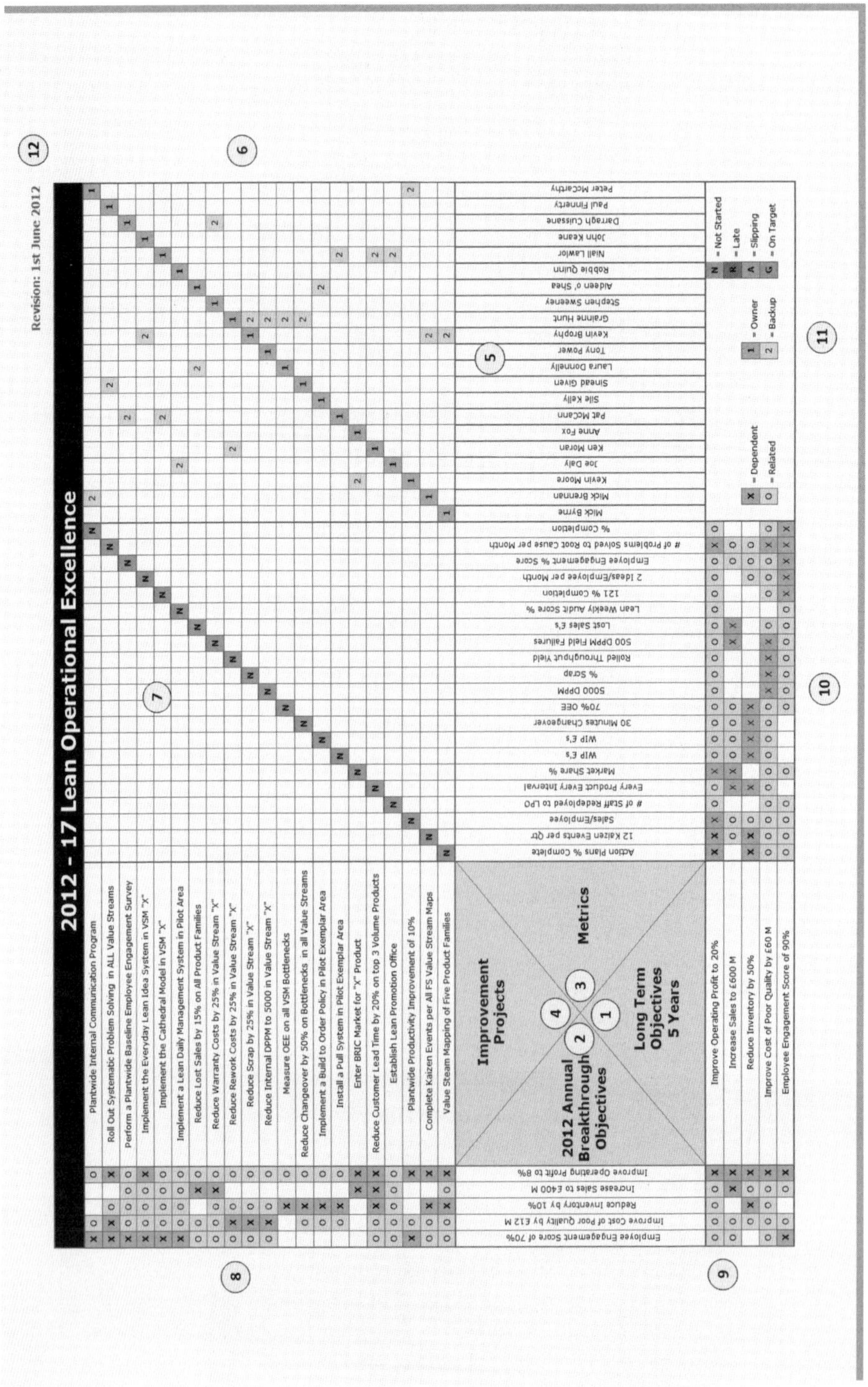

Figure 2.4   X-matrix manufacturing example (populated by the author for illustrative purposes only)

5. X-matrix development

The X-matrix is based on the work of Ryuji Fukuda[7], an authority on Japanese quality. It looks very complex at first glance, but it is actually quite straightforward in practice. It is a visual management template that merges the what, who and how much of the organisation's strategy onto one A3 page. The matrix is a great dialogue and consensus builder in the formulation of strategy and is another form of catchball. Hence I recommend that you print the template and populate it in pencil initially; there should be lots of changes as consensus is built! The matrix is reviewed as a part of the hoshin monthly review meeting. The primary focus of this meeting is on exceptions (red items) and putting a plan in place to bring these back on track. (Note that managing 'on green' is discussed in Chapter 10.) New objectives and initiatives can be added as the business environment changes and learning increases. The example shown in Figure 2.4 is a top level or mother X-matrix. Lower level X-matrix templates can be deployed per level, if needed, to make the objectives more detailed and meaningful. The extent and level of this are dependent on the size of the organisation. The X-matrix enables everyone to appreciate how the long-term strategy, annual objectives, improvement projects and metrics are integrated together as a system (Lean principle 2).

Filling in the X-matrix |

1   You populate your organisation's three to five year long-term strategy. A balanced scorecard approach should be applied to the critical few objectives, under cost, quality, delivery and people growth.

2   The portion of this strategy that you aim to accomplish in the forthcoming year is added here with specific targets for each breakthrough.

3   The metrics are formulated and added here, taking a blended approach to result, process and balancing measures.

4   The improvement assignments are agreed that will deliver your organisation's annual breakthroughs. There can be several projects undertaken per breakthrough.

5   Accountability is determined for each assignment.

6   This grid outlines the owners and back-up resource for the assignments. It is the responsibility of the owner to develop more detailed plans for each improvement project.

Filling in the X-matrix | **continued**

7   The improvement projects are correlated to the metric, and the traffic light system is updated monthly to monitor progress against the detailed plans.

8   The improvement projects are correlated against your annual objectives. They are assigned as being dependent on delivering the strategy or related to the strategy. Again this should involve a team-based conversation and catchball.

9   The long-term strategy is also correlated to your annual objectives, as above.

10   Correlation between the long-term strategy and the metrics is completed.

11   Detail the X-matrix keys.

12   The revision date for the X-matrix is recorded; this should be monthly or more often as required.

---

6. Implementation

Ultimately, it's the rubber meets the road time! The breakthrough plans are rolled out throughout the organisation. Lean is learned primarily by doing, or more precisely through repeated PDSA cycles. However, people still need supplementary training and coaching on the Lean principles, tools and methods, and the leadership required for successful application. A detailed discussion of the Lean tools and methods appears in Chapters 4 to 9. Chapter 10 deals with the important keystone of Lean leadership and cultural enrichment.

The preferred approach to training is: *learn – apply – reflect.* The appropriate tools and methods needed for the particular breakthroughs are taught in a just-in-time manner. This new learning is then applied straightaway to the implementation of a particular breakthrough. The 'reflect' element means that we study the outcomes and learning and adjust our approach for the next cycle of improvements, if and when required. This process of learning prevents the classic waste of training that happens way in advance of being needed, if indeed it is ever used at all.

Improvement muscle is required at all levels of the organisation to deliver the breakthroughs. There will be pressure to do the day-to-day job *and* to deliver the hoshin breakthroughs. Lean productivity improvements will free up people, but the tendency to make these people redundant must be resisted. This would violate the 'respect for people' pillar and kill off the likelihood of other areas making improvements. Another equally damaging impact of laying off freed up resources is that we cut the capability to release time for people to spend on improvement work. This stops the virtuous circle of Lean in its tracks. Why not use your freed up resources to create greater and greater gains, for ever, through everyday waste elimination? Note: this is another reason why you need to think about what you measure. If you (or your accountants) track labour utilisation in isolation, this may discourage taking time out for improvement as this metric will degrade. However, the increased capability of your people will actually increase efficiency in the longer term.

7. Monthly evaluation

The hoshin plans are reviewed on a monthly basis. The X-matrix and bowling charts are reviewed for exceptions (red and amber). Countermeasures are developed and rolled out to bring these back on track. The meeting is often closed with a reflection exercise. Finally, the lessons learned should be disseminated throughout the organisation.

8. Annual evaluation

The annual review is the assessment step that examines the year end results of hoshin in terms of:

- Were the breakthroughs achieved and if so are they sustainable?
- Were the action plans rolled out in an inclusive manner? Was catchball performed?
- How did the monthly review process go?
- Were the metrics adequate? What was not captured?
- Can the achieved breakthroughs be managed in future by the normal daily management process and KPIs (key performance indicators)?
- Did the hoshin process develop engaged Lean leaders at all levels?

- What Lean principles and methods were learned during the year and by whom?
- Were people overburdened with the workload?
- What can we do better for the next cycle of hoshin deployment?

A person of influential authority in the organisation should have ownership and accountability for the overall hoshin process. They are responsible for the entire rollout of the hoshin process (but not delivery of the individual breakthroughs, this is the responsibility of the local area managers) and synthesis of the documentation.

Review

There are countless examples of organisations that have jumped on the Lean 'bandwagon' and attempted to deploy Lean tools in a piecemeal fashion. Stopping to ask, 'What are we trying to accomplish?' is commonly skipped. In my experience this piecemeal approach never works in the long term, apart from some short-term, quick wins, followed by an inability to sustain the gains and continuously improve. Lean is a systematic approach to improvement where joined up thinking is required.

As Dr Deming profoundly advised us, need must drive change. The hoshin process addresses the needs of the business. It invites us to think about what we do need to change from being, towards what we do need to change to be. This requires that we examine past performance, reflect on why we are in business, what drives us and where we are going. Through numerous diagnostic methods and creative thinking we craft the near and long-term objectives that will get us there. Alignment and buy-in are nurtured throughout the organisation through the hoshin process. Hoshin packages your strategy concisely in a systems format on a single sheet so people can understand it profoundly and hence execute it successfully. Learning and adjustment are performed on the strategy on a frequent basis. This is a very different approach from the traditional practice of taking down from the top shelf a dust laden, upper management strategy once a year in order to develop the following years.

3

Value stream mapping

Introduction

Many of your business managers will probably be stunned when they are shown the initial results of the value stream mapping of your system(s). Mapping pre-Lean processes generally reveals that the actual work performed that your customers are willing to pay for is minuscule in comparison with the overall lead time to deliver your product or service. Regularly we perform more than 95% of work in our processes that adds no value to the end user. If businesses attack this 95% of non-value-added activity, enormous gains in productivity, quality, lead time and employee and customer satisfaction transpire.

A value stream is the series of activities required to produce a product or service family. Value stream mapping (VSM) is a visual method of showing both the physical and information flows in an end-to-end system or sub-system. The VSM illustrates, on one page, an 'x-ray' of the business that identifies waste and process obstacles at a glance to the trained eye.

The method is a different approach from that of studying each process independently. This practice makes improvements at the local department level but also has the potential – unintended – consequence of degrading the performance of the wider system. Taking the value stream view means looking at the big picture, not just individual processes. The objective is to improve the end-to-end system, not individual elements in isolation.

A VSM:

▪ visualises the entire product or service flow, rather than discrete processes

▪ reveals the symptoms of waste and disconnects in the value stream that are preventing flow

▪ provides a common language for improvements and helps to build consensus on real business priorities

▪ makes apparent the conditions needed to achieve process flow

▪ integrates Lean methods and tools so you can coordinate effective improvements

▪ provides the connection between information and material flow

▪ becomes a blueprint for Lean transformative change

▪ reveals hidden symptoms of larger problems – it is a diagnostic technique

▪ results in an implementation plan.

What flows in value stream maps?

In manufacturing, materials flow

In service, customer requirements flow

In software development, code flows

In healthcare, patients flow

Value stream mapping categories

There are three main types of VSMs. The map that shows the existing condition of your system is called the *current state*. The map that shows the perfect scenario is called the *ideal state*. This map is used to release improvement teams from their assumptions about what is possible. It is a 'backwards from perfect' viewpoint, and asks the team to design the perfect 'green field' situation, as if there were no constraints. The realistic or near-term vision that the team works back to is called the *future state*. This is normally a map of what the organisation wants to achieve over the next six to nine months.

Value stream mapping stages

These are:

1 Team formation
2 Create the current state value stream map
3 Create the ideal state value stream map
4 Develop the future state value stream map
5 Develop the improvement plan

1. Team formation

A core team normally assembles for up to three days to perform the value stream mapping workshop. The management team appoints the event leader and this person can be supported by an experienced external Lean coach (in the early phase of the transformation until internal capability is acquired). The size of the mapping team can range from 6–12 members depending on the scope and size of your value stream. The team's composition should be multidisciplinary, representing all the key stakeholders from the value stream under study. The inclusion of your customer in the workshop is also good practice as it is central to the Lean paradigm of viewing value through the eyes of the end user. Union participation (if applicable) in the workshop is important for building buy-in and consensus towards the process of change. All improvement means change and change is hard for many people. People support what they create. Hence if stakeholders are not a part of the solution, they will be a part of the problem! The event leader and external Lean coach as a rule facilitate the workshop, provide expertise, remove roadblocks and challenge team members' thinking and assumptions as required.

2. Create the current state value stream map

The Lean coach introduces the team to the basics of Lean and the value stream mapping methodology. The team divides into sub-teams, to study specific value stream loops and to track and visualise the physical, information and people flows.

Data collection in a busy environment is analogous to changing the fan belt while the car is still running; caution needs to be exercised so as not to interfere with the general running of the area and you need to be extra vigilant regarding safety compliance. Each area should be briefed beforehand as to what is going on and the reasons your team are performing the workshop. Generally speaking 70% data (what typically happens) accuracy is sufficient at the current state mapping stage. This enables fast collection of data on the move and more detailed data can be collected at a later stage if required. Remember that most of the current available data is on the relative minuscule 5% of value-adding activities; hence a greater opportunity lies in the obscured data for the 95% non-value-added 'white space' portion of your value stream.

Common process attribute data collected in the current state includes:

- cycle time (individual process durations)
- Lead time (equals the sum of cycle times plus delays)
- changeover time (can be physical and cognitive)
- quality data (percentage complete and accurate, defects and mistakes)
- direct and indirect labour, overruns and overtime history
- shift patterns
- split percentages (demand that diverges in the value stream to specific work centres)
- utilisation percentage (proportion of capacity used)
- DNA (did not arrive) rates (for service industry generally)
- queue times
- number of people working in each area
- travel distance (see the spaghetti diagram description in the Glossary)
- information flow (electronic, paper, verbal, visual, etc.)
- information deficits (no or poor communication, wrong information, etc.)

▓ historical demand information (demand profile over time, current numbers forecast, arrival rates and times, revisits, etc.)

▓ activity triggers (what instigates the next steps)

▓ off-the-cuff comments (can be extremely insightful and point
towards cultural issues)

▓ employee and customer satisfaction data.

Armed with cameras (a picture is worth a thousand words!), stop
watches, data collection forms, area layout plots, spaghetti diagrams
(to capture product/service and employee travel times) and waste category sheets (see Table 1.2), your team can build a rich picture of the
current state baseline.

After the data collection is complete the team generally reassembles
in a room to integrate the data onto a value stream map similar to
that shown in Figure 3.1 later in this chapter. Sticky notes written in
pencil and stuck on butcher paper or on a wall are used to construct
the map. This allows your map to be modified easily. The map can
then be transferred into electronic format as in Figure 3.1. A digital
photo can also capture the map to save time. The real purpose of
mapping is action, regardless of what form it is captured in.

It is important at this stage to restrain the team from jumping into
solution mode. The objective is to capture the 'as is' baseline snap-
shot of the existing system. Without a baseline it is impossible to
determine if things have improved in the future.

3. Create the ideal state value stream map

The ideal state value stream map shows us a blue sky view of what
we would do if we were starting over again without any resource
constraints. The intention of the exercise is to jolt people out of
their currently held beliefs about what level of improvement is possible. The Lean coach guides the team through the development of
this map by asking a series of questions about the current state map:

▓ Is the current state proficient to match customer demand?

▓ Is the customer lead time appropriate?

▪ What processes create value and which are non-value-added waste?

▪ How can we flow work with fewer stoppages?

▪ Where can we schedule the system at one point?

4. Develop the future state value stream map

After developing the ideal state map the team reconvenes to develop the future state map. The future state map is the 'backwards from perfect' approach. The objective is to examine the ideal state and formulate a map and a transformation plan that represent a realistic, but stretching, ambition to be achieved over a 6–9 month time horizon.

5. Develop the improvement plan

The improvement plan (see Figures 3.4 and 3.5 later in this chapter) is developed to deliver the future state map and it is normally integrated into the annual hoshin plan breakthrough objectives (see Chapter 2).

Case study

Outpatients' orthopaedic clinic

Global background

Healthcare is facing a stern crisis worldwide. Demand for services is increasing year on year owing to an increasing birth rate and people living longer. This is occurring while budgets and resources are being slashed. Simply put, we have to learn to do more with less or people will be denied access to healthcare.

There is another alternative to making 'cuts' in order to save money and ensure access to our nation's healthcare systems. The cure: eliminate costs that are waste (instead of *cutting value-added costs* such as closing wards, etc.), improve quality (better quality costs less) and engage frontline staff in everyday improvement. Lean supports the six dimensions of quality in healthcare, namely safety, effectiveness, patient centric care, timeliness, efficiency and equality. Lean capability is about the elegance to do more work with less, to ensure exceptional outcomes with intellect and ingenuity, not cash.

Outpatients' clinic overview

The outpatients' department has been a source of contention for some time at this hospital. In particular the orthopaedic department had been under mounting pressure to meet increasing demand. Patient satisfaction scores were at an all time low due to long wait times and the increasing frequency of sub-optimal medical outcomes. Staff morale was also extremely poor, the work environment was very stressful and nobody was getting home on time at the end of the day. Employees were too busy to step back from providing care to look at opportunities to break the vicious circle of declining performance.

An impromptu meeting by the hospital's CEO on a plane journey to a medical conference was about to change all this! He met the CEO of a medical device manufacturer who introduced him to the concept of Lean healthcare and the acclaimed benefits. At the end of the journey the hospital CEO was sold on the fact that Lean held the promise to turn around his outpatients' unit. Armed with this new knowledge he organised a pilot Lean event for the orthopaedic department, using value stream mapping as the initial improvement methodology.

Current state value stream map baseline discussion

The mapping team was assembled and mapped out the current state baseline which revealed a number of opportunities. The first experience for the patient on arrival was to wait on average 7.5 minutes at either registration or the front desk (newly referred patients must register first, 25% of the overall patient volume are first time visitors) to hand in their referral paperwork or appointment.

The data collection for the initial steps revealed two issues. Firstly there is a high historical DNA (did not arrive) rate of 25%. To counteract this potential loss of capacity the clinic deliberately overbooks by the historical DNA rate. When there are swings in this figure, chronic clinic overruns occur. The front desk resources of two receptionists are under pressure to match demand as their utilisation percentage is running at 114%. This leads to fluctuating wait times, working through breaks and frequent overtime. As the mapping team walked the process through the eyes of the patients they were surprised to observe the distance patients have to walk and that the clinic is located on two different floors. When the patients arrive on the fifth floor via the lift there is a further average waiting period of 7.5 minutes to register for the x-ray department. Errors in a patient's care plan, such as missing information on their clinical records, are commonly picked up on here. The x-ray department opens an hour later than the front desk, hence there is a large backlog of patients waiting for this service. The department is unable to catch up on this backlog throughout the day and the average wait time for diagnostic imaging is 50 minutes. There are also large overruns in the area due to the unlevelled arrival of patients and shared resources with other value streams. This is further exasperated due to the previously mentioned unsynchronised opening times with preceding processes in the clinic.

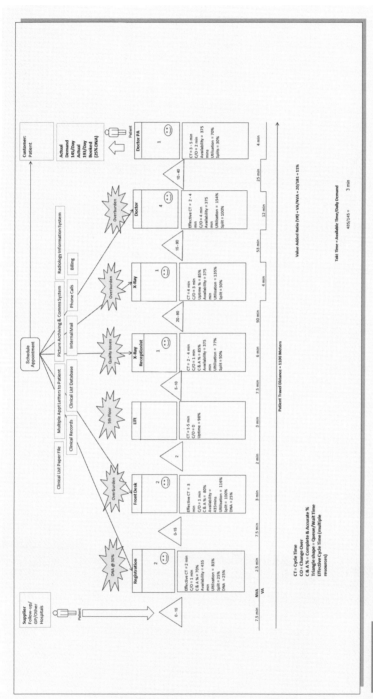

Figure 3.1   Current state value stream map

An additional average waiting time of 53 minutes to see the doctor is incurred, in large part due to poor coordination, variation in patient–doctor interaction times (complex consultations take longer) and changeover time between patients. When the patient is finished at x-ray they are free either to go or to make an additional appointment through the doctors' PA. The map also highlights the excessive travel distance of 1100 metres that mobility impaired patients walk due to the poor layout of the area. The value-added ratio for the clinic is 11%. (Note: in my experience the service value-added ratio is normally a little higher than in manufacturing.) This tells us that for the 181 minutes that the patient spends in the clinic they are receiving value-added care for just 20 minutes on average. The remainder of their time is spent either waiting for care or walking between departments.

Takt time refers to the tempo that the clinic should be operating at in order for the demand to be dealt with within the available time. The orthopaedic clinic should be discharging a patient every 3 minutes to prevent overruns and lengthy queues. Clearly the map shows that there are huge problems with meeting takt time in the current configuration due to excessive wait time and non-synchronised cycle times. The myriad information flows are detailed at the top of the map. The lines connecting each process conveys that each process is scheduled separately and without regard for the performance of upstream or downstream processes. At the end of day one of the workshop the team has built a detailed view of the current state. The current state is rarely a pretty picture and one of the key outcomes is building consensus on the problems through a common understanding of the end-to-end process. Perhaps for the first time the team sees this shared view. This helps to build tension and motivation for change.

Clinic ideal state value stream map discussion

The following questions are asked to structure the ideal state map.

1. Is the current state proficient to match the customer demand? The current state is not capable of meeting demand; clinic overruns and overtime are the norm. It is running above takt time in several processes, the worst being the doctors' consultation room. The process is currently running 54% above the available capacity.

2. Is the customer lead time appropriate? Due to the process running at overcapacity the patient lead time is excessive: the average visit lasts just over 3 hours for 20 minutes of value-added care.

3. What processes create value and which are non-value-added waste? The first three processes, namely registration, front desk and the lift, are clearly non-value-added when subjected to the following criteria:

▪ Does the process move the patient towards completion of their care plan?

▪ Is the patient willing to pay for this process?

▪ Is this process done right the first time?

The first two processes (registration and front desk) could be eliminated with a little ingenuity, such as having online web-based registration pre-visit and a new layout would eliminate the need to travel between different floors. A similar scenario could cover the requirement to register for x-ray, if the doctors' PA's work was streamlined and automated: this could be potentially merged into the doctors' consultation process.

4. How can we flow work with fewer stoppages? Figure 3.2 illustrates the ideal state map. The registration steps could be eliminated and replaced with an online system completed in advance of attendance at the clinic. The x-ray obstacle could be broken by reducing the changeover from 3 minutes to 1 minute using the SMED quick changeover methodology (see Chapter 7). The other remaining bottleneck, the doctors' consultation room, can be divided into two streams of flow. One stream would be for fast track, relatively straightforward consultations (analysis revealed 70% of overall clinic historical demand falls into this category). The other stream would be for more complicated consultations (30% of clinic demand). Streaming would eliminate the practice of a straightforward case being blocked by more complicated cases. Streaming would thus greatly increase flow in the system. The team worked on changeover time between patients in tandem with streaming. The hypothesis was that two of the four doctors from the current state could be redeployed to other value creating processes within the outpatients' department. Synchronising the doctors' start time with x-ray and running concurrent eight-hour shift patterns would also significantly facilitate flow. Astoundingly, half the physician resource would also be able to see 10% more patients per clinic without any overruns. Workplace organisation and visual management techniques, along with cellular layout within each department, would create the environment for flow through the elimination of nuisance factors such as search time and staff interruptions. Process mapping (examining all the micro steps in a specific process, see the Glossary) can be used to take a deeper dive into certain areas than the value stream map dips into. Other improvements such as sending a text message 48 hours before the patient's due arrival date would help to ease the blight of DNA failure demand (see the Glossary) and permit the clinic to be scheduled with real value demand.

5. Where can we schedule the system at one point? Scheduling at one point sets the required pace for all upstream processes. It is analogous to the accelerator pedal in your car: it either speeds up or slows down the entire system. This process is used to determine takt time, and all upstream processes are run in harmony with the pacemaker. The doctors' consultation rooms are set as the pacemaker and they regulate the entire system to enable a smooth, swift flow as patients are pulled into available processes.

Clinic future state value stream map discussion

When the team explored the ideal state they reached agreement that most of it could be implemented over the next nine months. The one exception was the relocation of the clinic onto the first floor. This proved to be too expensive in the near term: hence the ideal state was to be accepted as the future state with the exception of relocating the clinic.

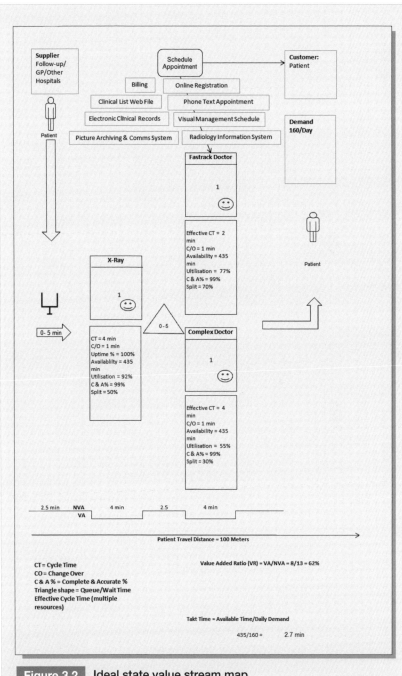

Figure 3.2 Ideal state value stream map

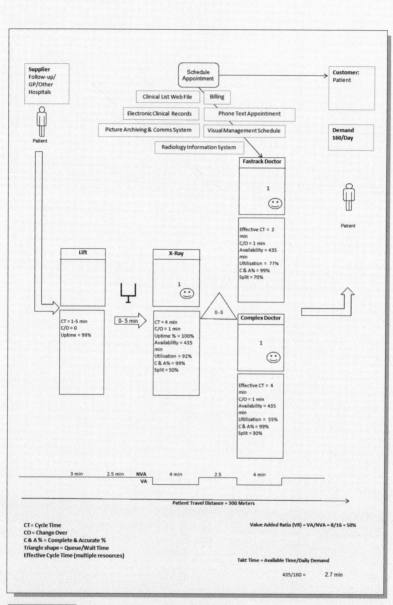

Figure 3.3   Future state value stream map

Activity	Responsible	Target Date	Comments
Management of Change Plan	RE	15 January 2012	Multiple media
Appoint Outpatients' Value Stream Manager	AB	30 January 2012	Overall responsibility for flow across departments
On-line Registration System	JT	01 February 2012	Leverage existing software used in pediatrics outpatients clinic
On-line Registration Education Material	AK	28 February 2012	Public awareness campaign, also onsite internet booking portal
Doctor/Personal Assistant Streamline Kaizen Event	TR	01 March 2012	Redeploy PA to Lean Promotion Office (LPO)
X-ray SMED Methodology	TT	15 March 2012	Reduce changeover by 75%
Introduce Patient Streaming	BG	15 April 2012	Visit pilot site to capture learning's
Test pre-48 hour clinic attendance text message	HS	30 April 2012	Integrate with current master scheduling software
Install pacemaker scheduling	WE	15 May 2012	Turn off point scheduling per department
Roll out 5S Workplace Organisation	RF	15 June 2012	Save one hour per employee/shift
Apply Visual Management Plan	IY	15 August 2012	Integrate with daily problem solving teams
Level Load Arrivals	WS	15 September 2012	Current state majority of patients arrive in batches making flow worse
Yokoten (sharing)	AB	25 September 2012	Spread the gains to two additional outpatient clinics using PDSA
After Action Review	RE	30 September 2012	What went well? What can we improve for the next cycle of yokoten?

Figure 3.4   Value stream improvement plan

Box Score

Metric	Current State	Ideal State	Future State	Future State % Improvement
Patient Volume	145	160	160	10%
Lead Time (mins)	181	13	24	754%
Value Add Ratio %	12	62	50	416%
Hours Worked	12	8	8	33%
# of People	11	3	3	366%
Patients Travel Distance (meters)	1100	100	300	366%
Capital Spend	As Is	£100,000	£5,000	N/A
Overtime Hrs/Year	2200	0	0	N/A
Revenue/Year	£253,000	£280,000	£280,000	10%
Revenue/Employee	£23,000	£93,333	£93,333	400%
Employee Engagement Score %	45	N/A	85	40%
Patient Satisfaction Score %	40	N/A	90	50%
Quality %	70	N/A	99	29%

Figure 3.5 Value stream box score

Box score discussion

The box score details the dramatic gains that are possible through successful application of Lean. Event type workshops such as value stream mapping lead to focused bursts of improvement that can deliver you sizeable gains in a short period. As can be seen from the box score for the clinic, future state, lead time has been reduced by more than seven times, travel distance has been reduced by more than three times, and productivity has been improved by a similar amount. These are truly striking one-off improvements to demonstrate a success-ful proof-of-concept for Lean. However, the greater gains will be realised not only by sustaining the current process but also by cultivating the shared culture where daily improvement becomes the new norm. Lean is a mixture of everyday incre-mental improvements that compounds into substantial long-term gains.

The seminal work of George Stalk and Thomas Hout[1] demonstrated the return on investment via the compression of lead time in busi-ness. They developed the 1/4:2:20 rule. This rule states that if you quarter your lead time you will double productivity and take 20% off your cost base. Clearly these scores, where the team has slashed the lead time more than seven times, will have a fantastic impact on both productivity and cost.

Review

Improving the capability of individual processes in isolation rather than end-to-end capability improvement is still all too common-place. Companies traditionally expend most of their resources improving the 5% or so of value-adding processes (think making an x-ray machine cycle faster) rather than going after the 95% waste (think waiting time, hand-offs, searching, walking, etc.). This is a large paradigm shift to make. The value stream mapping approach is a great mechanism to demonstrate the potential for improvement in all pre-Lean systems. It provides a common language and data for all to see. Some value streams can be quite complex and proc-ess multiple mixed products or services. Textbooks and case studies (including this one) are normally too simplistic to cover all com-plexities that arise from your own organisation's unique needs and process intricasies. However, the principles remain the same and the major learning and improvements come from the detailed dialogues that the mapping process stimulates.

Lean transformation practices

This part discusses the core Lean methods and tools that are used approximately 80% of the time by organisations on the Lean transformation journey. The top level methods illustrated are:

- 5S workplace organisation
- Visual management
- A3 problem solving
- Standard work
- Idea management system
- Kaizen
- Quick changeover
- Total productive maintenance
- Kanban
- Poka yoke
- Flow practices

(Many tools are nested within each individual method.)

4

Lean methods and tools (part I)

This chapter discusses 5S workplace organisation in Section 1 and visual management in Section 2.

SECTION 1: 5S WORKPLACE ORGANISATION

Introduction

5S is on the surface level a housekeeping practice, a deep spring clean. Untidy and cluttered workplaces are less productive. However, the deeper aim of 5S is to develop a team member's awareness and responsibility of normal and abnormal conditions in their immediate work area. It enables people to see problems and waste as soon as they surface and facilitates root cause problem solving. 5S creates the environment for Lean and supports many of its methods, for example standardised work depends on having equipment and tools always in the same place. 5S is, in essence, a visual communication of the workplace status. 5S also becomes an ongoing practice to help your people think about how their work area is laid out and arranged, and for them to act on all the small things that can make it better, safer, more ergonomic and easier to work in.

5S is a common starting point on the Lean journey as it is very employee centric and improvements are quickly visible. Jane Norman of Profound Knowledge Products Inc. uses the analogy of mowing the lawn to describe the impact of 5S: an immediate and distinct improvement in the work environment. Organisations that have successfully applied 5S are proud to have visitors tour their pristine facilities and learn from them.

Consequences of disorganised workplaces include:

- safety risks due to physical obstacles and concealed hazards
- lost time searching for materials and equipment
- defects and equipment breakdowns resulting from contaminated surroundings
- incorrect deliveries
- difficulty in distinguishing between what is and is not needed and in identifying problems.

The 5Ss are:

- **Sort** (remove all items and general clutter not used in the area)
- **Set-in-order** (arrange items so they can be found when needed within 30 seconds)
- **Shine** (clean and inspect the workplace and equipment to uncover issues and prevent problems)
- **Standardise** (make an organised workplace the norm for the area)
- **Sustain** (conduct audits to ensure continuous improvement and the prevention of back sliding).

In my experience, 5S that is well structured and supported is one of the most powerful methods for delivering a positive return on investment. This is because every one of your employees performs thousands of tasks every week in each of their areas, and seconds saved from wasted work such as searching, duplication and walking add significantly to the bottom line. These small savings grow appreciably when multiplied by hundreds of people on the shop/office floor each day of the year.

Waste (symptom) and 5S countermeasures

The potency of 5S is in attacking the sources of waste:

Waste (symptom)	An example of a 5S countermeasure
Transport	Locate equipment at point of use
Inventory	Inventory reduced on line due to kanban (see Chapter 8) racking
Motion	'Treasure hunts' for missing tools eliminated with shadow boards
Waiting	Machine changeover time is reduced with tool colour coding (set-in-order)
Over-production	Floor 'footprints' and visual management to prevent overbuild
Over-processing	Status of product at each stage is evident and handled only once
Defects	Abnormal conditions are surfaced in real time
Design	Changeover clamps are painted yellow to deter from leaving behind in the press
Overhead	Facility floor space is better utilised (less in-progress inventory)
Energy	Air leaks repaired during third S (shine)
Safety	5S is major safety enabler – loose cables, trip hazards, etc.
Ideas	Employees come up with ideas to remove waste
Technology	Find any file in your PC in 30 seconds! 5S is virtual here – think about the cost spent searching hard drives for files in your facility every day

How to apply 5S workplace organisation

Before rolling out 5S it is good practice to meet the work team in the pilot area. Start by asking what has wasted people's time over the past week. This will help people to connect with the benefits of 5S because it will be linked with the objectives of the organisation and identify with employee hassle factors such as searching for tools or continually solving the same problem day after day for the past 10 years! People will accept change when they are involved in the decisions and the outcomes are meaningful to them. This is no different with 5S.

Select a 5S champion who will drive the pilot rollout and prove the concept prior to a more extensive rollout. All employees in the area are given an overview of what 5S is and what deliverables are expected. The 5S champion and a small group of frontline employees conduct a baseline 5S audit and take photographs capturing the condition of the workplace at this precise time.

Sort

5S veterans will attest that approximately a third of items in any pre-Lean workplace are not required or are just general clutter or rubbish. The sort stage will address these excess items.

Unnecessary items are red tagged as a visual control cue that they are to be moved out to an interim holding area. The team will later make a decision on the items in this area. This approach encourages people to be ruthless about moving stuff out as the interim holding area provides a safety net. If the team decides that an item is needed again it can be returned. It is also a control against throwing out business critical items. Items are logged by an appointed person on a red tag log sheet (see Figure 4.1) at the red tag holding area, in real time, and an estimate of cost is recorded. Later this sheet is updated with the disposition decision.

A word of caution on sort: people's personal items are a sensitive issue, so adhere to the 'respect for people' pillar here. It will enable hoarders to move out more excess items in the long run. Examine the workplace three dimensionally, ground, walls and ceilings, and categorise all items in the area under one of the following classifications:

- excess (move out to the red tag holding area)
- obsolete (move out to the red tag holding area)
- defective (move out to the red tag holding area)
- not needed in the area (move out to the red tag holding area)
- used every day (store at point of use or carry with you)

Red Tag Log Sheet

Tag #	Description	Qty	Est € Value	Where	Reason Tagged	Disposition
1	Chairs	6	100	Office	Not needed	Use Elsewhere
2	6 x 7 Table	1	50	Office	Not needed	Use Elsewhere
3	Coat Hanger	1	10	Office	Not needed	Donate to Charity
4	Table Stool	1	20	Office	Not needed	Donate to Charity
5	Table 6 x 3	1	50	Stationary Room	Not needed	Use Elsewhere
6	Leather Chair	3	240	Office	Not needed	Donate to Charity
7	Step Ladder	1	20	Office	Not needed	Donate to Charity
8	Office Chair	2	50	Office	Not needed	Donate to Charity
9	Office Chair	1	25	Office	Not needed	Donate to Charity
10	Lockable Pedal Bin	2	120	Office	Not needed	Donate to Charity
11	File Box	1	0	Office	Not needed	Scrap
12	Oil Heaters	2	100	Office	Not needed	Central Storage
13	A3 Paper	5 Reams	50	Office	Not needed	Donate to Charity
14	Plastic Kanban Bin	1	25	Office	Not needed	Back to Stock
15	Copy Holders	2	20	Office	Not needed	Donate to Charity
16	Magazine Rack	1	5	Office	Not needed	Donate to Charity
17	Window Blinds	1	50	Office	Not needed	Scrap
18	Letter Trays	3	15	Office	Not needed	Donate to Charity
19	Screw Driver	1	5	Office	Not needed	Donate to Charity
20	Tape Gun	1	5	Office	Scrap	Central Storage
21	Heavy Duty Stapler	1	10	Office	Wrong Place	Donate to Charity
22	Pedestals	2	300	Office	Not needed	Use Elsewhere
23	Office Desk Dividers	1	40	Office	Not needed	Scrap
24	2011 Diaries	6	60	Office	Not needed	Scrap
25	High Vis Vest	40	80	Office	Not needed	Use Elsewhere
26	Lockers	3	150	Office	Not needed	Use Elsewhere
27	Floppy Drives	2	50	Office	Not needed	Scrap
28	Keyboard	6	120	Office	Not needed	Use Elsewhere
29	Printers	4	600	Office	Broken	Use Elsewhere
30	Speakers	5	50	Office	Not needed	Use Elsewhere
31	Monitors	4	400	Office	Not needed	Use Elsewhere
32	PC	5	1000	Office	Not needed	Use Elsewhere
33	Printer	1	20	Office	Not needed	Scrap
34	Mouse	3	30	Office	Not needed	Scrap
35	Brackets	18	180	Warehouse	Not needed	Scrap
36	Scanner Adapters	10	150	Warehouse	Not needed	Scrap
37	Telephone	1	25	Warehouse	Not needed	Scrap
38	Filing Cabinet	1	150	Warehouse	Not needed	Use Elsewhere
39	Laser Printer	1	200	Warehouse	Broken	Scrap
40	Paper Feeder	2	300	Warehouse	Obsolete	Scrap
41	Spot Light	1	10	Warehouse	Not needed	Scrap
42	Letter Tray	1	1	Warehouse	Not needed	Donate to Charity
43	Folder	1	1	Warehouse	Not needed	Scrap
44	Hand Sanitiser	5	50	Warehouse	Not needed	Central Storage
45	Steel Pole	1	0	Warehouse	Not needed	Scrap
46	Flip Board	1	1	Warehouse	Not needed	Central Storage
47	Kodak Developer	6	100	Warehouse	Not needed	Scrap
48	Box Rubber Bands	1	5	Warehouse	Not needed	Central Storage
49	Hand Truck	1	150	Warehouse	Broken	Repair
50	Lever Arch File	10	10	Warehouse	Not needed	Scrap
51	Laser Printer	1	150	Warehouse	Broken	Scrap
52	Stock Samples	1	50	Warehouse	Not needed	Scrap
53	CC TV Signage	15	75	Warehouse	Not Used	Hang Up
54	Fan	3	75	Warehouse	Not Used	Central Storage
55	Paper Shredder	1	100	Warehouse	Broken	Scrap
56	Phone Charger	1	5	Warehouse	Not needed	Recycle
57	Post-it Note Dispenser	1	5	Warehouse	Not needed	Scrap
58	Date Stamp	5	50	Warehouse	Not needed	Scrap
59	USB Cable	2	10	Warehouse	Not needed	Scrap
60	Floppy Drive	7	175	Warehouse	Not needed	Scrap
61	Cable	5	20	Warehouse	Not needed	Scrap
62	Gloves	1 Box	5	Warehouse	Not needed	Back to Stores
63	Phone	1	40	Warehouse	Not needed	Recycle
64	Notice Board	1	10	Warehouse	Broken	Scrap
65	Safety Pins	1 Box	30	Warehouse	Not used anymore	Scrap
66	Letter Holder	1	2	Warehouse	Not used anymore	Donate to Charity
67	Bulbs	12	12	Warehouse	Not used anymore	Scrap
68	Tray	1	1	Warehouse	Not needed	Donate to Charity
69	Pen Knife	1	2	Warehouse	Not needed	Scrap
70	Pen	20	10	Warehouse	Excess	Donate to Charity
71	PC Wipes	1 Box	10	Warehouse	Not used	Donate to Charity
72	Moisture Dispenser	2	20	Warehouse	Not used	Use elsewhere
73	Roll of cotton	1	10	Warehouse	Not needed	Donate to Charity

Figure 4.1 Red tag log sheet example

74	Index Book	1	10	Warehouse	Not needed	Donate to Charity
75	Fire extinguisher	1	50	Warehouse	Excess	Central Storage
76	USB Cable	1	2	Warehouse	Not needed	Scrap
77	Exit Sign	1	2	Warehouse	Not needed	Scrap
78	Notice Board	1	20	Warehouse	Excess	Donate to Charity
79	Christmas Decorations	5 Boxes	100	Warehouse	Used once per year	Central Storage
80	Oil Heater	1	50	Warehouse	Excess	Central Storage
81	Hand Foam Sanitizer	6	150	Warehouse	Excess	Use elsewhere
82	Gauze	1 Box	12	Warehouse	Excess	Scrap
83	Safety Boots	2	60	Warehouse	Excess	Scrap
84	Toner refill	1	50	Warehouse	Excess	Use Elsewhere
85	Fill SCHCID 46727	9	100	Warehouse	Excess	Back to Stock
86	Samsung Flat Screen	1	100	Warehouse	Not needed	Central Storage
87	Fuji Base & Monitor	1	100	Warehouse	Excess	Central Storage
88	Dell Monitor and Base(new)	1	500	Warehouse	Excess	Central Storage
89	Fire Assembly Sign	1	5	Warehouse	Excess	Scrap
90	IBM cartilages 38L1410	1	50	Warehouse	Excess	Central Storage
91	HP Laser 0923215 cartilages	1	50	Warehouse	Excess	Central Storage
92	Roll of labels	40	120	Warehouse	Excess	Scrap
93	Brother printer & fax	1	200	Warehouse	Not needed	Scrap
94	Signage	7	7	Warehouse	Excess	Scrap
95	Larynascope	1	100	Warehouse	Damaged	Scrap
96	Mop head	1	2	Warehouse	Not needed	Donate to Charity
97	Anti Glare Sign	1	5	Warehouse	Not needed	Scrap
98	Aluminum Picture Frame	2	10	Warehouse	Not needed	Donate to Charity
99	Calculator	1	10	Warehouse	Excess	Donate to Charity
100	Staples	10	50	Warehouse	Not needed	Recycle
101	Stapler	1	3	Warehouse	Excess	Donate to Charity
102	Large Paper Clips	200	20	Warehouse	Not used	Donate to Charity
103	Pen Holder	2	2	Warehouse	Not needed	Donate to Charity
104	Phone	7	60	Warehouse	Not needed	Recycle
105	Paper punch	7	70	Warehouse	Not needed	Central Storage
106	Folders	2	2	Warehouse	Not needed	Scrap
107	Carbon Paper	2	2	Warehouse	Not used	Scrap
108	Type writer	1	30	Warehouse	Not used	Scrap
109	Copy Holders	1	1	Warehouse	Not used	Donate to Charity
110	Laser Labels	12	60	Warehouse	Not used	Scrap
111	Telephone message pad	1	2	Warehouse	Not used	Scrap
112	Steel fixings	1 Box	50	Warehouse	Not needed	Scrap
113	Labels	4 Boxes	60	Warehouse	Not needed	Scrap
114	Bin		20	Warehouse	Not used	Scrap
115	Safety Boots	2	60	Warehouse	Excess	Scrap
116	Hand Truck	1	100	Warehouse	Broken	Repair
117	Old files	1 pallet	0	Warehouse	Obsolete	Shredder
118	Wire basket	1	5	Warehouse	Not needed	Donate to Charity
119	Heavy Duty Stapler	1	10	Warehouse	Not played anymore	Donate to Charity
120	PC Base	1	50	Warehouse	Not needed	Central Storage
121	Dot matrix printer	1	100	Warehouse	Obsolete	Scrap
122	Clip board	3	3	Warehouse	Donate to Charity	Charity
123	Dividers Pack	1	2	Warehouse	Excess	Donate to Charity
124	Kanban Cards	9 Packs	200	Warehouse	Excess	Back to hospital stores
125	Toilet descaler	12	60	Warehouse	Excess	Central Storage
126	Safety boots	1	30	Warehouse	Used	Scrap
127	Road hazard triangle	1	50	Warehouse	Not used	Scrap
128	Road Salt	2	20	Warehouse	Used in winter only	Central Storage
129	Dressings	1	30	Warehouse	Move out	Scrap
130	Castors	3	30	Warehouse	Excess	Scrap
131	Wall Rack	1	20	Warehouse	Not needed	Scrap
132	Ruler	7	4	Warehouse	Excess	Donate to Charity
133	Scissors	3	6	Warehouse	Excess	Donate to Charity
134	Floppy Drive	1	25	Warehouse	Obsolete	Scrap
135	Oxygen flow meter	1	100	Warehouse	Obsolete	Scrap
136	Blood pressure monitor	2	50	Warehouse	Obsolete	Scrap
137	Ball of string	1	2	Warehouse	Not used in area	Scrap
138	Safety Pins	2 Boxes	20	Warehouse	Not used in area	Back to stock
139	Black bags	4 rolls	10	Warehouse	Not used in area	Central Storage
		Total Value	**€ 9,354.00**			

Figure 4.1 Continued

- used about once a week (store where it can be located within 30 seconds)
- rarely used but needed (store off-line and label it for ease of retrieval)
- rarely used (store off-line and label for ease of retrieval or dispose of if cheaper)
- not known if needed (move out to red tag holding area).

Set-in-order

The objective of this phase is to arrange the remaining items so that they can be easily found and are in locations where they are needed to facilitate the smooth flow of work. Floor areas can be marked and labelled with stencilling to outline equipment and material 'home' locations (see Figure 4.2). Signage can also be suspended from the ceiling with strong fishing line to identify drop locations or kit locations, etc. Aisles and other location zones can be demarcated with colour coding using industrial grade floor tape or line paint marking machines.

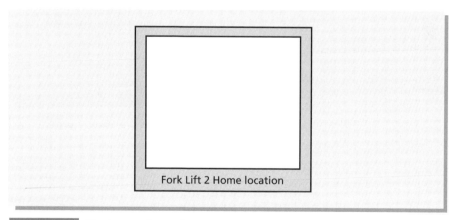

Fork Lift 2 Home location

Figure 4.2 Equipment home locations

Shadow boards are a very simple visual control that allow people to have easy access to the tools that they need to do their jobs. An outline of the tool or supply is drawn on a board and the tool or supply is attached with Velcro® or similar. If a tool is missing it is obvious. Some of the benefits of maintaining shadow boards include:

- time is not lost looking for equipment and parts; quick retrieval of tools is necessary for the job
- frustration of missing/no tools no longer affects employees, hence morale is improved
- makes it easy to see if parts are missing/worn out as it is a visual tool
- tools last longer (they are not misplaced or go missing)
- pressure is applied to replace missing/worn out tools, as it is obvious there is a deficiency
- clears up clutter and gives the workplace a tidy and orderly look, and improves safety
- financial savings as equipment does not need to be replaced as often
- a complement to high productivity (eliminates 'treasure hunts' for equipment) and quality (using correct tools/jigs, etc.).

However, all the above benefits are lost if boards are not maintained by all employees. Later, in Chapter 11, we discuss the Lean management system that enables Lean methods and tools such as shadow boards to be sustained.

Shine

Lean views cleaning as inspection or looking for non-conformances. When you wash and shine your car you notice if there is any damage or minor imperfections. The same philosophy applies to workplace equipment and products. Work teams should establish 5–10 minute routines for cleaning up every day. A deep clean can be performed periodically to restore areas to a pristine level. Teams also perform 'visual sweeping' to look for sort and set-in-order status. Refurbishment and painting are also often carried out during the shine phase.

The quality of an organisation's products or services is strongly mirrored by the condition of the workplace. 5S creates the environment

5S Cleaning Schedule (examples below for illustration only)

No.	5S Job	Sort	Set-in-order	Shine	Standardise	Sustain	Job Cycle A	B	C	D	E	F
1	Remove pallet/box over wrap @ put away	■				■	■					
2	Remove all strapping @ put away	■				■	■					
3	Sweep aisle ways with scissor brush			■					■			
4	Dust racking shelves			■						■		
5	Sweep under racking			■							■	
6	Remove Excess items to permanent Red-tag-cage	■				■	■					
7	Complete Red-tag Event										■	
8	Empty cardboard/plastic/strapping cages or bins				■			■				
9	Compact cardboard		■					■				
10	Bale plastic		■					■				

Job Cycle Code
A: Continuously
B: Daily (mornings)
C: Daily (evenings)
D: Weekly
E: Monthly
F: Occasionally

Figure 4.3 Cleaning schedule example

for excellence. Morale and stress will also be greatly improved in post-5S environments along with employee involvement in continuous improvement. It is unlikely that employees will step forward with ideas for improvement if their work environment is in disarray.

Standardise

You deploy standardise to ensure best practice in the sort, set-in-order and shine activities. A cleaning schedule is developed to make daily cleaning systematic and to put cleaning on the same stage as making the operational numbers. A sample cleaning schedule is shown in Figure 4.3.

Leader standard work is the glue that keeps 5S (and all the Lean methods) from falling apart and becoming another fad of the month. This forms a central element of the Lean management system discussed in detail in Chapter 11. Roles and responsibilities are cascaded down by level in a collaborative fashion. The 'who', 'what', 'why' and 'when' are detailed (see the hospital example in Table 4.1). The 'why' or purpose of any activity is particularly important. A good example from a hospital is cleaning: are we cleaning rooms or preventing infection? Bring out into the open the purpose of people's work to drive people's intrinsic motivation to improve.

Table 4.1 Leader standard work for 5S (leaders exist throughout the organisation)

Who	What	Why	When
Ward Sister	Assign owners to 5S weekly audit actions	Track audit trend & continuously improve	Wednesday @ 12 pm
	5S status and improvement actions @ shift handover	Sustained progress	7.30 am Daily
	Office 5S champion	Mirror ward progress	Weekly on Mondays @ 10

Who	What	Why	When
Charge Nurse	Conduct weekly audit	Track audit Trend and continuously improve	Wednesdays @ 11 am
	Maintain monthly before & after photos	Promotes improvements implemented	4th week of month
	Train & teach all staff on Lean/5S philosophy	Incorporates into normal work culture	Continuously
Staff Nurses and area champions	Return equipment to 'home' locations when finished	Prevents backsliding	Continually
	Maintain and repair 5S labels etc. as required	Makes job easier	Continuous
	Action assigned activities from audits as appropriate	Prevents backsliding	Weekly
	Implement improvement opportunities	Improves ward performance	As appropriate
	Complete zone daily task checklists	Prevents ward workplace deterioration	Daily
Nurse Auxiliaries	Return equipment to 'home' locations when finished	Prevents backsliding	Continually
	Maintain and repair 5S labels etc. as required	Makes job easier	Continuous
	Action assigned activities from audits as appropriate	Prevents backsliding	Weekly

Who	*What*	*Why*	*When*
Nurse Auxiliaries (cont)	Implement improvement opportunities	Improves ward/ performance	As appropriate
	Complete zone daily task checklists	Prevents ward/ workplace deterioration	Daily
Patient experience	Return equipment to 'home' locations when finished	Prevents backsliding	Continually
	Maintain and repair 5S labels etc. as required	Makes job easier	Continuous
	Action assigned activities from audits as appropriate	Prevents backsliding	Weekly
	Implement improvement opportunities	Improves ward performance	As appropriate

Sustain

The final 'S' is the element that enables stability and further continuous improvement. The audit detailed in Table 4.2 conducted on a weekly basis highlights that non-conformances, along with countermeasures, should be driven through the 5S storyboard (see Figure 4.4). To compare the before and after conditions of your workplace, photographs should be taken monthly and compared with the previous month's photos. This will visually demonstrate improvement or deterioration. A permanent red tag area is helpful so that unneeded items can be removed on the go and not just in periodic clean-ups. This prevents the rebuilding of clutter. 5S supplies such as tapes, stencils, cameras and signage materials should also have their own readily accessible home location (see Figure 4.5). The supervisors of each area are a critical resource in driving and sustaining the 5S improvement agenda and for making time for 5S. The 5S storyboard

Table 4.2 5S audit

Rating	Sort	Set-in-order	Shine	Standardise	Sustain
5	There is evidence that team members by themselves are red tagging on a daily basis	There is evidence of everyday improvement for storing items and tools etc.	Problems uncovered through shine are captured & auctioned in the visual mgt area	5S improvements are reflected in the workplace employee engagement scores	# of problems solved to root cause per month from 5S is tracked
4	Virtual red tagging has been performed on PCs	Floor markings, signage, shadow boards are in place where needed and maintained	Visual sweeping captures non conformance in sort and set-in-order with countermeasures	5S is integrated in management and team gemba walks	Recognition system is in place for performance excellence in 5S
3	There is an active process in place for red tagging 'in real time'	Min and max quantities have been identified and visually controlled	The cleaning schedule is visibly displayed at the workstations	Leader standard work is in place for 5S and is followed at all levels	5S audit is performed weekly and posted on the 5S storyboard and actions are countermeasured
2	Excess items have been red tagged and removed to disposition area	Needed items are stored at point of use and visually controlled, including 5S items such as tapes, etc.	The cleaning schedule is followed by all team members, cleaning stations are in place	5S storyboard is in place, up to date, and team stand-ups occur there	Area champions have been appointed and roles are being carried out
1	The area is badly cluttered with excess items	Items are haphazardly placed throughout the workplace	The odd spring-clean occurs but not systematically	There are no routines practised daily to maintain an organised workplace	Monthly before and after photos are taken and displayed on the 5S storyboard

should be the nerve centre of sustaining the gains. This is where the monthly before and after photos are displayed, area champions are recognised and audit activity is tracked (see Figure 4.4).

It is when things are busiest and people are under pressure that compliance with 5S is most important. It facilitates smooth work flow and prevents problems. Dr Maxwell Maltz in his groundbreaking book *Psycho-Cybernetics*[1] noted that it took 21 days for amputees to stop feeling phantom sensations in an amputated limb. From further research he found it took 21 days to create new habits in general. Therefore the first month or so of a newly rolled out initiative needs strong and visible management support to hardwire the newly required behaviours.

5S review

As with Lean, 5S never ends. If it takes people more than a few seconds to find something, your employees should ask themselves 'Why?'. A decade after Toyota's Kentucky plant began 5S training management say that employees are still coming up with approximately 6,500 5S ideas alone each year. The beauty of problems discovered via 5S is that they are usually implemented quickly (as they are small problems) and have a positive effect on employee irritations. Productivity is also greatly improved. For example post-5S activity shadow results from the nursing profession reveal that between 1–2 hours of time can be released back to caring at the bedside per nurse per shift.

5S improves morale and ownership of the workplace, encourages involvement and continuous improvements. 5S mitigates what is referred to in the field of social science as the 'broken windows theory'. Once one window in a derelict house is broken, soon they are all broken due to the abandonment perception. You can observe the same effect when streets start to be littered at large social occasions, etc. The same applies to our workplaces and 5S is the countermeasure. 5S hits all four True North metrics. The subtle hidden benefit of 5S is that it builds discipline – the discipline to lay the foundations for excellence – and Lean is all about disciplined execution of the basics, just like any good team in sport.

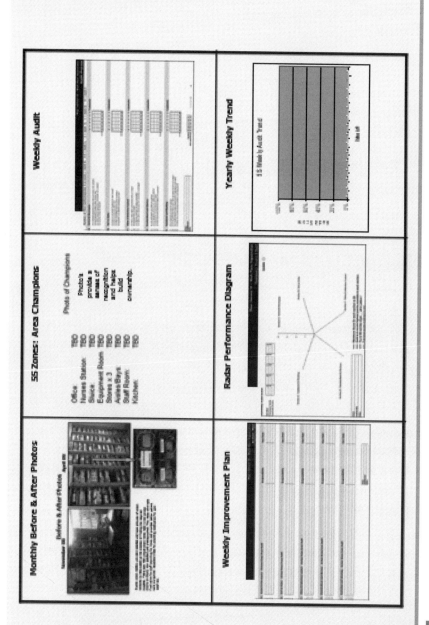

Figure 4.4   Paediatric Ward 5S: workplace organisation storyboard in office

```
┌─────────────────────────────────────────────────┐
│      5S Items for Sustaining Workplace Organisation │
│                                                   │
│                   Red Paper                       │
│                  Yellow Paper                     │
│                Double Sided Tape                  │
│                 Insulation Tape                   │
│               A4 Plastic Laminates                │
│                    Velcro                         │
│                Thermal Laminator                  │
│                  Audit Sheets                     │
│                  Stencil Set                      │
│  Floor Tape (blue, red, green, yellow, and black & amber) │
└─────────────────────────────────────────────────┘
```

Figure 4.5   Sustain equipment home location

SECTION 2: VISUAL MANAGEMENT

Introduction

One hallmark of managing in a Lean culture is quick response to deviations from the standard process. Two elements are required to realise this in the workplace: a defined, agreed upon standard (that works well and is followed by all) and a method to quickly determine departures from that standard. This is the purpose of visual management.

With visual management, a quick walk through the workplace is all that is needed to determine the status of the area – is it a good day, a bad day – and if intervention is required. Hence organisations must strive to design a workplace that almost talks to you, one where problems become immediately apparent.

By responding to issues at the time they occur and asking 'Why?' five times (more or less), root cause(s) can be quickly identified. The causal trail is still warm and process corrections can be made relatively quickly before the problem escalates.

About 80% of our brains is dedicated to visual processing. We need to recognise and incorporate this fact into our workplace design. A visual workplace is devised of mechanisms that are purposely created to communicate information at a glance and without the need for verbal intervention. An example of visual management is the departure screen at an airport. Visual systems can share information not just through the sense of sight, but also through sound, touch, smell and taste. In tandem with 5S (5S prepares the way to workplace transparency), visual management lays the foundation so that the basics are performed flawlessly. Without the basics, operational excellence is unattainable.

To create a visual workplace you need to ask:

■ What decisions do employees need to make?

■ What do they need to know in the area to make those decisions?

■ What would an employee need to know if it was their first day working in the area?

The deliberate design of the workplace removes the need for decision making based on unspoken tacit knowledge. It is proven that the fewer decisions a person has to make whilst performing a job, the fewer mistakes are likely to occur due to reduced ambiguity and cognitive workload.[2]

To check if a workplace is satisfactorily designed from a visual management perspective you could ask if a stranger could walk into the workplace and be up to speed with the workings of the area within five minutes.

Examples of good visual management include: transparent machine covers and guards, colour coding, floor marking to designate areas for different tasks, shadow boards for supplies and tools, work team storyboards with charts and metrics, location signage and equipment labels.

Why use visual management?

The purpose of visual management is:

■ to make problems immediately visible

■ to prevent having to ask avoidable questions

■ to enable somebody to see if things are missing

■ to help workers and management stay in contact

■ to clarify targets for improvement

- to promote communication (from my experience communication is one of the major root causes of defects and errors)
- to promote employee involvement and inclusion through maintaining the visuals
- to reduce errors (well-designed systems reduce baseline error rates by approximately one third)
- to reduce search time in the workplace
- to make everyone's jobs easier and less stressful
- to recognise achievements and improvements.

Levels of visual management

There are four levels of visual management, each level building on the ones below.

Table 4.3 Four levels of visual management

4. Visual management (sustaining levels 1–3)	Daily practice of the three techniques below to manage the workplace and quickly detect issues, hence triggering root cause problem solving.
3. Visual controls (defect prevention)	To detect abnormal conditions at a glance before they become a defect. Examples include floor marking and signage to outline locations, mistake proofing devices (think three-pin plug), production status andon systems (refer to the Glossary), and colour coding.
2. Visual display (information sharing)	All the information for workplace decision making such as standards and status storyboards are available at a glance and kept up to date.
1. 5S workplace organisation (process transparency)	Area is designed for optimum performance, safety and immediate exposure of non-conformances.

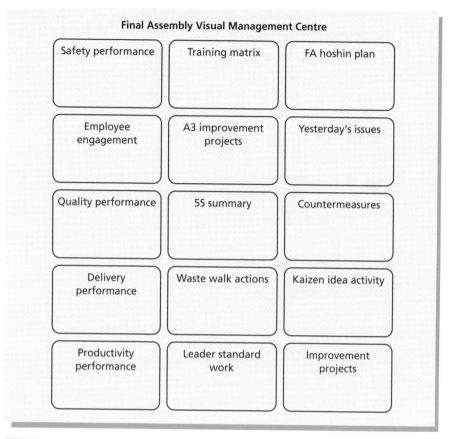

Figure 4.6 Visual management centre

Visual management centre (VMC)

A VMC (see Figure 4.6) is the central repository of the visual displays in the workplace. The purpose of the VMC is so that anyone in the workplace, even those who are unfamiliar with the detail of the processes, can rapidly see what is going on, and distinguish what is, and is not, under control.

You can use the VMC in your organisation to:

▪ be the focus area for your daily stand-up meetings to understand and indicate work priorities

▪ see whether daily, weekly and monthly performance metrics are on or off track

▪ identify abnormalities or when something is going wrong or not happening in your workplace

▪ display hoshin kanri (refer to Figure 2.3) plans, A3 problem-solving activity (covered in Chapter 5), leader standard work (see Chapter 11), waste walk activity (see Chapters 1 and 11), 5S audit, skills versatility matrix, etc.

▪ communicate to everyone what performance measures are in place

▪ provide real-time feedback on all aspects of your workplace performance

▪ cut down on ad hoc meetings to discuss work issues.

VMC success factors include: a daily assessment of information; timely problem resolution; and an identification of the drivers behind the numbers.

Operational tracking at the gemba

Operational tracking at the gemba refers to visual display of real-time, manually updated records of the actual outcomes from a process versus the defined target performance level. An example is shown in Figure 4.7 where actual production numbers are entered on an hourly basis in the columns corresponding to each day of the week. When the number is below (or indeed above) the target the reasons for this are recorded. This then triggers real-time problem solving and countermeasures to correct problems. This board is updated by the frontline staff running the process and provides both a tempo to the work environment and a mechanism for employees to highlight problems that are hindering them in achieving their target numbers.

A useful template, illustrated in Table 4.4, can be used to audit the level of visual management in your own workplace and address any gaps.

Time	Target	Monday		Tuesday		Wednesday		Thursday		Friday	
		ACTUAL	REASON	ACTUAL	REASON	ACTUAL	REASON	ACTUAL	REASON	ACTUAL	REASON
8:00 - 9:00	7	ACTUAL	REASON	ACTUAL	REASON	ACTUAL	REASON	ACTUAL	REASON	ACTUAL	REASON
9:00 - 10:00	11	ACTUAL	REASON	ACTUAL	REASON	ACTUAL	REASON	ACTUAL	REASON	ACTUAL	REASON
10:00 - 11:00	11	ACTUAL	REASON	ACTUAL	REASON	ACTUAL	REASON	ACTUAL	REASON	ACTUAL	REASON
11:00 - 12:00	11	ACTUAL	REASON	ACTUAL	REASON	ACTUAL	REASON	ACTUAL	REASON	ACTUAL	REASON
12:00 - 1:00	11	ACTUAL	REASON	ACTUAL	REASON	ACTUAL	REASON	ACTUAL	REASON	ACTUAL	REASON
1:00 - 2:00	6	ACTUAL	REASON	ACTUAL	REASON	ACTUAL	REASON	ACTUAL	REASON	ACTUAL	REASON
2:00 - 3:00	11	ACTUAL	REASON	ACTUAL	REASON	ACTUAL	REASON	ACTUAL	REASON	ACTUAL	REASON
3:00 - 4:00	11	ACTUAL	REASON	ACTUAL	REASON	ACTUAL	REASON	ACTUAL	REASON	ACTUAL	REASON
4:00 - 5:00	11	ACTUAL	REASON	ACTUAL	REASON	ACTUAL	REASON	ACTUAL	REASON	ACTUAL	REASON
5:00 - 6:00	11	ACTUAL	REASON	ACTUAL	REASON	ACTUAL	REASON	ACTUAL	REASON	ACTUAL	REASON
Total	101										

Countermeasures	Countermeasures	Countermeasures	Countermeasures	Countermeasures
1	1	1	1	1
2	2	2	2	2
3	3	3	3	3
4	4	4	4	4
5	5	5	5	5

Figure 4.7 Week by the hour report[3]

Table 4.4 Visual management assessment (manufacturing example)

Description	In place	Needed	Comment
Health and safety			
Health and safety regulations and signage			
Spill and eye wash stations			
Chemical storage cabinets			
Lock-out, tag-out visuals			
Days since last incident displayed			
5S workplace organisation			
5S storyboard			
Floor marking and stencilling			
Signage and labelling			
Tool and supplies shadow boards			
Cleaning schedule displayed			
Cleaning stations			
5S audit			
Permanent red tag area			
Colour coding			

Visual display

Visual management
centre

Work standards
displayed

Visual control

Quarantine area

Day/week by the hour
boards

First article off board

Limit samples

Kanban system

Changeover
storyboard

Error proofing devices

Location demarcation

Andon system

Visual management review

Visual management is not about the area looking attractive; it is
about working better through non-verbal sharing of information
and operational status. It is management by sight and what gets
measured, gets improved. In my experience once your employees
experience the positive benefits they will be asking for deeper and
broader applications. As with all communication channels the key to
a positive delivery is to make metrics meaningful at each level of your
organisation. You must make sure that the increased transparency
through information sharing and posting of operational metrics is
not perceived as punitive to people. Demonstrate through communication and actions that the intention of visual management is to
provide a strong focus on the process, resulting in improvement of
the system. The intention is not to blame people: Dr Deming advised
us that 94% of problems are system not people related.

5

Lean methods and tools (part II)

This chapter discusses A3 problem solving in Section 1 and standard work in Section 2.

SECTION 1: A3 PROBLEM SOLVING

Introduction

> *'No one has more trouble, than the person who claims to have no trouble.'*
>
> Taiichi Ohno

Problem solving is central to Lean management and is the primary method of realising improved performance. The quotation above, from Taiichi Ohno (Toyota's principal Lean sensei), shows that problems are welcomed in a Lean environment. In many businesses a culture of hiding problems is commonplace and this is extremely destructive to organisational success. In your organisation you should be pleased if you come across problems as they are the seeds of improvement.

A problem is defined as any obstacle that prevents the attainment of the target condition (the gap between the current and desired state). A problem usually presents itself as a symptom of an underlying, more deeply concealed, root issue. It is commonplace across industry to put a sticking plaster on problems or to solve the surface causes or symptoms.

The root cause of problems can be generally classified into three categories:

1 No standard work.

2 Standard work exists but is not followed.

3 Standard work exists, is followed, but is not adequate.

A3 problem solving is the Lean methodology used to build consensus and mentor people in problem solving. A3 assists people to observe current reality, present facts, propose working countermeasures, gain agreement and follow-up with a process of checking and adjusting the actual results. It works through a large and smaller nested PDSA (see Chapter 1 for a definition) cycles. It is called A3 as it is confined to a single sheet of A3 paper for maximum conciseness and clarity. The format also reduces management communication time and nurtures deep thinking. It enables an intense vigilance on the problem through its structured approach and encourages collaborative team-based conversations about the problem.

It is common for A3s to contain both hand-written text and sketches. A picture is worth a thousand words and engages creative right brain creativity. At the outset you and your team should spend adequate time properly clarifying and defining the problem. From my experience the problem often goes through numerous iterations as you proceed through the phases of the A3 and your understanding increases through the diagnosis stage in particular. However, spending time to define the problem to your best level of current knowledge at the outset is a key factor for successfully addressing root cause(s) later in the process.

A3 is not a linear form of problem solving and teams should move backwards and forwards through the steps (just as in the problem definition above) to update the A3 sheet as the knowledge about the problem expands under each section. A3 problem solving should be performed at the gemba (the place where the actual problem occurred – also known as the point of cause) involving those who work in the process. This enables the maximum number of relevant ideas to surface and fosters local ownership required for successful problem resolution. If you do this, it is likely that successful problem-solving activity will spread through your organisation as frontline employees directly see the benefits. Blind copying is not encouraged though; solutions that work in a particular set of circumstances and time often need to be modified when leveraged elsewhere in the organisation.

A3 problem solving consists of nine steps (see Table 5.1). Note that the challenge is to work diligently through all the nine steps. For many people it is tempting to skip steps 1–3 and go straight into the analysis phase and then stop at step 5 or 6 when a certain comfort level is reached through problem containment. One of the major building blocks for the creation of a Lean culture is for your management team to commit to following *all* nine steps of this process. The goal should be that the nine steps evolve to be the way that people in your organisation think conceptually about issues in their heads as well as on paper. The one thing that distinguishes the elite performing Lean organisations is their diligence in working through all nine steps involved in A3 systematic problem solving.

A3 will foster dialogue and communication in your organisation. It's not just down to one person; A3 is a team endeavour. The authority to make changes is built through the A3 owner building consensus with stakeholders. You will see that this is a shift from the traditional practice of authority being viewed as the entitlement of those of power or higher rank in the organisation. In a Lean culture, developing an A3 and taking ownership is encouraged at all levels. It is a powerful persuasion technique to help influence other people. Leaders with authority to make changes that solve problems that result in improvements should be independent of hierarchy.

It is critical that problem surfacing and solving takes place against a backdrop of a non-penal culture. By this I mean that you have to foster a blame free culture, or even better a just culture. James Reason, a former Professor of Psychology at the University of Manchester, popularised the concept of a just culture (in my view stronger than a blame free culture as 'blame free' carries the inference that nobody is accountable). A just culture is one where an atmosphere of trust exists and people are encouraged and even rewarded for providing essential safety related information. This need not be limited to safety concerns, in my view. Inadvertent errors that people make due to poor system design (> 90% of all mistakes) must not be used to blame or reprimand people. Such errors should be exploited as a way of improving your organisation's systems. However, errors that are caused by negligence, recklessness and intentional policy breaches must never be tolerated. A just culture ultimately results in problems not being masked as they might have been in the past due to fear of reprisal or humiliation. Problems are best viewed as gaps in your current knowledge about your processes and as opportunities for evolution. This demands that you view problems impersonally and that the focus is on the concern not the person or team. In my experience the irony of a problem receptive culture is that more problems will be surfaced and dissolved in comparison with a culture that strives to keep quiet about problems at all costs.

Why A3?

- It builds alignment as to what the real problem actually is and the path to resolution.
- It builds consensus to make changes all the way across the organisation.
- It develops problem-solving capability at all levels.
- It exposes lack of agreement (through consensus building) that can undercut progress.

A3 document

The structure of the A3 document is detailed in Table 5.1. The intent is to work through each section in sequence and these can then be updated throughout the problem-solving process as your knowledge of the problem deepens through analysis and tests of change. The A3 should be assigned an owner who is responsible for implementation and a mentor to guide the owner through the phases in a way that raises their skills. This practice uses the process both to improve the process and to develop your people.

Table 5.1 A3 document template

1. Clarify the problem	2. Background (context setting)	3. Current situation
'If I had an hour to save the world I would spend 59 minutes defining the problem and one minute finding solutions'. Albert Einstein	What is the business case for working on this problem?	Articulate the gap that details the extent of the problem.
Define the real problem, not the symptom to get effective countermeasures. (Note: the problem can be revised as our knowledge deepens throughout the nine-step process.)	What metric(s) need to be improved?	What do we currently know about the problem in terms of the what, where, when and how much?
Good problem statement format: Verb (action word) (target) by X (amount) by XX/XX/XX (date)		Have you collected real facts at the gemba, not just perceptions of reality?
To better define the problem try some of the following: looking at it from a higher or a lower level or both; rephrasing it; reversing it; challenging the assumptions behind it; and asking, 'What if?' to open up possible avenues to the real problem.		Include visuals such as charts, graphs, etc.

Table 5.1 Continued

4. *Target setting*	5. *Root cause analysis*	6. *Develop countermeasures*
What are we trying to accomplish? What specific improvements do we need to realise?	Use the simplest problem analysis method that shows the relationship between cause and effect. Use the seven QC tools (see below) or other tools as required. Test the cause/ effect logic by asking 'Why?' downward and 'therefore' upward.	What are the potential options to test to improve performance towards the target condition? Have multiple alternatives to test for each potential root cause. How will the countermeasures address the root cause(s) of the gap and why? Run experiments on the proposed changes using multiple PDSA cycles to understand, develop and test the countermeasures.

7. *Implementation plan*	8. *Follow-up*	9. *Standardise, after action review (AAR) and spread plan*
The implementation plan addresses the what, how, when and who of execution. Countermeasures that tested successfully are rolled out on a wider scale again using PDSA cycles. Has consensus been built with the people doing the actual work? What are the metrics that indicate progress? What resources are required to support the implementation actions?	Verify that the implementation actions have been a success. Have there been any unintended consequences? Are there any remaining issues to be closed out? Is there a contingency plan in place? Improvements reveal new problems! What is the next A3?	Document and standardise successful changes. Train the relevant people in the new methods using TWI (training within industry). What other actions are required to sustain the gains? What went well? What could have been done better? What did we learn for the next cycle of improvement? What other areas could benefit from sharing this improvement?

The seven basic quality tools

The Japanese quality authority Ishikawa was heavily influenced by Dr Deming, the American statistician, professor, author, lecturer and consultant, who was heavily involved in the transformation of the Japanese manufacturing industry in the mid-1900s. Ishikawa formalised seven basic quality tools that Deming argued could solve over 90% of quality problems. These are used throughout the A3 problem-solving process, some as diagnostic tools, in the analysis step and include the cause and effect diagram, Pareto chart and process map. Others are deployed as hold the gains/sustaining tools, for example using a run chart to monitor data over time and to detect if the process drifts beyond the specified stability limits.

The seven tools are:

1 cause and effect diagram

2 Pareto diagram

3 process map

4 tally chart

5 scatter plot

6 run chart

7 histogram.

1. Cause and effect or fishbone diagram

This is a visual team tool used to brainstorm possible root causes to a problem with your employees. The potential causes are written in the diagram. It is common to use the six 'Ms' to label the initial bones: Man (person), Machine, Methods, Materials, Measurement and Mother Nature. The contributing causes are tested to see if they are root cause(s) through the repeated asking of 'Why?'. This tool is known as '5 Why?' as five is generally accepted as the number of times we need to ask 'Why?'. (Not always the case in practical use however!)

Example problem statement: |

Customer orders are consistently delivered late.

Why?

The press machine frequently breaks down. *(Identified contributing cause under Machine section)*

Why?

The ram seizes and trips out a fuse.

Why?

The ram wasn't adequately lubricated.

Why?

The lubrication pump was clogged up.

Why?

The dispenser on the pump was broken.

Why?

Grime and grit entered the pump shaft.

Why?

The pump motor was designed without a filter. *(Deep root cause)*

You can have as many levels of 'Why?' as the situation demands. Continue asking 'Why?' even when you think that you have revealed the root problem. To test the last core root cause, work your way back up the 'Why?' ladder asking 'therefore' to verify if each 'Why?' holds true. In practice, each 'Why?' can often lead to several branches. You may for that reason have to prioritise, go down one branch, and then return to the branching point to explore other possibilities. One caveat to be aware of with '5 Why?' is that different people solving the same problems can derive different root causes, so it is sensible to use a number of tools to complement and reinforce each other. An example would be to use a cause and effect diagram (see Figure 5.1), prioritise the primary potential causes, and then use '5 Why?' to investigate if these causes are symptoms or root cause(s). You would finally run a small test of the change using PDSA to ground your theory into facts.

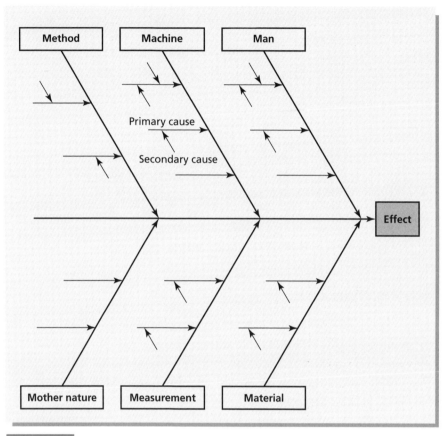

Figure 5.1 Cause and effect or fishbone diagram template

2. Pareto diagram or 80/20 rule

This principle is named after Alfredo Pareto, an economist who noted that a few people controlled most of a nation's wealth. It is viewed by many as the single most powerful management technique of all time. It gives recognition to the fact that a small number of problems (< 20%) account for a large percentage (> 80%) of the effect of the overall number of problems. That is, the vital few cause you 80% of the pain! You should aim to solve these first before the trivial many. A principle worth remembering is that this rule also applies within the top 20% bracket – 20% of the top 20% has 80% of the impact! An example Pareto diagram is shown in Figure 5.2.

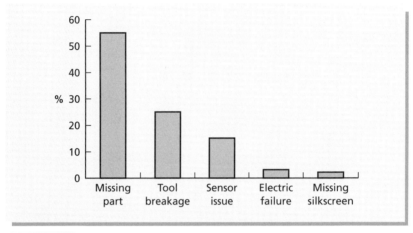

Figure 5.2 Pareto diagram of defect categories

3. Process map

The process map (see Figure 5.3) lists every step that is involved in the manufacture of a product or a service delivery. It helps to identify value and waste. It is also powerful for standardising processes after problem-solving activity has led to improvements in the original 'as is' process map. The mapping should be done at the actual workplace of the process under study, not remotely or relying on people's perception of how they think the process works. Once the map is complete the individual steps can be brainstormed into those that add value, those that are pure waste and should be eliminated as soon as possible, and those which are necessary but non-value-added (they are needed to support the process in the short term). Each step is challenged using the criteria discussed previously:

Value-adding task

An activity is 'value-added' if, and only if, *all* these three conditions are met:

1 The customer must be willing to pay for the activity.

2 The step must either physically move the product or service towards completion, or be an essential precondition for another step.

3 The step must be done right the first time.

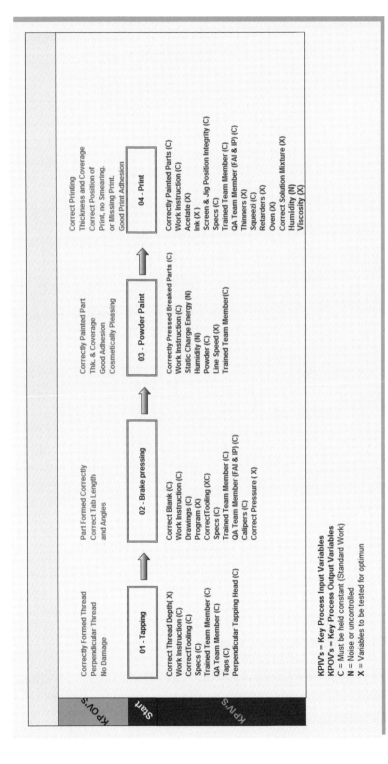

KPOV's

| 01 - Tapping | 02 - Brake pressing | 03 - Powder Paint | 04 - Print |

Correctly Formed Thread
Perpendicular Thread
No Damage

Part Formed Correctly
Correct Tab Length
and Angles

Correctly Painted Part
Thk. & Coverage
Good Adhesion
Cosmetically Pleasing

Correct Printing
Thickness and Coverage
Correct Position of
Print, no Smearing.
or Missing Print.
Good Print Adhesion

KPIV's

01 - Tapping
Correct Thread Depth(X)
Work Instruction (C)
Correct Tooling (C)
Specs (C)
Trained Team Member (C)
QA Team Member (C)
Taps (C)
Perpendicular Tapping Head (C)

02 - Brake pressing
Correct Blank (C)
Work Instruction (C)
Drawings (C)
Program (X)
Correct Tooling (XC)
Specs (C)
Trained Team Member (C)
QA Team Member (FAI & IP) (C)
Calipers (C)
Correct Pressure (X)

03 - Powder Paint
Correctly Pressed Breaked Parts (C)
Work Instruction (C)
Static Charge Energy (N)
Humidity (N)
Powder (C)
Line Speed (X)
Trained Team Member(C)

04 - Print
Correctly Painted Parts (C)
Work Instruction (C)
Acetate (X)
Ink (X)
Screen & Jig Position Integrity (C)
Specs (C)
Trained Team Member (C)
QA Team Member (FAI & IP) (C)
Thinners (X)
Squeezi (C)
Retarders (X)
Oven (X)
Correct Solution Mixture (X)
Humidity (N)
Viscosity (X)

KPIV's = Key Process Input Variables
KPOV's = Key Process Output Variables
C = Must be held constant (Standard Work)
N = Noise or uncontrolled
X = Variables to be tested for optimun

Figure 5.3 Process map example

Non-value-adding task

An activity that is neither required by the business nor one the customer is willing to pay for. These activities fall into the TIM WOOD DOES IT (see Chapter 1) categories of operational waste.

Value-added enabling task

An activity that is required to operate the business but one the customer is unwilling to pay for (e.g. inspection, regulation, budget tracking).

4. Tally chart

How often are certain events happening in your organisation? Tally charts (see Table 5.2) turn opinions into facts. Simple but powerful, you can place them next to your processes and use them to check the occurrence of issues. They are useful for identifying trends or signals such as a particular day of the week, shift, etc.

Table 5.2 Tally chart

Defect category	Tally	Total
Missing part	IIIIIIIIIIIIIIIIIII	19
Tool breakage	IIIIIIIIIIII	12
Sensor issue	IIIIII	6
Electric failure	II	2
Missing silkscreen	I	1

5. Scatter plot or measles chart

Each defect occurrence is plotted on an existing defective part or engineering drawing at the location where the problem occurs (see Figure 5.4). If the accumulation density is concentrated in one area it gives an excellent indication of where the problem lies. Some companies use this method to identify which areas in the organisation are generating the most ideas for improvement.

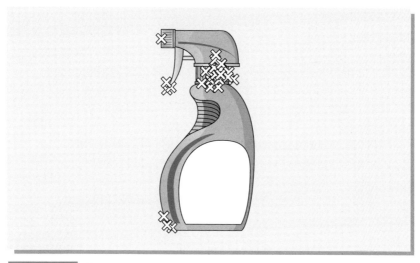

Figure 5.4   Scatter diagram signalling a strong defect problem area

6. Run chart

A run chart (see Figure 5.5) is a simple visual representation that displays data in the sequence that it occurs and shows a process's characteristics over time. For example, a run chart in a café could plot the number of customers served against the time of day or day of the week. The data might illustrate more customers arrive at 1 p.m. than at 5 p.m. and even more during the weekend than on weekdays. This might lead to improvements in the staffing levels at particularly busy times to improve the customer experience.

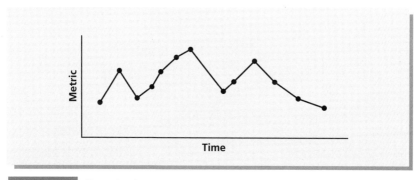

Figure 5.5   Run chart

It is very important to capture the performance of a process over time and under a wide range of conditions. This helps us to make informed decisions regarding the condition of the process with respect to common and special cause variation. Common cause variation is deviation caused by unknown factors but the process still remains stable. In the café example this might be a slight variation between the number of people who sit for lunch on a Tuesday or Wednesday. An example of a special cause variation might be that there is a football final in the town and the café is booked out from 3 p.m. to 7 p.m. that evening. The cause and effect diagram discussed earlier is often used for investigating special cause variation.

7. Histogram

A histogram (see Figure 5.6) represents the frequency and distribution of data. It allows large data sets to be graphically displayed in a concise chart where trends and outliers can be quickly spotted. Generally the more bell shaped the graph contour is, the more stable and in control the process is.

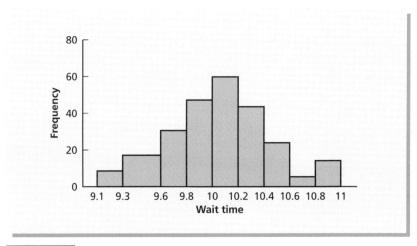

Figure 5.6   Histogram

Four ways of using A3s

1 *Problem solving*: a problem-solving A3 is used for structured systematic root cause problem solving (see Table 5.1 earlier).

2 *Proposal*: a proposal A3 is focused on the future, expressing where and how you want to improve the situation in a particular area (see Table 5.3).

3 *Status report*: a status A3 communicates the progress of a medium- to long-term project (see Table 5.4).

4 *Strategic*: a strategic A3 develops the path to the achievement of a hoshin breakthrough goal (see Figure 2.1).

Table 5.3 Proposal A3 outline

Proposal:	*Date: To*	*From*
Theme:	Plan:	
Proposal detail:	What How Who When	
	Open issues:	

Table 5.4 Status A3 outline

Status report:	*Date: To*	*From*
Theme:	Implementation Status:	
Background:	Total Effect:	
Objectives:	Open Issues/Next Actions:	

Categories of problems

It is useful to classify problems into four categories, namely A, B, C and D problems.

'A' problems

The cause is known. Countermeasures can be implemented immediately using PDSA cycle(s).

Team members can usually solve these problems directly; these problems are often related to non-conformance to standard work or no standard work. Standard work is one of the primary methods used in Lean to make problems visible. About 60–70% of problems encountered in your organisations in all probability fall into this category. These problems do not require the level of analysis provided by A3. Instead these problems can be tracked using a 3C board as in Table 5.5. This visual management board is a good method for sharing concerns and successful solutions within your local areas and with other value streams.

Table 5.5 A 3C board

Concern	Cause	Countermeasure
1.		
2.		
3.		

'B' problems

The root cause(s) are known, countermeasures are not known.

These problems are normally solved using the A3 methodology. They can be a re-occurrence of an 'A' problem when the incorrect cause(s) had been countermeasured. The frontline supervisor often mentors their team members during the process. In parallel with this comes the progression of your team members' problem-solving capability. Developing the correct thinking through PDSA is integral to the process along with deeper knowledge of the process under analysis. Approximately 20% of problems encountered in an organisation are 'B' problems.

'C' problems

Cause is unknown.

These problems also require an A3 and deeper analysis using the basic quality tools such as cause and effect diagrams and '5 Why?' analysis to arrive at a proposed set of countermeasures to be tested. Approximately 10% of problems encountered in an organisation are 'C' problems.

'D' problems

This is intentionally creating a problem through removal of precaution contingencies – the proactive creation of problems to stress the system. An example of this would be the lowering of an inventory buffer between workstations in order to reveal problems (that would otherwise be concealed by the comfort of extra inventory) due to small machine stops, etc. Tightly linked processes without excess cushions, be that extra inventory, time, people, etc., force you to tackle the source of disruptions rather than mask the causes by adding extra resources.

A3 problem-solving review

A3 is a powerful method for solving problems and communicating within the organisation. Due to its concise and standard format it obliges everyone in your organisation to think about and view the problem or project with an aligned approach. It pushes people to go to the actual workplace and interact directly with frontline employees. The process also subtly develops people's 'hard' and 'soft' skills. The 'hard' skills are developed through problem definition formulation and root cause analysis. The softer people skills are nurtured through the process of dialogue and building persuasion and consensus with the various stakeholders. Alignment is built through the coaching process of Socratic questioning (open ended questions of what, why, when, where and how). This questioning approach rather than telling (reduces accountability) develops the other stakeholders through allowing them to learn through experimentation rather than directives. (This is developed further in Chapter 10 through deployment of the Cathedral model.) The process of problem solving is used not just to solve problems, but also to create leaders in Lean organisations. Over time A3 has the power to change the cognitive thinking of people, as this structured approach evolves into a habitual way of applying shared thinking to problems.

SECTION 2: STANDARD WORK

Introduction

> *'Today's standardisation...is the necessary foundation on which tomorrow's improvement will be based. If you think of "standardisation" as the best you know today, but which is to be improved tomorrow – you get somewhere. But if you think of standards as confining, then progress stops.'*

Henry Ford[1]

Stability is the foundation of Lean, and in order to create stability it is necessary to describe, document and teach standard work to employees. Standard work is the current best known documented way to safely, effectively (satisfies customers' needs) and efficiently (least wasteful way) carry out a job. It also needs to meet the required level of quality in the allotted time. The very act of documenting the work highlights obvious improvements. You should view standard work as a continuous improvement method that removes operational waste and allows supervisors to audit their processes (deviations from being able to follow the standard raises problems). Without standards there is no baseline for performance comparison. Standards are most effective and bought into when developed in collaboration with your people doing the everyday work. Standard work improves process discipline, which is the heart of Lean transformation.

Standard work supports the True North aspirations of quality, cost, delivery and people growth (we discuss True North in Chapter 1). Quality is improved through the removal of variation and more consistent delivery of customer requirements. Performing work steps by the same method each time improves quality across all industries. When a problem does occur, comparing the standard work method to what is currently happening in the process can quickly identify the root cause(s). Hence standardisation enables non-conformances or quality issues to be highlighted immediately. The root cause of practically all problems in your organisation – as stated previously – can be traced back to three broad categories:

1 There was no standard work for the task.
2 There was standard work for the task but it was not followed.
3 There was standard work for the task, it was followed, but the standard was inadequate.

Cost is enhanced through the removal of waste and defining the current best known method that most effectively meets your customer requirements. Standard work supports delivery through the specification of the current best-known work sequence, standard work in progress and takt time (see Chapter 3). Takt time paces and staffs the value streams in synchronisation with customer demand. This means that all processes are paced at the rate that your product and services are being sold. Standards help define the theoretically correct number of people required to staff the organisation to meet customer demand. People growth is also cultivated with standardisation through the acknowledgement that standards are just the current temporary best known method that we recognise today. The expectation is that people should challenge all standards on a continuous basis in order to improve upon them. You should strive to have a robust change management process in place that allows making changes to standards to be as seamless as possible.

Standard work is often frowned upon as it raises the idea that the workplace will become regimented and stifles creativity as people will be expected to mindlessly conform to policies and rules. The opposite should be true in a Lean organisation. Standard work should not be top down. Standards should never be set in stone, instead they should be developed in collaboration with those doing the work. People will generally follow standard work when they are involved in developing it (they then identify with it and ownership is fostered). Standard work does in fact free up time for improvement and creativity. This is because in a stable environment people spend less time fire-fighting. If work is deferred to individual choices there is no consistency in outcomes. When properly applied (visible and reviewed frequently) standard work will help sustain and lock in improvements and also expose concealed waste in your workplace.

As Figure 5.7 shows, standard work is a reflection of the current best known method. The target condition or desired state must be defined. This is the magnet that is pulling people to improve the current condition and to reduce the difference that exists between the two states. The target condition is a powerful waste removal concept. The difference is closed through repeated turns of the PDSA wheel in the form of tests of change. These changes should be reflected in each new version of standard work and can be viewed as the means that prevents backsliding against the force of entropy.

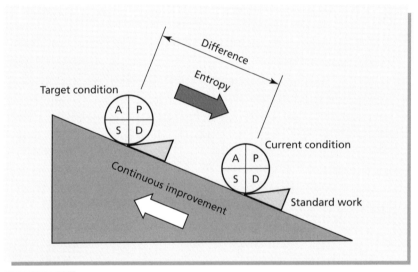

Figure 5.7   The target condition creates a pull for improvement

'Continue the cycle, over and over, with never-ending improvement of quality, at lower and lower cost.'

W. Edwards Deming[2]

There is no end game or 100% stable process; problems are inherent in every system. How will you know if you are reaching the target that you set? A clue might be that you are seeing only common cause variation over a number of months. In other words the process has reached stability, and you are in the position to 'challenge' this capability by setting an even higher standard of operation.

Standard work and job classifications

Charles Perrow[3] classified jobs into four categories:

1 *Routine work*: these are highly repetitive jobs such as assembly line tasks or transactional office work, for example, processing application forms. These tasks are prime targets for standard work. However, the expectation is that the employees are on the look out for shortcomings in these standards and will come forward with ideas that they can contribute towards improving the work.

2 *Technician work*: there is a wide variety of tasks and the order can change depending upon the situation. An example of technician work would be a person overseeing the operation of a complex automated machine, or a person running an MRI scanner in a hospital. Their activities can be supported by standard work for repetitive daily tasks such as productive maintenance, or reference procedures for equipment settings.

3 *Craft work*: there are an almost infinite number of different tasks involved in this job classification. Expertise and practice are significant factors for the attainment of high levels of competency. There are very high levels of autonomy in this job style, but standard work is deployed in a limited fashion so as to aid fundamental skills such as problem solving, safety policies, quality acceptance levels and the workplace layout.

4 *Non-routine*: this type of work is concerned with one-off type projects where decisions must often be made without prior knowledge. The engineer performing research and development would be classified in this category. Formal standard work is implemented sparingly such as the sharing of best practice, following good design protocol and adhering to specifications. The emphasis is more on proficient training and extensive experience under the guidance of a mentor.

The standard work chart (see Figure 5.8) makes the job content explicit and is usually but not always combined into one A3 page. Its primary purpose is to ensure that the defined standard is followed; this is accomplished through daily support from the area supervisor. Takt time and cycle time are derived through direct observation of the work over a wide range of users and market conditions over time. Cycle time divided by takt time gives a feel for the theoretical number of staff needed in a process area. This puts a science behind the correct levels of staffing required for an area which is often very loosely calculated or based on people's perceptive judgements. If demand changes significantly, takt time will also change and this should trigger changes to standard work. The capacity of the process must be understood in order to develop effective standards as this will determine factors such as staffing, cycle times and indeed takt time itself. The work elements detail the what, how and why of the job. The 'why' or purpose of the process should also be made explicit in order that people understand the benefits of their job to the end user. In general, employees will resist what they do not understand, and are unlikely to comply if they do not see mutual benefit (or the why) in doing so. Key points are detailed (in a participative manner between the area supervisors and the frontline people running the

Product		Drafted by:	
Value Stream		Approval:	
Operation		Date:	
Takt Time: Cycle Time:		Revision #:	
#	Work Elements (what, how, &, why)	Key Points (safety, make easier, make or break)	Picture/Diagram

Figure 5.8   Standard work chart example layout

process) for work elements that make the job safer, easier or are of critical importance. Failure to perform the key points successfully can lead to safety concerns, make the job harder for employees and/ or can make or break the job's desired outcome.

When you are implementing standard work practices, remember that key points should be stated in a positive manner. For example, avoid stating, 'Do not use too much wrapping'; instead be specific and say, 'Use 350 mm of 3 micron polyethylene wrapping'. Of course, not all work elements require key points. Often the description is complemented with photos, sketches or diagrams to enhance clarity or to place emphasis on critical quality checks. A better understanding of the purpose of standard work will help to determine the appropriate level of detail. Standards are sometimes populated in pencil to ease the bureaucracy of change control and the supervisor stamps and initials changes to provide a safety net against uncontrolled changes.

Improving standard work

In order to focus on the current version of standard work you will need to study the process in detail. The way to do this is by using a form called a standard work combination chart; this will remove waste in each of the TIM WOOD DOES IT categories. A sample chart is shown in Figure 5.9. This chart will help you consider the micro details of processes and factor in all the minute details that can have serious consequences if they escalate. It is very useful to combine this chart with a video analysis of the process so that you can later play it back for detailed analysis. Show it to all the process stakeholders so that you can examine the details in an unbiased manner. The renowned parable below reminds us of the importance of attention to detail:

> 'For the want of a nail the shoe was lost; For the want of a shoe the horse was lost; For the want of a horse the battle was lost; For the failure of battle the kingdom was lost; And all for the want of a horse-shoe nail.'[4]

Standard Work Combination Chart

Process:		Available time:		Takt Time:		Manual = ————
		Daily Demand		Studied by:		Automatic = ••••••••••••
						Walk = ————

#	Description of Step	Time			Time																	
		Manual	Automatic	Walk	5	10	15	20	25	30	35	40	45	50	55	60	65	70	75	80	85	90	95	100
1																						
2																						
3																						
4																						
5																						
6																						
7																						
8																						
9																						
10																						
11																						
12																						
13																						
14																						
15																						
16																						
17																						
18																						
19																						
20																						
					Totals																	

Figure 5.9   Standard work combination chart

From Figure 5.9 and the expected level of detailed analysis, you will see that standard work is much more than documenting the work, it is a vigorous waste reduction practice. Once standard work has been created and everyone is trained, it is time to start the process and make observations. This is the time to look for yet further improvements.

Bringing standard work to life

When the process has been documented your work is not complete! Once you have knowledge of work practices you then need to transfer this to the people doing the work. It is necessary to obtain a structure that will transfer the information in the standards to the people performing the work. This is where the programme known as training within industry (TWI) is invaluable.

Employees often do not follow standard written procedures because they do not understand them, they are impossible to follow as written, they are incomplete and offer either insufficient or superfluous information, or a different method is known that will increase quality, productivity, safety or cost. In short, they need to be trained on the what, how and why a job must be performed in a particular way.

TWI is a four-stage programme for training employees. It involves:

- how to do the task – called job instruction (JI)
- how to continually look for ways to improve the task – called job methods (JM)
- guidance on treating and managing people with respect, as detailed in the job relations programme (JR)
- job safety (JS) so that the effectiveness of both the JI and JM programmes is maximised (this relates to the 'respect for people' pillar).

Job instruction is used to impart the knowledge in standard work to employees. It should be done directly by the supervisor who in turn should be wholly proficient in performing the task. The job is broken down in a job breakdown sheet where the specific what, how and why of the job are outlined (see Figure 5.10 below). A job breakdown sheet is user friendly and has more specific job details than standard work charts (which are used primarily for auditing by the supervisor).

The supervisor works through the four steps on page 109 to explain the job standard. These four JI steps are commonly carried by supervisors in credit card sized memos that serve as a visual cue for correct application. This time tested method is extremely effective for training in all types of industries from manufacturing to software development and beyond. Its origins date back to World War II when over 1.6 million personnel were trained through TWI to support the manufacture of war equipment. TWI is arguably the most proven and effective training programme in existence today.

Task						Org Logo	
Part #							
Equipment & Supplies Required:							
Safety Equipment							

Important Steps		Key Points		Reasons	Photo(s)/Diagram(s)
WHAT?	Work Elements	HOW?	Things in important steps that will: 1. Assure safety 2. Make or break the job 3. Make the job easier	WHY?	Reason(s) for the key points
1					
2					
3					
4					
5					
6					

Key point reminders:	◊ Quality check	Φ Quantity check	✚ Safety	☒ Makes the job easier	Prepared By:	Rev:
						Date:

Figure 5.10   Job breakdown sheet

Job Instruction Method[5]

Step 1: Prepare the student

▪ Put the student at ease.

▪ State the job name.

▪ Find out what the student already knows about the job.

▪ Get the student interested in learning the job.

Step 2: Present the operation

▪ Teacher demonstrates one major step at a time as the student observes.

▪ Teacher demonstrates again as the student observes each major step and key point.

▪ Teacher demonstrates again as student observes each major step, key point and reasons for the step.

▪ Explain clearly, completely and patiently.

▪ Present no more than the worker can master.

Step 3: Try out performance

▪ Have the student try the job while you correct mistakes.

▪ Student explains the major step as the job is done again.

▪ Student explains the key points as the job is done again.

▪ Student explains the reasons as the job is done again.

Step 4: Follow up

▪ Assign the person a task.

▪ Tell the student where to go for help.

▪ Check their progress frequently.

▪ Encourage them to ask questions.

▪ Gradually reduce the coaching follow-up.

Standard work review

Standard work ensures reliable, capable and repeatable work outcomes. Standard work is perhaps the hardest work of Lean but one of the most critical elements. It can also be the least engaging work in Lean as it requires meticulous attention to detail. You probably even found reading this chapter arduous and tough going! We work in organisational cultures where heroic fire-fighting is generally rewarded over preventing problems. As mentioned previously, the major cause of almost all your work problems can be traced back to deficiencies in standard work. We are time and again rewarded for workarounds rather than preventing problems. However, we have to live with the consequences of not following standard work and the subsequent fire-fighting and losses that ensue. Hence it seems obvious that it should never be optional to perform work in the correct way through standard work. The wisdom that the right process will yield the right results is very true.

We all have experienced the benefits of standard work in our daily lives from, say, our consistent customer experience whilst visiting Starbucks to the pilot's standard safety checks before departing for take-off at the airport. Even highly variable work can benefit from a degree of standardisation, for example in a stressful service recovery situation, loose scripting can help ensure that all the customer sensitive touch points are covered. Even creative work (yes, creativity is a process too!) can have elements standardised such as the various phases of the creative process, knowledge management portals and references to required information. Standard work is not a set up and forget exercise: it needs to be observed, audited and nurtured by your local area supervisors.

Note: non-value-added failure demand work placed on your organisation should not be a target for standard work; the goal is to eliminate this category of work.

Standard work also greatly reduces the learning curve to job proficiency. (In my experience proficiency levels are reached in half the time in cultures that have embedded standardisation into the daily work routines.) Thus the possibility of job rotation and flexibility is greatly enhanced.

Standards can never cover everything that can happen and good standards should factor in criteria to handle variation in local conditions. Standards should however look after the estimated vital 20–30% or so of tasks that should be consistently delivered across all industries. As J.W. Marriott, CEO of Marriot Hotels, stated:

> *'What solid systems and SOPs [standards are often called standard operating procedures in service industries] do is nip common problems in the bud so that staff can focus on uncommon problems that come their way.'*[6]

6

Lean methods and tools (part III)

This chapter discusses the idea management system in Section 1 and kaizen events in Section 2.

SECTION 1: IDEA MANAGEMENT SYSTEM (IMS)

Introduction

Many organisations find that one of the principal challenges during their Lean transformation is engaging employees in the *daily* routine of continuous improvement. Respect and humility are good starting points. Management must recognise that their frontline employees see problems and opportunities every day in their immediate work areas that they do not.

Long-established methods of attempting to capture ideas, such as suggestion boxes, do not work. There is a story about a suggestion found in the suggestion box: 'Can you remove the suggestion box? Nobody ever uses it!' Suggestion systems get stuck in their own red tape. There are long implementation times, low participation rates (typically < 5% of workforce), and high rejection rates, partly because some are duplicate suggestions which have already been considered. Most traditional suggestion systems fall victim to ideas for other people to do something about, rather than the originator of the idea. If all you have to do is suggest an idea for someone else to implement you can state whatever you like. Often the suggestion box thus simply becomes a grievance box.

In contrast to traditional suggestion systems that are typically hierarchical in control and approval, the idea management system (IMS) gives authority to people on the frontlines. The area supervisor acts as the catalyst and coach for ideas and manages the infrastructure for implementation. The focus is on the many, small, daily annoyances and minor problems that associates can resolve themselves that will lead to a smoother workplace. A hidden benefit of the implementation of many small ideas over time is that competitors cannot copy these compounded small improvements. The intention is that problems are nipped in the bud prior to escalating into bigger issues.

Emphasis on employee involvement over cost savings explains most of the difference between the two systems. Despite not focusing on cost savings, typically financial returns are about ten times greater than the traditional systems such as the suggestion box.[1]

The three primary aims of the IMS are as follows:

1 Employee inclusion in local decision making – the intention is to increase engagement and the sense of belonging in the organisation, leading to increased intrinsic motivation and active involvement.

2 Training and skills development – the IMS improves problem solving, kaizen proficiency and speeds up on-the-job training. Move away from the concept of simply harvesting ideas from employees to promoting the IMS as a mechanism to improve and develop people. Focus on the people and the results will follow.

3 Positive effect – improved efficiency of operations, and reduced cost of poor quality along with intangibles such as improved safety, morale, and the creation of an environment of increased trust and teamwork are aimed for.

Employees should be coached to put forward ideas that make their work easier, can be implemented quickly, eliminate the cause of problems, save money, and do not cost too much to implement. The implementation rate for improvements proposed by those closest to the problem is very high. Your people at this level know the intricateness of their processes and have a stake in seeing their ideas successfully utilised. I have spoken to Toyota veterans and they say that there is a greater than 95% implementation rate for ideas as many of them are not implemented in their original form, but are enriched in collaboration with employees. People enjoy carrying out their own ideas (we support what we create) and are committed to seeing them work. It gives them a feeling of having a direct impact on the running of the workplace and a sense of accomplishment. *Hence getting the person who raises the idea to implement it or to participate in implementation is crucial to the success of the system.* This concept is formally known as kaizen teian. Self-implementation is the cornerstone of successful idea systems and the big differentiator between these and standard suggestion systems.

This level of empowerment will not happen overnight and at the outset people may need support in implementing their ideas, but this investment will develop more capable employees over time. This leads to a virtuous cycle where employees become more and more capable in problem solving and idea implementation. In the early stages management can seek ideas that are very basic. This stage is to get employees involved, thinking about and questioning their work. It also allows ideas put forward to be implemented (as they are basic) and this builds momentum. In the intermediate stage, management places emphasis on up-skilling, so that employees can provide better ideas. In order for the workers to provide better ideas, they should be trained in problem solving and in the use of basic creativity tools. This requires education. The hidden benefit is that the work becomes much more engaging as people use their thinking skills on a daily basis. Ultimately, in the advanced stage, after the workers have become more educated, involved, and hence engaged, management then starts to be concerned with the financial return on ideas.

Documenting ideas is crucial

You may find that one of the hardest things to instil during implementation of the IMS is to ensure that *all* ideas are written down.

We commonly hear: 'That's already happening here, we just don't write the ideas down.' However, is there anything else that is important, for example, your recruitment policy, that you do not have a process for? Ideas are too important to be left to chance and in the absence of a defined process they will be pushed to the back burner due to urgent day-to-day pressures.

It is vital that the reasons for having to write down *all* ideas are communicated to employees:

■ When ideas are written down you can see what has changed and where, and who is involved in stimulating this type of improvement. The objective is that ideas will be shared and spread across different areas of the organisation.

■ The process gives employees personal pride about being allowed to fully participate in the improvement process.

■ You write things down to sustain the activity. It is the constant doing and sharing that motivates others to get involved.

■ Ideas are forgotten and lost trying to keep up with the pace and fervour of the daily work demands, so need to be noted down 'on the job'.

■ Sharing ideas often leads to another cycle of ideas by triggering other ideas and cross pollinating additional uses for the idea.

■ By sharing ideas the originator has self-expressed accountability to their peers to implement the change.

■ By sharing ideas, people naturally recognise that everybody has opportunities to improve.

The intention is that the idea is written down, concisely detailing the before and after situation, along with the effect, on an idea card (see Figure 6.1). The idea originator fills in their name and classifies the impact such as 'better process', along with a quick educated guess of cost savings from predefined guidelines. It is also good practice to include pictures or simple sketches of the before and after condition to enhance clarity. Finally the card is posted on an idea board for sharing (see Figure 6.2).

Idea card					
Idea #		Area ref:			
Date		Originator		Supervisor	
Picture/sketch of current condition			Picture/sketch of target condition		
Description of current condition			Description of target condition		
Team member/supervisor to complete together					
Estimated impact			What we learned by implementing this idea		
Impact verified by			Spread/leverage opportunities		

Figure 6.1 Idea card format

Idea metrics

In sport, if we are not keeping the score we are just practising. So it is in business and a small number of metrics are needed to monitor and improve the IMS. Some popular metrics include:

■ *Participation*: the number of people who have submitted an idea over a certain time period. A person is only counted once, regardless of the number of ideas submitted. Best-in-class organisations achieve greater than 80% participation.

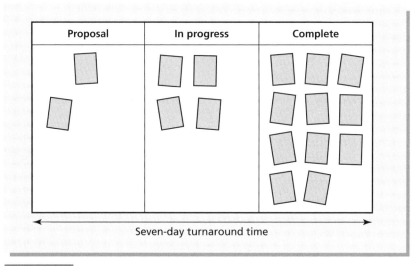

Figure 6.2   Visual idea board format

- *Ideas/employee*: total number of ideas implemented for the time period divided by the total number of employees at the end of that time period. Best-in-class organisations realise over 24 implemented ideas per employee per year. To put that in perspective this equates to one small implemented idea per employee every two weeks. Do you think that this is a realistic target for your organisation to release the vast untapped ideas residing within your employees?

- *Savings/employee*: total savings for the time period divided by the total number of employees at the end of that time period. Savings normally should be net, that is gross savings minus recognition and administration costs. Best-in-class organisations save over £2000 per employee per year. If an organisation of 500 people was trading on a 5% profit margin this would be the equivalent contribution to the business of winning a contract worth £2 million in revenue per year. However, as stated previously, the radically greater concealed benefits are the substantial increases in employee engagement and skill levels and the subsequent increases in discretionary efforts of employees.

▪ *Average turn-around time*: the total time of processing the idea from being put forward to implementation. Best-in-class organisations have a turn-around time of less than seven working days.

Reward and recognition

When organisations pay monetary rewards for ideas there are winners and losers. To overcome this you should make ideas and creativity an expected facet of everyone's job. Coming up with an idea is often the easiest part. There are many stages to be fulfilled and people involved to bring an idea into realisation. Hence paying the originator for proposing the idea often results in stifled teamwork and usually bottlenecks in the process. Rewards substantially increase the cost, time and effort needed to evaluate and implement ideas. The best systems rely on recognition and non-monetary items (Chapter 10 discusses a unique form of recognition under the Cathedral model that is highly applicable to idea systems).

Intrinsic motivation is the natural desire that people have to do a good job, better themselves and make a positive difference. It is the wholesome and fulfilling feeling a person gets from making improvements to their work. Intrinsic motivation is the difference between saying 'You couldn't pay me enough to do that', and 'I can't believe I'm getting paid to do this!' According to Alfie Kohn[2] only intrinsic rewards motivate over the medium and long term. Nurturing intrinsic motivation is crucial to the success of the IMS.

Extrinsic motivation is work done in expectation of a monetary reward. Paying for ideas can be extremely harmful to the IMS. Extrinsic rewards fade fast, become an entitlement, and may often lead to destructive behaviour. The process to implement the idea can be driven entirely by the anticipation of the reward and hence is open to dysfunctional behaviours such as cheating, withholding information and discouraging teamwork. It is important to communicate the reasons why monetary rewards are not employed to avoid the impression that the organisation is merely being tight-fisted.

Research studies have concluded that non-cash recognition is more effective than direct cash awards. A survey of 1600 companies by The American Compensation Association on productivity concluded that:

▪ Non-cash awards offered a 3:1 return on investment in comparison with cash awards.

▪ Successful non-cash initiatives cost 3–5% of an employee's annual salary while successful cash programmes must equal 5–15% to be successful.

The recognition has to be something that the employees want – which is different in various cultures.

This following popular parable demonstrates the perils of paying out rewards.

A parable

'An old woman lived alone on a street where boys played noisily every afternoon. One day the noise became too much and she called the boys into her house. She told them that she liked to listen to them play, but her hearing was failing and she could no longer hear their games. She asked them to come along each day and play noisily in front of her house. If they did, she would give them each a quarter.

The youngsters raced back the following day, and they made a tremendous racket playing happily in front of the house. The old woman paid and asked them to return the following day. Again they played and made noise, and again she paid them for it. But this time she gave each boy only 20 cents, explaining that she was running out of money. On the following day, they got only 15 cents each. Furthermore, the old woman told them that she would have to reduce the fee to a nickel on the fourth day. The boys then became angry and said they would not be back. It was not worth the effort, they said, to play for only a nickel a day.'

Rewarding employees for ideas is dependent on each organisation but some typical recognition examples include:

▪ a newsletter announcement for all winners

▪ monthly raffles for idea participants

▪ attendance at conference and training courses

- polo shirts for prolific idea participants
- praise – a personal 'thank you' means a lot
- cinema tickets – this promotes family involvement
- gift vouchers or 'Idea £s'– employees can pick from a catalogue the items that have a special meaning to them.

Recognition takes little or no money; the most important component is that it must be genuine. We are all motivated by different things so the best policy is for supervisors and team leaders to discover what motivates each individual on their team, then use a variety of recognition methods tailored to enhance each individual's motivation to participate. As long as the intended recognition has meaning to people it can cause them to do extraordinary things. Often the greatest recognition for employees is seeing their ideas have been listened to and used. Think what people will go through to win coveted sporting medals (that cost a few pounds each!). How can you create that coveted value for your organisation's recognition symbols?

Idea process flow

This has the following steps:

1 Challenge all employees to come up with two improvement ideas per month to make their work easier or more interesting, reduce costs, improve quality, improve throughput, improve safety, improve customer service, etc.

2 Encourage employees to write down ideas on an idea card every time they find a problem, make a slip-up or see an opportunity for improvement, and post them on the 'Proposal' area of the visual idea board. Whenever possible take photos or draw pictures of the before and after situations. Viewing a picture is easier than words and establishes clarity. A picture quickly explains the improvement idea and stimulates other people to do the same thing. We want people to copy each other to accelerate the continuous improvement engine and get everyone involved. Copying stimulates even more and greater ideas.

3 The idea generator evaluates and filters their idea via their peers to ensure it is suitable. (This saves supervisor evaluation time and improves the quality of ideas.) The supervisor then responds to the originator within 24 hours of the idea being forwarded. The supervisor should mentor and teach people who submit weak ideas so that they are able to submit better ones next time. Weak ideas are valuable as they unearth existing training gaps. Always remember that if you reject the idea with no reason the person feels rejected and worse still they may never bring forward ideas again! Strive to enrich the ideas with the originator and if this is not possible be tactful and explain the reasons why it is not feasible at this time. Also be welcoming of issues and problems that are brought forward, even if they are not accompanied by a solution yet, as these are also great potential opportunities. Remember the underlying goal of Lean is to ensure that all problems are surfaced on a continuous basis. Consider also the ripple effect (spread or yokoten – see the Glossary) for all ideas and the leverage impact that these may have across the entire organisation.

4 The person who comes up with the original idea should implement the idea themselves or with their work team. If additional help is needed from maintenance, technology, etc. the idea originator should coordinate the completion of this work.

5 Record implemented ideas in an idea log and/or electronically into an idea tracking software package. The electronic version is useful as the system grows and can be used as a knowledge database for intra- and cross-site spread. Software can also be utilised for automatic metric report generation. Data mining also becomes important once you get to several hundred ideas, to establish trends, etc.

6 Develop monthly metrics to ensure that the goal of two ideas per month is reached and display the results visually at the gemba. It is preferable if the local frontline Idea Champion maintains these to build buy-in and area ownership.

If this six-step cycle flows smoothly the improvement activity will also flow slickly, one idea will lead to another and continuous daily improvement will translate into improved performance and higher employee engagement. The intention is that this cycle will be used countless times daily and simplicity is all! In summary the essential elements of high-performing idea systems are:

- It is easy to put forward ideas.
- The evaluation/enrichment process is swift.
- The idea originator coordinates the implementation of their idea.

Idea management system review

To exploit the vast latent potential of employee ideas, roles and responsibilities for the idea system must be outlined at all levels. Ideas should be visually displayed on boards, implemented fast and recognised. Fresh skills are learned by employees through interacting with support functions when implementing their ideas. People are coached to recognise 'hidden' waste, and the idea system is integrated into everyday problem solving. Idea activity should also be measured. The employee's direct manager should mentor and support the idea originator during implementation. Small ideas do not take vast time and resources to put into practice and are not a drain on management: the opposite in actual fact.

Employees hate to see money wasted and the IMS gives them the motivation and authority to stamp out waste. Even occasional 'bad ideas' should be viewed as training opportunities; the intent behind the idea should be teased out with the employee or team (yes, team ideas are welcome too!) and put forward again. Peer accountability is expressed through employees posting their ideas in the local work area. In advanced systems, ideas are often tested and implemented prior to being put forward into the idea system.

SECTION 2: KAIZEN EVENTS

Introduction

The Japanese word kaizen translates as change for the better. Kaizen events or rapid improvement workshops are improvement blitzes with specific stretch targets that last typically between three to five days. These are sometimes referred to as kaikaku (large-scale change events) or jishuken (management-based events) or accelerated improvement workshops (common in healthcare where engineering language can be bewildering).

Kaizen events should be deployed strategically to improve a specified value stream. The future state value stream map, as discussed in Chapter 3, will highlight systemic problem areas in the value stream and significant improvement projects to close these gaps are often tackled using a kaizen event workshop. Additionally, organisations often choose to run an event as a proof point to demonstrate the potential of Lean.

The most successful Lean companies in my view use kaizen events (for both management and frontline staff) as the primary mechanism for learning about Lean. Lean is not learned in the classroom (although you can introduce the concepts here), it is learned deeply by physical practice just as an athlete cannot be taught how to perform their sport from the dressing room, instead they have to practise daily. Kaizen pulls in all the Lean tools over a period of extended practice and really flicks on the light bulbs as to the potential for improvement for both management and team members. Kaizen events are classified as either maintenance kaizen (to resolve issues such as downtime, etc.) or improvement kaizen (to raise the level of performance closer to the fourth True North Lean principle of perfection). Kaizen has the potential to give an organisation an excessive competitive advantage and really compresses traditional project lead times.

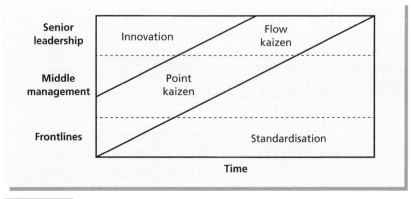

Figure 6.3   The kaizen flag

The kaizen flag concept[3] (Figure 6.3) is a good barometer for where focus should be at the various levels in your organisation. At the senior leadership level approximately one-third of time and energy should be spent on strategic activity designing waste out of future processes and developing innovation opportunities for the organisation. Another one-third of the time should be spent directly participating in flow kaizen events that improve the overall system-wide value stream velocity of current operations. The remaining third is spent on day-to-day operations, people management and facilitating the improvement of standardisation through gemba walks, etc. At the middle management level approximately one-third of time is spent coaching and developing people in improvement work, problem solving and point kaizen (local changes such as through the idea management system). The remaining two-thirds of the time is spent running the day-to-day operations, auditing standard work and on personnel activities. The frontline is where money is made and services are delivered, hence the greatest proportion of time here is spent delivering value to customers. However, crucially the Lean paradigm calls for the dual focus of doing work *and* spending time every day on improvement work and point kaizen to incrementally raise the bar.

These workshops are team-based process improvement bursts that are highly action oriented. In general, more than 50% of the identified improvements during the workshop are implemented within the week and the vast majority within 30 days of the workshop's end. This represents a new departure of getting things done fast versus the conventional project mindset that can span months. Significant improvements in the range of 50% or more on the baseline metrics are realised over a period of one week or less.

The events are powerful engines for change as cross-functional teams of people with deep and distinct process knowledge are brought together for a highly focused period to analyse their processes and realise improvements. For example, in an event with a team of 12 people with an average of 15 years' experience each this would bring 180 years of accumulated knowledge, experience and wisdom to the table for an entire week. Kaizen events are also often used as an action oriented method to systematically deploy the hoshin strategy.

Common results that can be achieved include:

▪ throughput time reduction of 50–90%

▪ productivity improvements of 15–25%

▪ work-in-progress reductions of 20–85%

▪ set-up time reduction of 30–85%

▪ defect reduction of 50–100%

▪ material/supplies/people travel distance reductions of 50–85%.

Kaizen event stages

Do not underestimate the time needed for preparatory activities to ensure that you run a successful event. As a rule of thumb, 40% of the time should be spent on preparing for the event, 20% of the time on the actual event week itself, and the remaining 40% on close-out and follow-up activity.

Pre-event preparation

The cycle time for a kaizen event is typically seven weeks and then two further monthly checkpoints are carried out after 60 and 90 days from the event week to lock in the gains. Preparation for the 3–5 day workshop normally starts three weeks before the event (see Figure 6.4). When the area for improvement is identified the management and Lean facilitator (externally appointed or internal expert) normally walk through the process and construct a high-level process map. The following tasks need to be considered by the event leader and Lean facilitator in preparation for the week-long event.

Three weeks before

▪ Schedule the week event.

▪ Select the event sponsor (authority to remove potential road-blocks).

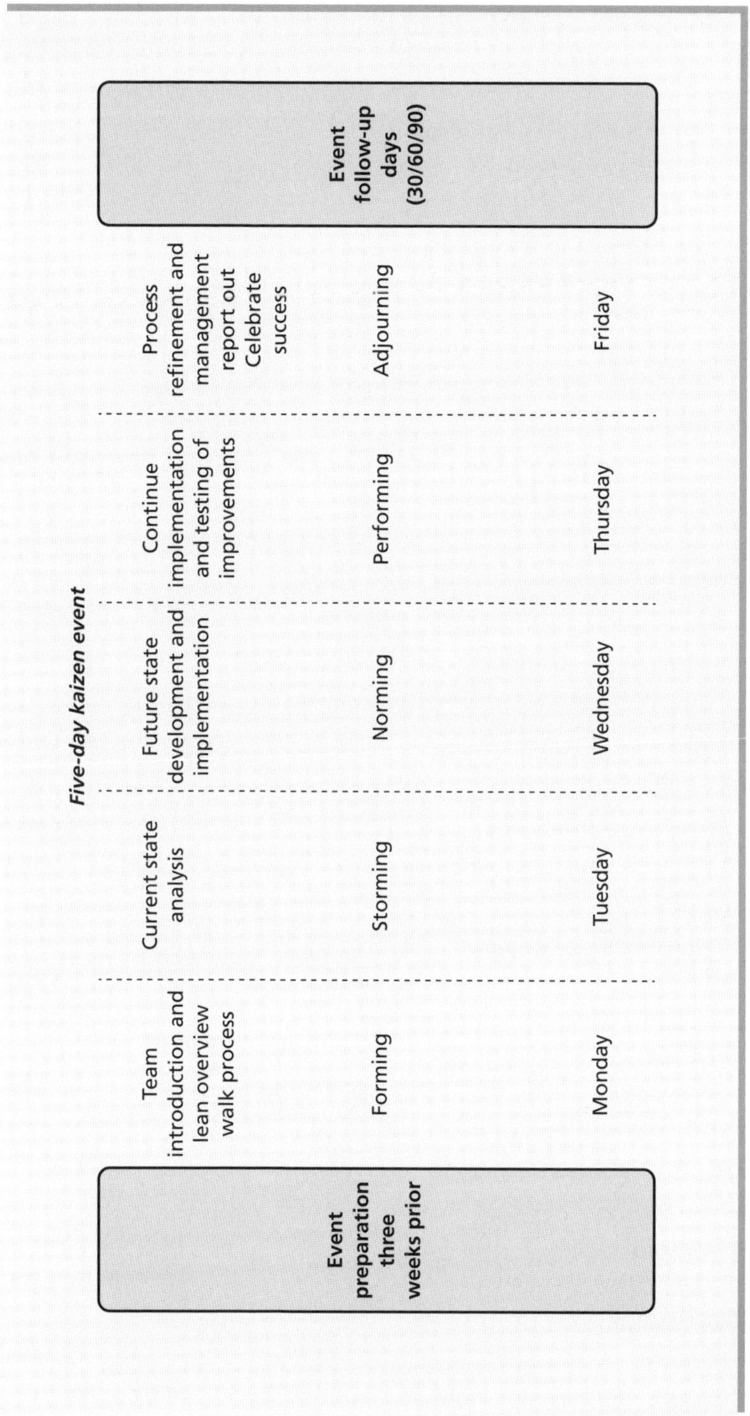

Event preparation three weeks prior	Team introduction and lean overview walk process	Current state analysis	Future state development and implementation	Continue implementation and testing of improvements	Process refinement and management report out Celebrate success	Event follow-up days (30/60/90)
	Forming	Storming	Norming	Performing	Adjourning	
	Monday	Tuesday	Wednesday	Thursday	Friday	

Five-day kaizen event

Figure 6.4   Kaizen event outline

▪ Draft the kaizen charter. This document sets objectives for the event, targets for improvement (for example, productivity, quality, cost, lead time, set-up time), scope of the event, process start and end points, constraints (financial, etc.), event leader, core and extended on-call team members. The charter is personally signed by the area management team as a sign of commitment to the process and to give the team authority to make changes.

▪ The composition of the team's stakeholders is a critical ingredient for success: the majority should be from the area under improvement, they should have particular knowledge of the area operations, be respected and viewed as leaders in the area. Often sceptics can be transformed during the event, a pair of fresh eyes on the team can bring new perspectives and unions should be represented on the extended team at least.

▪ Typically the optimum size of the kaizen team is between eight and twelve core team members (a full-time presence on the week event) but this can vary widely depending on the scope of the undertaking.

▪ Gain alignment and discuss expectations with area management.

▪ Perform a Lean assessment of the area (see the Appendix).

▪ Develop a data collection plan to be completed before the workshop such as process attributes like takt time, cycle times, staff numbers, overtime, process flows, layout, changeover time, shift patterns, demand data, inventory information, current standard work documentation (if it exists) etc.

▪ Book a conference room or equivalent for the week and schedule the event week in people's diaries (including the presence of management for event report outs).

▪ Draft the communication plan to be deployed before, during and after the event. (Note: this is one of the most commonly omitted tasks and is of extreme importance.)

▪ Meet with the kaizen team to present the kaizen process and to discuss the event objective. Also involve downstream and upstream internal customers and external customer representation if appropriate.

▪ Walk through the process with the core event team and record observations as required.

▪ Implement week three communication plan.

Two weeks before

- Work with the area supervisor to identify people who will be attending the week event and ensure that all shifts will be represented at the event week.

- Arrange for support staff such as maintenance, IT, facilities, etc. to be available for the week on-call if required to help with implementing changes such as fabrication work or software changes.

- Arrange logistics and directions, etc. for external staff attending the event week.

- Gain approval for the rapid purchase of supplies and equipment during the course of the week (if required).

- Select and prepare the appropriate Lean training materials (as required by the event objectives).

- Develop and distribute the event agenda.

- Train the team and management in the philosophy and basics of Lean and probable methods that will be utilised during the event week (if required).

- Conduct a meeting with the kaizen team to review readiness for the event and select sub-teams as required, for example one team might examine material flow, one information flow and another people flow.

- Update the management team on the preparation status.

- Order catering (if required in-room to facilitate the continuity of the event).

- Implement week two communication plan.

One week before

- Prepare event materials such as training booklets, order flipcharts and sticky notes/markers etc., book the projector, make name cards, organise the room layout.

- Conduct the weekly team meeting to review progress and address any concerns.

- Check in with all team members to arrange any last minute substitutions if required.
- Perform a dummy run of the week and test training materials.
- Check on catering (if required).
- Present the event pre-collected data in a user friendly format for participants.
- Implement week one communication plan.

Event workshop

Bruce Tuckman proposed the popular model of team development in 1965 based on forming, storming, norming and performing. In 1977 he and Mary Ann Jensen added 'adjourning' to the model. This model is very appropriate to describe the development of the event team over the course of the week together.

Team development

Monday

Forming – participants are polite but guarded and test other participants' motives and commitment. There is a high dependency on the kaizen facilitators during this stage to intervene to nurture team dynamics.

Tuesday

Storming – facilitators need to be ready for confrontation and social loafing (holding back) at this stage and there can be resistance to new ideas.

Wednesday

Norming – resistance is melting and the team is gaining competence and accepting feedback.

Thursday

Performing – teamwork and resourcefulness are now the norm and implementation is generally moving ahead at full steam.

Friday

Adjourning is concerned with closing out actions and terminating roles. Participants can experience a sense of loss as they prepare to go back to the 'day' job. The seasoned event facilitator will help participants see that this is just the beginning of a never-ending improvement journey.

The attitude and culture required for success are encapsulated in the 12 golden rules below. These are conveyed to the team throughout the week with the expectation that they are adhered to. Team members are also strongly encouraged to use the 'challenge anyone concept' when adherence to any of the rules is violated.

Kaizen spirit golden rules

1   Core team members must be present for the entire event, no outside interruptions, phones off.

2   Be open to change and new ideas, view problems positively as opportunities.

3   Think of how to do it, not why it cannot be done; excuses have no place.

4   Challenge everything! Ask open-ended questions. There are no sacred cows, so ask, 'Why?' five times to uncover root causes, not symptoms.

5   Blame has no place – focus on the process or lack of process and attack problems not people.

6   Speak with data, then add experience and instinct into the discussion.

7   Do not seek perfection. Do it now even if not flawless, but aim to make it better.

8   Spend ideas and ingenuity, not pounds. Kaizen is a no-cost or low-cost solution.

9   Abandon department thinking or turf battles – value flows across departments. The 'stripes come off' in kaizen – all team members have an equal standing and say.

10   Seek the wisdom of many people rather than the knowledge of a few.

11   Improvement ideas are infinite.

12   Avoid scope creep.

Schedule

The schedule below is for a week-long event. (Note: the duration of the event can change depending on the size of the undertaking.)

Monday

■ Check that the room is in order prior to the scheduled kick-off.

■ Sponsor introduces and frames the event's importance to the business need.

■ Introductions, expectations and an ice breaker game.

▪ The week's agenda is given.

▪ Deliver the Lean training as per the needs of the event.

▪ Reconfirm commitment to following the golden rules.

▪ Break into identified sub-teams, walk through the process and document current state observations.

▪ Implement the day-one communication plan including updating the area under analysis when the kaizen team will be onsite.

Tuesday

▪ Review objectives and today's agenda.

▪ Divide into sub-teams and go to the gemba to map the current process in detail and collect the relevant process attribute data per sub-team.

▪ Observe and record operational waste in the area using the TIM WOOD DOES IT form (see Table 1.2).

▪ Take pictures as required (worth a thousand words!).

▪ Talk with the frontline associates as required to get actual facts.

▪ Observe opportunities for Lean methods such as 5S workplace organisation, etc.

▪ Interact with the area supervisor and keep them informed of findings.

▪ Observe staffing levels and customer demand over the period of observation.

▪ Return to the conference room and document the data analysis using sticky notes.

▪ Brainstorm and perform analysis of the maps and other documentation.

▪ Challenge every step in the process. Look to eliminate non-value-adding activities, use alternative methods and streamline current value-adding activities.

▪ Perform systematic problem solving as required.

▪ Use creativity techniques such as SCAMPER to break people out of pre-conditioned patterns of thinking.

> *'Discovery consists in seeing what everyone else has seen and thinking what no one else has thought.'*
>
> Albert Szent-Györgyi (physiologist and Nobel Prize winner)

SCAMPER |

SCAMPER is a checklist of provoking questions you would not normally ask that helps you to think of changes you can make to an existing process or product/service, or to create a new one. The questions were developed by Alex Osborn and later rearranged by Bob Eberle into SCAMPER. The questions SCAMPER stands for are detailed below and you can add and expand with your own additional questions (see Table 6.1).

Table 6.1 SCAMPER table for idea provocation

Substitute	Can I substitute something else? Who else? What else? Other ingredients? Other material? Other power? Other place?
Combine	What can be combined? Combine materials? What other products can be merged with this?
Adapt	What else is like this? What other ideas does this suggest? Does the past offer a solution? Whom could I copy or draw inspiration from?
Magnify/Modify	What can be magnified, made larger or extended? What can be exaggerated? What can be added? More time? Stronger? Higher? Longer? How can this be altered for the better? What can be modified? Is there a new twist? Change meaning, colour, motion, smell, form, shape? Change name?
Put to other use	What else could this be used for? Are there any other ways to use as is?
Eliminate	What are the opposites? What are the negatives? Should I turn it around? Up instead of down? Down instead of up?
Reverse/ Rearrange	What if it were smaller? Understated? What should I omit? Delete? Subtract? What is unnecessary? Streamline? Make miniature? Condense? Compact? What other rearrangement might be better? Interchange components?

▪ Develop the improvement plan to deliver the improved future state process.

▪ Determine where support is needed from other departments for implementation and organise this for days 3 and 4.

▪ Sub-team debriefing report disseminated to entire kaizen team and management (5 minutes each).

▪ Implement the day-two communication plan and convey the plans for day three.

Wednesday

▪ Review yesterday's findings.

▪ Review golden rules and today's agenda.

▪ Conduct further root cause analysis and problem solving as required.

▪ Plan the implementation activities.

▪ Begin implementation using PDSA cycles.

▪ Plan overnight work and deliveries (if required).

▪ Sub-team debriefing report disseminated to the kaizen team and management (5 minutes each).

▪ Implement the day-three communication plan and convey the plans for day four.

Thursday

▪ Review yesterday's accomplishments.

▪ Continue implementation.

▪ Run improved process and fine tune as needed.

▪ Develop new metrics.

▪ Prepare standard work (what is being done? in what order? how long should it take? what clearly defined measurable outcomes are required?).

▪ Prepare area for management walk through.

▪ Plan overnight work and deliveries as required.

▪ Sub-team debriefing report disseminated to entire kaizen team and management (5 minutes each).

Friday

- Develop management final report presentation.
- Meet with area supervisors to communicate changes and possible effects.
- Develop 30-day actions for items not finalised during the event week.
- Send kaizen results summary to sponsor.
- Perform a dry run of the final presentation.
- Final presentation detailing improvements achieved, work to do, infrastructure to sustain the gains, and question and answer forum.
- Management and kaizen team walk through of the post kaizen area.
- Schedule weekly update meetings until the 30-day action plan is complete and improvements sustained.
- Plan 60- and 90-day checkpoints.
- Conduct an after action review or hansei (see Chapter 13 for more detail) of the event to consolidate learning and to review (what went well?, what didn't go well, what helped?, what hindered?, lessons learned?) how the kaizen process itself worked (not just the results that were achieved, remember the right process will always deliver the right results).
- Look for spread and leverage potential of the gains achieved in other areas.
- Review alignment with the site's annual hoshin plans (see Chapter 2).
- Implement the day-five communication plan.
- Recognition (ideally by the CEO, see Chapter 10 on the Cathedral model) and celebration event.

Confirmation phase

The confirmation phase ensures that improvements made in the event week are sustained and yet further cycles of improvement are progressing. There is a detailed follow-up meeting each week for one month after the event where the primary focus is on closing out the actions at the 30–day checkpoint. Standard work and training constitute a lot of the heavy lifting in this phase. Two further checkpoints are organised for 60 and 90 days after the event to cement in the improvements.

Kaizen review

Key success factors for a successful event include:

▪ through preparation, post-event follow-up and support

▪ a dedicated, internal, Lean facilitator for the workshop

▪ an external Lean coach for early events

▪ cross-functional team selection representing all stakeholders from the affected value stream

▪ management kick-off and active involvement throughout the entire kaizen cycle

▪ finance department verification that the claimed 'hard' cost savings are real and that there is a plan in place to exploit the savings (for example, released capacity to do more should be translated into increased demand)

▪ just as important as the actual physical results from the event is the way people have developed and grown as leaders as a result of their participation.

There should be acute recognition that kaizen events alone will not be sufficient to transform your organisation. For example, if you run 50 kaizen events per year in your company that may have hundreds of processes then you will only get to revisit a process every second year or so and entropy will have pulled its performance back down. For Lean to be fully effective it must be deployed as a system; the mindset and methods applied together are greater than any single method. Kaizen events are certainly powerful for step change improvements but the real gains emerge when everyday incremental improvements are implemented by those working the processes (see section 1 of this chapter and Chapter 11's Lean daily management system). Everyday improvement is possibly the most powerful tactic to ensure that Lean gains are indeed sustained.

7

Lean methods and tools (part IV)

This chapter discusses quick changeover in Section 1 and total productive maintenance (TPM) in Section 2.

SECTION 1: QUICK CHANGEOVER

Introduction

Changeover is defined as all the activities involved between delivering the last good product or service to delivering the next good product or service at the specified level of efficiency. Changeover is relevant across all industries: from the changing of a mould on a plastic injection machine, to setting up for the next procedure in a hospital's operating theatre, to a software engineer getting up to speed on a new application having switched tasks from another project. The last is known as cognitive changeover and is a common predicament in the knowledge economy.

The quick changeover, or SMED process as it is commonly known, was formulated in the 1950s by Shigeo Shingo.[1] The acronym SMED refers to single minute exchange of die (tool) where the single minute refers to a sole digit or, in effect, changing over in less than ten minutes. It is common to achieve reductions in changeover of 50% or more with very low capital expenditure. Achieving quick changeover is an ideal candidate for the kaizen events discussed in the previous chapter.

The classic approach to moderating the impact of changeover in a business is to perform as few changeovers as possible and keep equipment or people producing large batches when the equipment is running well. But there are many unintended consequences of this practice, perhaps the worst being inflated lead times (time is money!). One reason for this is because in large batch processing there is an increased risk of quality write-offs due to extended feedback loops on quality conformance, and lead time is increased when we work with large batches (see Chapter 9 for further discussion on lead time and its impact on cost and other factors).

Why quick changeover?

The benefits are as follows:

■ *Reduced inventories*: in manufacturing and services, batch sizes can be reduced as the time for changeover is reduced. This in turn allows smaller inventory quantities to be carried and overall product lead time is reduced through smaller transfer batches. To reduce changeover time by 50% while at the same time doubling the number of changeovers inventory can be reduced by up to 50%. So the deeper reason for changeover improvement is to be able to conduct more changeovers and reduce lead time. A metric called every product every interval (EPEI) measures the time interval that your complete range of product offerings are cycled through. The smaller this interval the leaner your organisation will become and the greater its potential to offer product diversity as a strategic tactic. Inventory holding costs include obsolescence, theft, damage or spoilage, insurance, handling (equipment and labour), cost of money tied up in inventory, space and racking allocated to inventory, and cost of updating inventory control systems such as SAP. Depending on the industry these costs can amount to a yearly holding cost of 50–80% of the value of the inventory. For example, if you are carrying on average £100,000 of inventory at any given time, it may be costing you an additional £50,000 to £80,000 per year to hold this (depending on the industry type). So you should give your full attention to the levels of inventory that you are holding and that they are the appropriate amounts, in the appropriate place, at the appropriate time.

▪ *Higher quality levels*: when inventory levels are lowered product is moved faster through the value stream and potential non-conformances are discovered more quickly. This leads to an increased probability of finding the true root cause of faults.

▪ *Improved flexibility*: reducing set-up time frees up capacity and the capability to offer and deliver more products or services.

▪ *Improve frontline employee capabilities*: involving frontline people in problem solving and kaizen leads to the development of new skills and increased levels of engagement.

▪ *Lower costs*: operational capacity improvement leads to increased output and the potential avoidance of further capacity and facility expenditure to meet demand.

> *'One of the most noteworthy accomplishments in keeping the price of Ford products low is the gradual shortening of the production cycle. The longer an article is in the process of manufacture and the more it is moved about, the greater is its ultimate cost.'*
>
> *Henry Ford[2]*

It is important to have a strategy for exploiting improvements in changeover performance. This ranges from increases in capacity to the potential to serve niche markets that demand small batches of diversified products. Many companies are using quick changeover as a way of differentiating their business. One excellent example is Southwest Airlines. It leads the industry in terms of cost and customer satisfaction through its speed at emptying one aircraft on the ground to having the aircraft loaded and back in the air. It takes the airline between 20 and 30 minutes for a 137 seater aircraft.[3] For its competitors the turnaround time is approximately one hour. Ground time is non-revenue generating for aircraft companies; consequently changeover improvement has immense implications for profitability.

Quick changeover does not mean rushing through the steps to achieve the changeover; quality will be improved through the removal of waste and hence process steps (fewer process steps means fewer potential opportunities for errors). Most pre-SMED changeover processes contain 80% waste: this is because they are often not deliberately designed as a process. They are frequently seen as a necessary burden and changeovers are hated by team members in general due to the hassle factors involved. Fewer steps and better teamwork allied with simplified decision making actually enable superior quality in less time.

A powerful example of quick changeover is the pit stop process in Formula 1 racing. When the car stops at the pit, preparation is first class, with the right quantity of equipment and material in place and in working order. There is no searching for items and the team is in position and ready to go. In business this is often not the case. For example, the production line or operating theatre may sit waiting for people to be available to work on the changeover and when they do start to work the roles and responsibilities for changeover are often unclear. Added to this is often the availability of equipment and supplies. Frequently they are not in place and time is wasted searching for them. In the pit stop, teamwork is first rate and everybody has defined roles and rehearses the routine regularly. Economies of repetition lead to increased competency. As a result the changeover in Formula 1 can be performed in less than five seconds; just a few years ago this remarkable feat was ten seconds but never say that good is good enough!

Figure 7.1 shows the approximate breakdown of typical changeovers and the opportunity for improvement: 80% of the time is generally in the preparation and ramp-up stages.

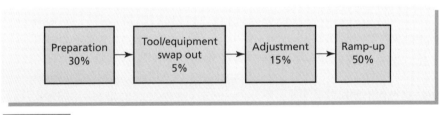

Figure 7.1   Changeover stages

Ways to implement SMED methodology

Set objectives

Reduce changeover by 50%.

Team selection

Cross-functional team: frontline associates, supervisor, technician, engineer and Lean coach (usually a team of 5–8 people).

Train stakeholders

In why the improvement is being sought and what the benefits are for the business and the people themselves, the SMED process, process mapping, standard work combination chart, TIM WOOD DOES IT waste categories (see Table 1.2), and A3 problem solving.

Collect data and study the existing changeover

A number of roles are required to study the changeover process. The scribe documents the process. The timer clocks each task. Sometimes these two roles can be performed by the same person depending on the pace of the changeover. The pacer outlines the motion of the changeover person on a spaghetti diagram (see the Glossary). A video camera is very valuable for studying the process because it provides irrefutable evidence as to the current state. The waste observer records all instances of operational waste that have been detected. Ideally an individual scribe, timer, pacer, video recorder and waste observer should follow each person performing the changeover.

A typical changeover analysis sheet is shown in Figure 7.2.

SMED four-step process

The team meets after the data collection and develops a theoretical reference changeover sequence and time. A reference changeover is the time that a waste free changeover would take. The SMED stages are shown in Figure 7.3 and detailed as follows:

1 Separate internal activities (equipment must be stopped to do this activity) and external activities (this activity can be done whilst equipment is operating). For example, ensuring that all the required equipment is in position for the changeover is an external activity. An example of an internal activity would be cleaning a hotel room between guests.

#	Start Time	Event	Task Description	Internal	External	Eliminate	Improvement Actions

Figure 7.2 Changeover analysis sheet

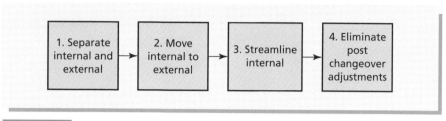

Figure 7.3 SMED stages

2 Move internal to external: brainstorm ways to enable activities that are currently performed when the equipment is stopped to be done when the equipment is running.

3 Streamline internal: identify ways to enable faster application of internal activities. An example of this would be the replacement of bolts with toggle clamps (if appropriate) on a hydraulic press machine.

4 Eliminate post-changeover adjustments (time to return to the normal rate of working and quality checks etc.): look for ways to maximise the speed that the operation is returned to normal efficiency after the changeover has been completed.

Figure 7.4 shows the four-step SMED process in action.

> '... many companies have set up policies designed to raise the skill level of the workers, few have implemented strategies that lower the skill level required by the set-up itself.'
>
> *Shigeo Shingo[4]*

Develop an improvement action plan that includes both 'soft' organisational changes and 'hard' design led changes. Your team can then move into the implementation stage to deliver the improvements.

Figures 7.5 and 7.6 illustrate the impact of SMED on changeover time when tasks are performed externally when the equipment is running, performed in parallel, streamlined and/or engineering and design methods are deployed to reduce the time of ramp-up to defined levels of efficiency. Using these techniques you will generally see a 50% reduction in changeover time.

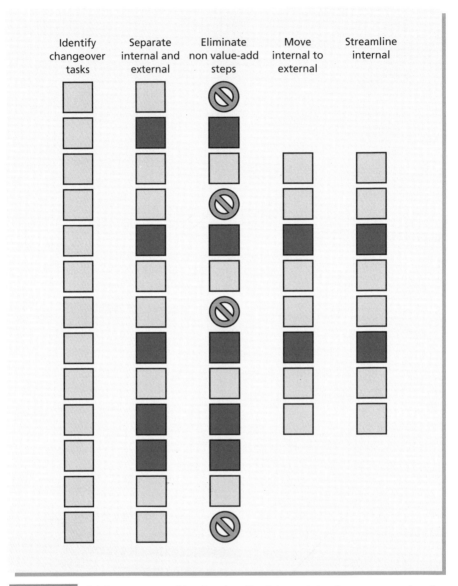

Figure 7.4 Sticky notes used to develop the future state changeover using the four-step SMED process

SMED improvement prompts

- Conduct tasks in parallel
- Break task interdependencies
- Use quick release couplings
- Use power tools
- Use location pins
- Use hydraulic lifters
- Use magnetic clamps
- Use overhead lifting aids
- Eliminate adjustments
- Replace bolts with wing nuts
- Apply 5S to the area (see Chapter 4, Section 1)
- Provide instructions at point of use
- Use visual controls or cues to reduce cognitive orientation (knowledge work)
- Redistribute tasks to obtain a better flow
- Open up tolerances
- Heat treat parts that wear
- Light weighting – replace steel with aluminium
- Use magnets
- Use gravity to good effect
- No changeovers during break times

When the process improvements have been implemented, the process needs to be verified. Re-time and video the process and study it for yet further improvements. Write and adopt new changeover standards and build consensus across shifts. It creates buy-in if you involve associates in designing the standard work and then train people according to the new standard. Sustaining the gains is fostered if you include a changeover time metric in your operational review meeting. It is good practice after the SMED event to conduct a review with your team members to maximise what has been learned.

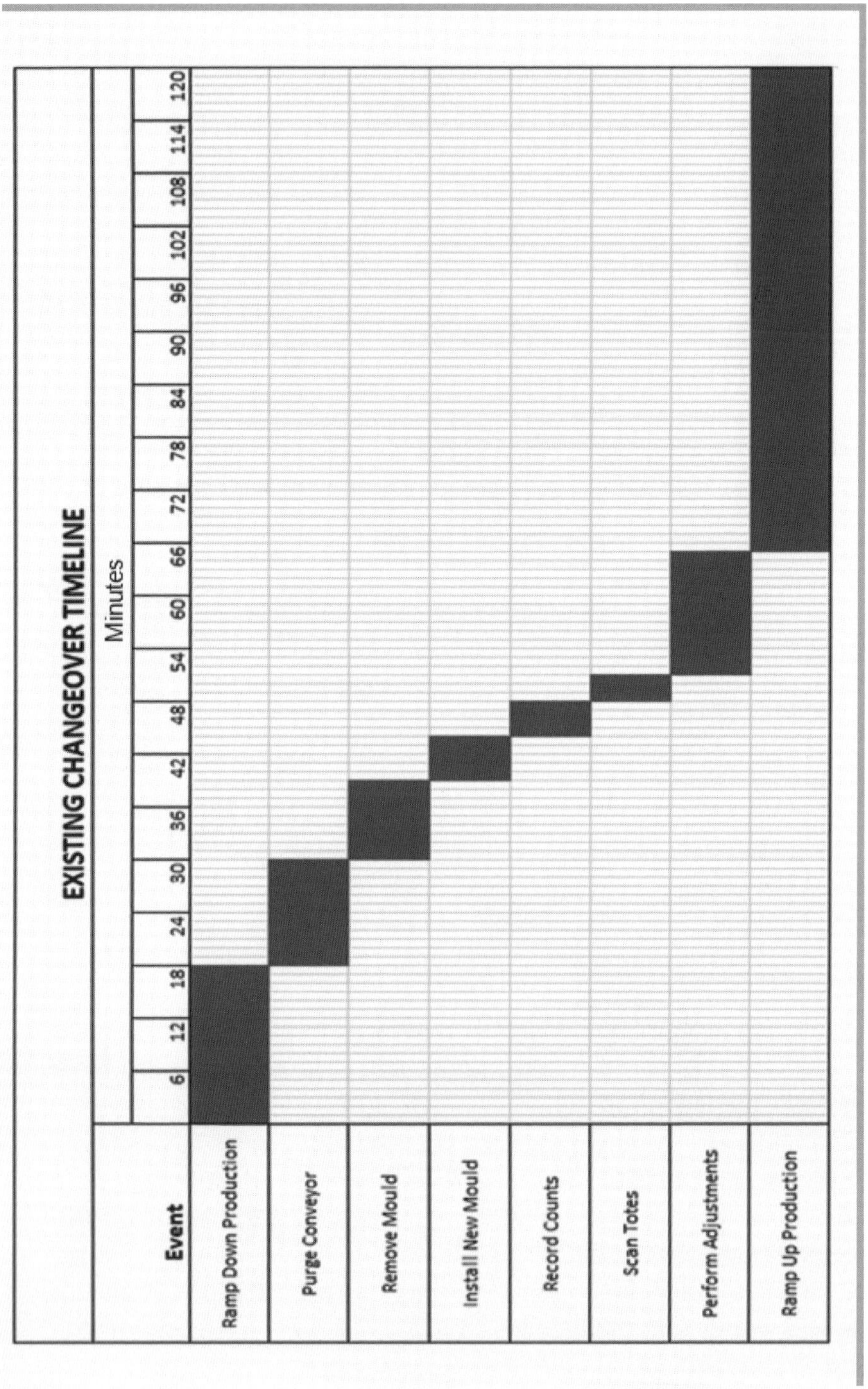

Figure 7.5   Pre-SMED changeover example

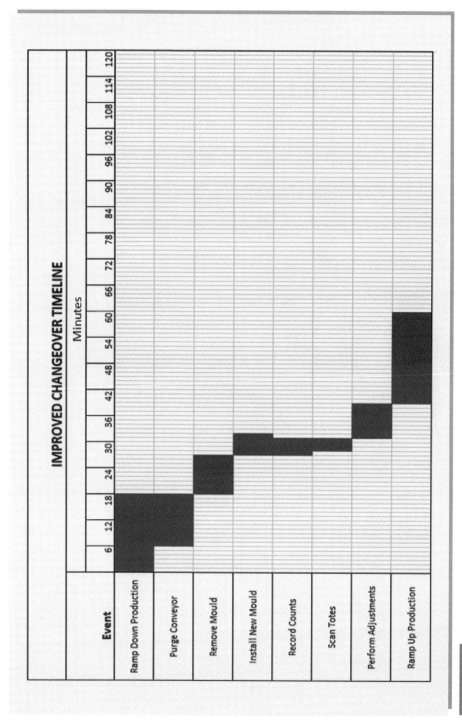

Figure 7.6   Post-SMED changeover example

Using a visual management board (see Figure 7.7) is also an extremely effective way of sustaining gains from the initial SMED event and driving further, daily, continuous improvement. The board depicts the analogy of the racing pit crew to demonstrate the philosophy of quick changeover. The post-SMED standard work procedure for the improved changeover is displayed. The old adage of 'tell me how you will measure me and I'll tell you how I will behave' is very true. The fact of measuring and reviewing change-over performance will evoke what is known as the Hawthorne effect, which instantly improves performance significantly. (If you have not heard of this, the Hawthorne effect is a form of reaction where people improve or adapt their behaviour from simply being measured.)

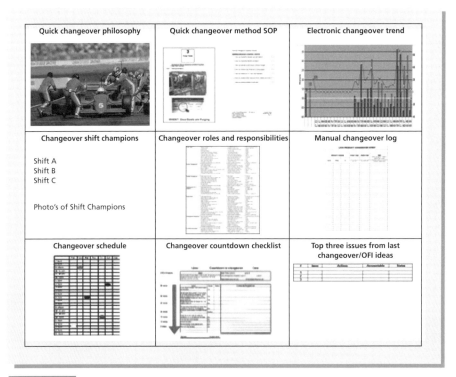

Figure 7.7   Visual changeover board at the gemba

The board displays both an automated electronic metric and a manual version. This forms a good reference for comparison and also enables the frontline workers to interact physically with the visuals. To help to build ownership, photos of changeover shift champions can be displayed and also roles and responsibilities are outlined in the leader standard work (see Table 7.1). The schedule of changeovers is displayed and magnets are used to populate daily and hourly timeslots where changeovers are scheduled. This helps to inform the team when they need to start preparation for changeover (consider that approximately 30% of changeover time is preparation). The countdown to changeover checklist details the tasks that need to be completed (see Table 7.1). Finally the board has a section that captures issues from each changeover so that continuous improvement is practised between every changeover, leading to everyday incremental gains in performance.

Quick changeover review

Quick changeover is one of the most rewarding but amazingly absent methods deployed across most businesses today. Every day we come across examples of poor changeover, from waiting for a hotel room to be ready for occupancy, to waiting in line to board a plane at the airport. The benefits of slick changeover include lower inventories, on-time deliveries and improved efficiency. Achieving quick changeover will ultimately result in improved productivity, more satisfied customers and staff, and increased profits.

Table 7.1 Changeover leader standard work

Who	What	Why	When
Production manager	Bi-weekly process waste walk and board reading	Sustain the gains and show support	Monday and Thursday @ 3pm
	Review audit metric at ops meeting (target C/O 35 mins)	Monitor progress	Tuesday 12 pm
	Planned vs. unplanned C/O ratio review metric	Highlight % of unplanned events	Tuesday 12 pm
Supervisors	Determine product changeover time	Communication to line	3 hours before changeover
	Verify that we have materials	Prevents line interruptions	3 hours before changeover
	Supervisor informs techs about changeover and time	Time to prepare internal equipment	3 hours before changeover
	Inform coordinator and team associates of exact changeover time	Time to prepare external equipment	3 hours before changeover
	Update changeover board magnet schedule	Communication	Daily
	Drive resolution of 'Top 3 Issues' log on board if required	Resolve daily issues and sustain the gains	At daily huddles @ 11:30 am/pm and 3:30 am/pm
Technicians	Attend daily huddles (8:15, 11:30 and 3:30)	Communication	8:15, 11:30 and 3:30
	Maintain and repair shadow boards, etc. as required	Reduce time retrieving and searching	As required
	Complete actions assigned from 'Top 3 Issues' log as required	Resolve daily issues	As assigned
	Follow 'Count Down to Changeover' checklist (external tasks)	Ensure external tasks are prepared	3 hours before changeover
	Follow changeover standard sequence (see posted Gantt chart)	Ensure current best way is followed	3 hours before changeover

Who	What	Why	When
Shift coordinator	Follow 'Count Down to Changeover' checklist (external tasks)	Ensure external tasks are prepared	3 hours before changeover
	Follow changeover standard sequence (see posted Gantt chart)	Ensure current best way is followed	3 hours before changeover
	Log changeover start/stop time and 'Top 3 Issues' sheet	Track changeover times	Every Tuesday @ 12pm
	Order materials from warehouse	Ensure no part shortages	As required
	Complete SAP if required and workbooks on-line	Inventory accuracy	3 hours before changeover
	Reset quality insurance station	Inventory and quality accuracy	Every changeover
	Replenish shadow boards as required	Reduce time retrieving and searching	As needed
	Perform physical changeover as required	Reduce cycle time and flexibility	Per changeover
Frontline staff	Follow 'Count Down to Changeover' checklist (external tasks)	Ensure external tasks are prepared	3 hours before changeover
	Follow changeover standard sequence (see posted Gantt chart)	Ensure current best way is followed	3 hours before changeover
	Order materials from stores	Track changeover times	3 hours before changeover
	Complete SAP if required and workbooks on-line	Ensure no part shortages	Per changeover
	Maintain shadow boards as required	Reduce time retrieving and searching	As needed
	Perform physical changeover as required	Reduce cycle time and flexibility	As scheduled
	Ensure purged material is labelled correctly	Ensure no product mismatches	As required

SECTION 2: TOTAL PRODUCTIVE MAINTENANCE (TPM)

Introduction

True Lean transformation is unattainable in your organisation if you have low equipment reliability. Total productive maintenance (TPM) takes a holistic view of equipment including concepts that cover availability, performance, quality, safety and capital investment.

Why TPM?

The importance of TPM becomes critical as organisations become leaner and hence more exposed to:

▪ shorter lead times

▪ lower levels of inventory

▪ tightly linked processes.

Hence machine stoppages can be extremely disruptive and effective maintenance is vital to achieving output targets. A great deal of capital expenditure is classically wasted on new equipment rather than making the best use of existing equipment. TPM tackles these issues at the source.

TPM will bring maintenance into focus as a necessary and vitally important part of your business. Scheduled time for maintenance is integrated into the routine work day. The idea is to have emergency and unscheduled maintenance become a thing of the past.

In the 1950s, equipment maintenance was not practised to be preventive; it predominantly involved just the act of repairing a piece of equipment after it broke down. It was, in effect, breakdown maintenance: react only when the equipment has failed. In due course management came to realise the importance of preventing equipment breakdowns in order to boost productivity. Thus, scheduled maintenance activities in order to prevent unforeseen breakdowns (preventive maintenance) gradually became popular. Under this approach equipment maintenance was the sole responsibility of technical personnel in the maintenance department.

In the 1970s, the concept of productive maintenance became popular. This combined into one system: preventive maintenance, equipment reliability engineering, equipment maintainability engineering, and equipment engineering economics. In this system, the technical or engineering group still had the foremost responsibility for equipment maintenance.

The concept of 'true' TPM in which everyone from the frontline people to senior management own equipment maintenance evolved shortly afterwards. TPM embraces various disciplines such as 5S, inspecting for early failure warnings, and frontline equipment ownership. This creates the environment where everyone has a stake in and responsibility for keeping equipment running and productive.

The frontline workers are no longer restricted just to running the equipment and calling a technical specialist when a breakdown occurs. They are actively involved in monitoring, cleaning, lubrication, adjustments, and also perform basic calibrations on their respective equipment. This will free your technical workforce for complex preventive maintenance activities that require more of their technical expertise. Management should also show interest in data concerning equipment uptime, utilisation and efficiency. In short, everyone understands that the concepts of zero breakdowns, maximum productivity and zero defects are goals to be shared by everyone under TPM.

Aside from eliminating equipment downtime, improving equipment productivity and defect reduction, TPM has the following goals: improvement of personnel and team effectiveness through the sense of ownership of performance targets, and a reduction in operational costs and throughput times. However, TPM cannot be implemented overnight. Normally it will take your organisation at least two to three years to establish an effective TPM system.

TPM pulls in many other Lean methods including:

- 5S (workplace organisation)
- SMED (set-up reduction)
- problem solving
- poka yoke
- team coaching and facilitation.

(Note: the success of your Lean transformation will be dependent upon how the philosophy, principles and methods all work holistically together as a system.)

Application of TPM

Your leadership team should set definitive annual objectives for the TPM programme (ideally through your hoshin planning process, as described in Chapter 2). The objectives might address specific performance measures such as MTBF (mean time between failure), MTTR (mean time to repair), equipment availability, performance efficiency, quality, safety, percentage of employees participating, and growth in employee skill versatility.

The implementation should begin with just a few target or pilot areas. The purpose of the pilots is to minimise risk by limiting the rollout to a controlled area and to build a showcase example to encourage the spread of these local success stories across your organisation.

A pilot area should be selected based on:

▪ a high probability of success
▪ an area that has important but resolvable maintenance problems
▪ where employee–manager relations are good
▪ where employees are open and willing to try new ideas.

TPM improvement plan

Only the critical equipment and/or bottleneck or near bottleneck processes should be subjected to the following rigorous care plan. A bottleneck occurs when the capacity of your organisation is limited by a specific resource. Without increasing this resource the performance of the overall system cannot be improved as this is the 'pinch point'.

The care plan

This consists of the following steps.

1. Current state analysis

Through observations, interviews, and analysis, the team gathers data about the current state of the equipment in terms of production losses, downtime, MTBF, etc. The team assesses current skills of your personnel, other skills they will need for TPM, and their motivation to learn additional skills. The assessment can be done with the assistance of small groups of team members. The team assesses all matters relating to maintenance – 5S, productive maintenance, procedures for scheduling and managing productive maintenance and repairs, etc., and the organisation's culture and ability to adapt to change. A TPM visual management board can be established at the gemba to show progress along the improvement journey (similar in concept to the changeover storyboard, see Figure 7.7). Collect manuals and drawings covering mechanical, hydraulic, electrical, and pneumatic aspects of equipment. Assemble available data on history – installation records, working patterns, performance rates, replacements, and planned maintenance records. Also identify any accident black spots or other safety risk areas.

2. Calculate current overall equipment effectiveness (OEE) and address losses

The True North target condition for your equipment is to operate 100% of the time it has demand (availability) at 100% of the designed capacity rating (performance) and with 100% perfect yield (quality). OEE measures the achievement of this ideal.

$$OEE = availability \times performance \times quality$$

OEE helps to really focus on the potential of a process and to highlight previously obscured problems. If a set of process metrics was reporting, for example, availability at 93%, performance at 90% and quality at 97% then many managers would be satisfied that things were going pretty well. However, when these metrics are aggregated together through multiplication a different picture emerges.

$$OEE = availability (93\%) \times performance (90\%) \times quality (97\%) = 81\%$$

This means that if the equipment is running around the clock then 32 hours are being lost every week to mainly concealed and non-obvious losses!

There are six losses associated with the calculation of OEE: for *availability* these are breakdowns and excessive length of time to changeover; for *performance* these are minor stops and running at reduced speed; and for *quality* these are yield losses and start-up defects (see Figure 7.8).

Your team should identify and Pareto (80/20 rule) the most important losses and perform systematic problem solving to address the root causes.

Another modification of OEE is a metric called total effective equipment performance (TEEP). TEEP is a financial tool for management rather than a frontline focusing metric. It is a measure of capacity loading on an asset and can alert management to opportunities to improve sales or the volume of work that comes into a facility. You could have a high OEE for two shifts whilst there are no orders for the third shift, and TEEP will highlight this.

There are however several concerns you need to be aware of when using the OEE metric:

▪ OEE says nothing about schedule attainment. It is useless having a high OEE if you are making the wrong products.

▪ You can improve OEE in good and bad ways. Good ways are to reduce minor stoppages and decrease the duration of change-overs. A bad way is to do fewer changeovers (remember the EPEI metric discussed earlier). OEE is not an end in itself. This is where the balancing metrics introduced in Chapter 2 need to be deployed to prevent potential unintended consequences of what you measure.

▪ Do not measure OEE organisational wide. Combining machine performance is meaningless. Target only critical machines such as bottlenecks.

3. Initial clean up and condition evaluation

Photograph the current state of the equipment. Systematically inspect every part of the machine in great detail. Discuss and understand the role of each component and their interdependencies – not superficially but in detail. Discuss the optimum conditions for the operation of each critical component (such as temperature,

Goal	OEE	Eliminate the six losses due to		Countermeasure examples
Maximising overall equipment effectiveness by establishing and sustaining the optimal relationship between people and their equipment	Availability	Breakdowns		Maintain basic equipment conditions (autonomous maintenance)
				Adhere to correct op conditions (regular checks)
				Restore deterioration
				Address design weaknesses
				Improve skills at all levels
				Record and analyse downtime
		Excessive set-up and adjustments		Address with rapid changeover techniques
				Introduce SOPs for set-ups and changeovers
				Apply 5S
			X	
	Performance rate	Idling and minor stoppages		Record problems on tally sheet and identify and address key issues
		Reduced speed		Identify underperforming processes – address using team-based improvement techniques
				Achieve and surpass established speeds, leading to new standards
			X	
	Quality rate	Reduced yield		Collect and categorise defect data
				Identify key problems with Pareto analysis
				Apply team-based problem-solving techniques
		Start-up losses		Introduction of a warm-up cycle
				Rigorous application of SOPs
				Enhanced training against SOPs
				Mistake proofing applied to set-ups and changeovers

Figure 7.8 OEE metric and equipment loss countermeasure

lubrication, cleanliness and sharpness). Clean and inspect, capturing all problems found. At the end of the cleaning, fill in an appraisal form for each component covering mechanical, hydraulic, electrical and pneumatic categories. Develop a cleaning and inspection programme. Identify sources of contamination (internal and external) and develop a plan to eliminate the source of the contamination, and if necessary clean. Develop the restoration plan and ownership to include quick changeover tooling and poka yoke devices (see Chapter 8, Section 2) to eliminate the source of potential errors if required.

4. Develop asset care

Clearly define the roles and maintenance tasks for the frontline staff. Produce a cleaning schedule for the equipment. Develop a kamishibai (Japanese term that loosely translates as 'sequence of events') board. This is a visual management mechanism for the completion of routine daily activities. When the activity is completed the card is turned backwards. It is colour coded: red to indicate that the task is due, green to indicate that the task has been completed. Identify, mark and colour code all gauges, pipe work, lubrication points, levels and sight glasses, and nut positions, etc. Label all components and tools – with cross references to their specific equipment. Indicate flow directions and motor rotations. Install transparent inspection windows and covers over critical components so that they are visual.

Figure 7.9 illustrates a visual prompt to alert people that the bolts have worked loose; the line will no longer match up to form a continuous straight line. Can you think of any situations where this simple practice could really improve reliability and safety in everyday life?

Asset care is applied using a seven-step process known as autonomous maintenance:

1 Initial cleaning and inspection (often using yellow tags to highlight areas requiring attention).

2 Eliminate sources of grime and facilitate cleaning (enclosures, etc.), improve accessibility and make inspection easier through the use of transparent equipment covers, etc.).

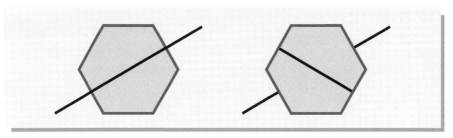

Figure 7.9   Scribe a line across a nut and onto the mounting casing

The first two steps re-establish and control basic conditions and prevent deterioration.

3 Prepare standards for cleaning, lubrication and tightening (single point lessons, etc.).

4 Carry out technical inspection (audit against newly prepared standards).

5 Coordinate maintenance activities.

The above three steps develop equipment knowledge and check and correct deterioration.

6 Organisation and visual management (standard work, poka yoke devices, storyboarding, etc.).

7 Sustain and improve (employees gain confidence and competence through team-based improvement activities). TPM becomes 'business as usual'.

The last two steps ensure that the continuous improvement embeds into the culture and that the gains are held.

A good analogy to autonomous maintenance is Heinrich's Law. Herbert W. Heinrich[5] proposed the following concept that became known as Heinrich's Law (see Figure 7.10).

In a workplace, for every accident that causes a major injury, there are 29 accidents that cause minor injuries and 300 near misses that cause no injuries. And so with equipment, before one serious breakdown occurs, there were 29 minor disturbances and 300 malfunctions that caused no downtime. Frontline, employee-driven, autonomous maintenance is the engine which addresses potential signs of equipment breakdowns and is therefore an important

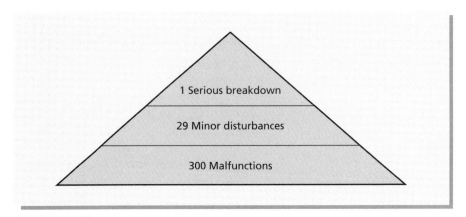

Figure 7.10 Heinrich's Law applied to equipment failure

mechanism to prevent prolonged and costly equipment downtime or total failure. It also greatly expands the lifecycle of equipment through daily preservation.

As part of TPM employees' roles will change (see Table 7.2).

5. Consolidate best practice

Taking all that's been learned in previous steps, you develop a best practice manual. Develop single point lessons (see Figure 7.11) where necessary to encapsulate best practice routines. Review standard work and amend where necessary including pictures, in consultation with frontline employees, and display the results at the gemba. Review the maintenance instructions. Review equipment spares – what needs to be kept, where, and how much? Index the spares and cross reference with manuals and SOPs. Develop a spares catalogue associated with each machine. Locate the manuals appropriately – not in the office, but at point of use.

TPM review

Most people have minds of gold ... harnessing the latent potential of your people through involvement in TPM is good for business. People are the best condition monitors of equipment that were ever invented! TPM has an extremely positive impact on culture and workers love to have a say in decision making that affects them.

Table 7.2 Changing roles as part of TPM

The new role of frontline staff	The new role of maintenance
Run equipment	Perform complex maintenance tasks (skill/task alignment)
Identify potential problems (use of five senses)	Solve complex maintenance problems
Keep equipment clean and tidy	Monitor and predict machine performance
Perform autonomous maintenance tasks	Plan and implement predictive maintenance
Collect performance data	Coordinate the development of standard work, single point lessons and checklists
Put forward improvement ideas and coordinate implementation	Train frontline staff in autonomous maintenance using the training within industry (TWI) programme
Participate in kaizen events	Participate in kaizen events

You cannot become an enduring Lean organisation without the foundation of operational basics and TPM is about looking after the basics. The key message is that the quality of your maintenance is the preservation of your customers' quality. TPM makes it easier to do things right and difficult to do things wrong.

OEE is a particularly harsh metric but extremely effective (the aggregate effect highlights the existence of concealed problems) in that it encourages the 'best of the best' historical performance. I recall hearing one of the world's foremost TPM experts, Peter Willmott, say that if your OEE is 60% this means that you are, in reality, effective only three days of the week! Other metrics such as yield and efficiency miss this reality. OEE is best measured at bottleneck resource points but also provides the hidden benefit of driving down work in progress as reliability increases at non-bottleneck resource points (as the bottleneck is broken). This enables a complementary shift towards other Lean metrics such as EPEI and improved customer responsiveness.

WASTE WALK SINGLE POINT LESSON

1. What is a waste walk?

The waste walk is a way of learning. It will help you gradually establish a new, lean way of seeing and thinking.

You are developing people's lens to be able to spot 'visible and hidden' waste. The further you develop this lens within the area, the better people spot waste on an everyday basis. But by doing the waste walk you are developing this lens together. You are aligned in your thinking which turns into aligned decision making and action.

It drives improvements in small, simple steps. You aren't trying to transform an entire process in one giant swoop. You are eliminating one identified waste at a time.

2. Why perform a waste walk?

You be more aware of the work that is being done.

You will see beyond the reports to actually see the results or work in progress.

Workers will appreciate that you do come around to see the work they are doing.

You will find ways to improve the work that is being done.

You will take away something each day that you can use to improve the workplace or the work being done.

3. What factors are critical to doing a successful waste walk?

Perform the exercise in an open and non punitive manner. The focus is on the PROCESS or lack of process/standards, not to blame employees.

Identified actions must be closed out in the agreed time lines; these have equal priority to shipping the product out the door.

View the workplace processes via the following rules:
- Is the work content specified as to sequence, timing, and desired outcome?
- Is there direct connections and clear communication at process handoffs?
- Is all the non value added steps and waste being removed from the process steps?
- Frontline staff are involved in daily problem solving activity within their work processes?

4. How do you perform a waste walk?

Conduct the waste walk with the area supervisor and a different frontline employee(s) each time to utilize the exercise as a coaching session for employees.

Pick a dedicated time. Pick a process or an area to walk.

Example Dialogue Questioning:

Is this a normal situation?

What would be the ideal situation?

What is the employee's opinion on this? Have we asked him/her?

What is the problem?

Why? Why? Why?

Do we all agree on this? Who else needs to be involved in this discussion?

As you walk the area, identify examples of waste. Don't filter them on what you can fix and what you cannot. Use the 13 waste categories to describe and identify them. It's not just waste, but the specific example of waste. Remember also that the waste categories are symptoms, dig deeper for the underlying causes of the waste using the 5 Why? questioning.

Finally pick one or two things that you can eliminate and do it. Do it immediately. Post the completed waste walk sheet and improvement actions in the Visual Management Center.

Waste Category	Waste Category
1. Transport (excessive movement of product, people, information, poor layout)	8. Design (equipment not designed to support ease of use etc)
2. Inventory (excessive raw material/supplies, batches, finished goods, stock-outs, obsolescence)	9. Overhead (larger facility or equipment and resources than necessary, idle rooms or machines)
3. Motion (excessive employee or customer walking, poor ergonomics, searching for items)	10. Energy (wastage of electricity air, light and heating, poorly performing equipment)
4. Waiting (waiting for equipment, material information, queuing, watching automated machines run)	11. Safety (adverse incidents, near misses, not reporting concerns, injuries)
5. Over-processing (general inefficiency due to machine condition etc, duplication, doing more than is necessary, unnecessary services, excessive legacy testing)	12. Ideas & Talent (customer and employee ideas not captured on a continuous basis, not sharing best practice, not engaging or listening to your employees)
6. Over Production (producing before needed or in greater quantities than required)	13. Technology (I.T issues, scanner problems, excessive manually systems, training needs)
7. Defects (errors and rework, customer returns/complaints)	

Figure 7.11 Single-point lesson example for a maintenance process waste walk

8

Lean methods and tools (part V)

This chapter discusses kanban in Section 1 and poka yoke in Section 2.

SECTION 1: KANBAN

Introduction

Kanban is a visual management concept to facilitate the flow of work. It is another Japanese term that has made its way into the language of Lean management. The English translation is 'signboard' or 'signal card'. The concept was developed by Taiichi Ohno in the 1950s to regulate production. He was inspired by the shelf stocking practices of US supermarkets when he saw that they created a system to replace products only as the supply of each product began to run low. The core concept here is to produce product only to replenish product consumed by the next downstream process or customer. It is a use one–make one policy. Hence the system is based on actual usage rather than forecasted usage and replaces the traditional daily or weekly production schedule. It is not an inventory control system, it is a scheduling system that conveys what to make, when to make it and how much to make. Kanban is often a physical or electronic signal that triggers the fact that more materials or supplies are required.

Many of the core Lean concepts need to be bedded down to make kanban work, including 5S and standard work, and demand must be smoothed to ensure a levelled schedule. Successful execution of kanban thus requires stability. Everyday kanban examples include your pocket tissue pack and your cheque book; there is a coloured reminder sheet to order more when you get down to the last few.

Why kanban?

Benefits include the following:

■ Reduces inventory through the calculation of quantities based on real end user demand and replenishment time.

■ Improves flow through reduced inventory levels and the high-lighting of problems in relative real time.

■ Prevents over-production by placing restrictions on the amount of work and material that can be constructed. Over-production is the worst of all the TIM WOOD DOES IT categories of waste as it potentially causes all the other waste types in one form or another. One example of kanban deployment is kanban squares on the floor. When these are empty this is authorisation for the preceding process to produce the exact quantity to fill them and then stop. Kanban essentially improves EPEI (every product every interval), which is really a measure of batch size.

■ Kanban places control at the frontlines as the kanban design tells people what to run, how much to run and in what sequence to run it. Hence schedulers and production control personnel are freed up to move on to other activities such as waste elimination in the supply chain.

■ Production is based on real demand and the risk of obsolete inventory and spoilage is greatly reduced over traditional MRP forecasting systems.

■ Competitive enhancement is obtained by sequencing deliveries to customers (exactly what they want, when they want it, in the order they require).

Types of kanban

■ *Production kanban*: authorises and provides instructions such as the type and quantity for the production of a product.

▪ *Withdrawal kanban*: authorises the movement of goods.

▪ *Kanban square*: an enclosed area – when empty then fill, when full then cease production.

▪ *Signal kanban*: a triangular kanban used to signal production at the previous workstation that is a batch operation (due to long set-up time, etc., such as a metal stamping machine that needs to produce a batch of parts due to the nature of the process). Note the batch size should be kept as small as possible through improvements in changeover time, etc.

▪ *Material kanban*: used to replenish material and supplies (see the hospital example later in this section).

▪ *Supplier kanban*: triggers replenishment between a customer and externally located supplier. The supplier sequences parts in reverse order for truck loading.

A typical kanban schematic is shown in Figure 8.1.

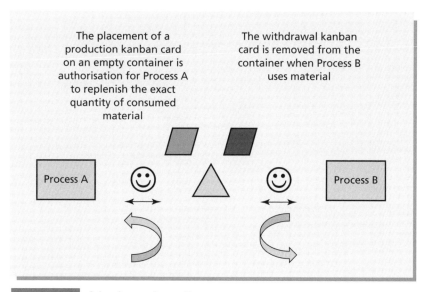

Figure 8.1   A kanban schematic

Kanban sizing formula |

N = (D × LT + SS + BS)/Q

where:

N = number of kanban cards required

D = daily demand per day in units

LT = lead time per day to replenish the buffer

SS = safety stock (to provide protection against variation in demand)

BS = buffer stock (to mitigate against the risk of internal disruptions such as equipment breakdown, etc.)

Q = container quantity

(Note: safety stock and buffer stock are distinguished separately here but they are often aggregated. The reason why they should be set apart is to make the process more transparent. If demand becomes more stable over time we can reduce the level of safety stock and as reliability of internal operations is improved the level of buffer stock can be reduced.)

Example

How many kanban cards (see Figure 8.2) are required in a process loop if the daily demand is 7500 units, each container holds 1000 units, the lead time is 2 days and the customer specifies 1 day of safety stock and 1 day of buffer stock?

Part Number	123
Part Name	Widget, LHS
Supplier	ABC Corp.
Vendor Number	2341
Container Type	Plastic Tote 120 × 140 cm
Container Qty	1000
Delivery Interval	Daily
Storage Location	B 012
Production Operation	Final Assy
Bin Location	C – 04
Delivery Location	Dock 4B

Figure 8.2   Example of a kanban card

Using the formula:

$$N = (D \times LT + SS + BS)/Q$$
$$N = (7500 \times 2 + 7500 + 7500)/1000$$
$$N = 30 \text{ kanban cards}$$

Culture and people implications

Kanban systems are one of the simplest systems to operate but they do require a change of mindset. Namely that it is no longer acceptable to produce unwanted inventory or to leave the work at your workstation rather than where it is needed next. Ignoring the human aspects of kanban implementation will doom your efforts to failure. Rules must be clearly communicated and Lean simulation games help to build understanding.

Kanban rules

These are as follows:

▪ Authorisation to produce is triggered by the kanban card only, otherwise do not produce.

▪ Standardise the process.

▪ Do not pass defective products to the next process.

▪ The succeeding process withdraws only what is needed.

▪ Produce only the exact quantity withdrawn by the downstream process.

▪ Level the production (kanban card quantities need to be modified if the takt time changes).

▪ Kanban should be fine-tuned as the processes improve (start loose by allowing some slack or excess inventory in the system and withdraw inventory as problems reduce over time so as to stress the system and see if further underlying problems surface). This is a manifestation of 'D' type problems discussed as a part of A3 problem solving in Chapter 5, Section 1.

Supplier kanban in a hospital setting

In hospitals it is common practice for clinical staff time to be consumed on medical supply management. These tasks include filling out manual requisition forms, ordering supplies, cycle counting, dealing with obsolete medications, stock de-trashing and put away, etc. To compound this poor skill–task alignment situation, repeated studies point to huge losses in clinical care giver time due to searching for supplies that are poorly organised and also commonly located long distances away from their point of use. There is a saying in manufacturing circles that the more inventories you have, the more likely it is that you will not have the actual correct part that you need to complete a build. This is because transparency is poor when a workplace is swamped with inventory and it becomes very unclear as to what is actually in stock. The same situation applies to healthcare, but the risks are even more critical as we are dealing with people's lives and a stock out of a critical supply can have life threatening consequences.

Hospitals on the Lean transformation journey are now turning around the scenario described in the previous paragraph through the adoption of a material kanban system to control and self-regulate the replenishment of medical supplies. Procurement staff manage the system for the entire hospital to ensure that the right stocks are available in the right quantity, date and location at the right time.

The benefits of kanban for patients, hospitals and staff include:

▪ Faster patient response time to requests for medication, etc. as all items are now grouped by medical category usage and in alphabetical order.

▪ Less stock out risk as the visual management two-bin kanban system provides a cue when stock needs replenishment.

▪ Reduces or eliminates ward staff time devoted to stores activities.

▪ Savings in inventory holding costs are, on average, 30% over traditional push-based supply order systems.

▪ Reduces or eliminates stock obsolescence.

▪ Improves stock rotation.

▪ Frees up space on the wards.

▪ Improves communication and feedback due to the visual nature of the system and the increased interaction with onsite logistics personnel.

▪ There is more time to care at the bedside as time spent searching and walking for parts is significantly reduced.

▪ Cycle counting is virtually eliminated.

▪ The hospital is often not charged for inventory until it is actually used (consignment stock).

▪ Better housekeeping due to the systematic arrangement of supplies and a kanban audit system.

▪ Hoarding of supplies by clinical staff (for fear of running out) becomes a past practice as the availability of supplies becomes a systematic process.

After kanban implementation, similar care items used for certain care procedures are grouped together and in alphabetical order (see Figure 8.3). Items are labelled and anything can be found within 30 seconds, even by agency staff unfamiliar with the area.

The individual racks have two bins inside. When the front bin is empty it is swapped with the full bin at the back and the card on the front is turned (see the barcode in Figure 8.4) to alert the logistics team that this is to be scanned and that signal is then sent electronically to central supplies to trigger replenishment.

Locating small quantities of supplies at the point of use where they are needed saves literally thousands of wasted hours of valuable clinical staff time across the hospital walking to centralised storage rooms for supplies each day.

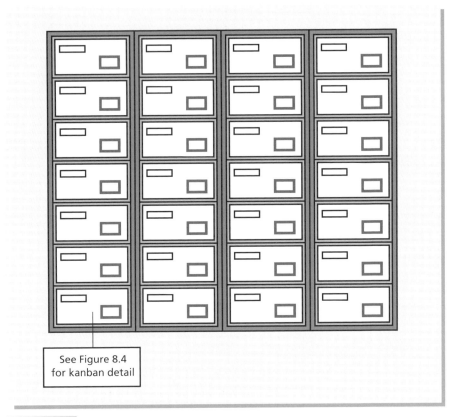

See Figure 8.4
for kanban detail

Figure 8.3   Example of a kanban supply system

Kanban review

Kanban enables organisations to have the correct inventory, in the correct quantity, at the right time when needed. This is achieved by calculating quantities based on real end-user demand and replenishment time. It also improves flow through acceptable inventory levels and highlights problems in real time as process steps are more tightly connected. The methodology also places decision making with those doing the work as the kanban design tells employees what to run, how much to run and in what sequence.

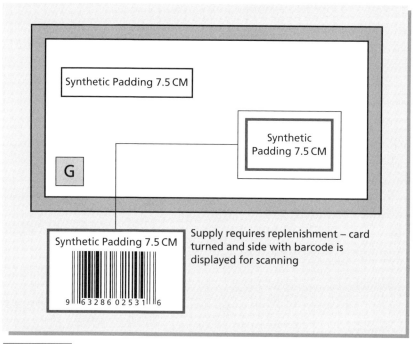

Figure 8.4   Example of a hospital kanban supply system

SECTION 2: POKA YOKE

Introduction

The late Shigeo Shingo, Toyota's initial external consultant, codi-fied the concept of poka yoke in the 1960s. The English translation of poka yoke means to avoid inadvertent errors. It was originally called fool-proofing but this violated the 'respect for people' pillar due to the 'fool' implication. It is now most commonly called mis-take proofing. Quality can be built into products and services at the source through the application of mistake proofing. It is important to recognise that the potential for failure cannot be totally elimi-nated; failure modes can combine, stack up and interact, and result in errors. The art of management is to prevent these errors and mis-takes resulting in customer defects.

Employee errors are, as a rule, unintentional. Remember Dr Deming and the wisdom that the root cause(s) of almost all problems are sourced in inadequate system design. To err is human, hence mistakes are inevitable. How often have we gone to the shop and come back without the very item that we went there for in the first place! Mistake proofing devices help to avoid defects, even when accidental errors are made. This is the establishment of a culture that depends on the development of a system for quality assurance rather than relying on the vigilance of people to inspect quality. This also nurtures the 'respect for people' pillar by freeing the cognitive load on employees so they can pursue value-added activities. The customary way to react to mistakes was to reprimand the worker, provide retraining and bestow motivation talks telling them to be more careful. This approach is ineffective at best. Additionally, reliance on inspection is a flawed strategy. In my experience of performing inspection repeatability studies, 100% inspection is between 60–80% effective in finding product or service deviations depending on the varying complexity of defects.

The Dana Corporation reported employing one device that eliminated a mode of defect that cost $5 million a year. The device, which was conceived, designed and fabricated by a production worker in his garage at home, cost $6.00 to implement. That is an 83,333:1 ratio of return for the first year. This type of saving will occur each year that the process and the device remain in place.[1]

Mistake proofing devices surround us every day. Filling your car with petrol is made safer and more reliable through the use of three mistake proofing devices:

1 The insert on the dispenser nozzle prevents diesel being dispensed unintentionally.
2 There is a release coupling that disengages from the petrol pump and shuts off fuel delivery should you drive away with the dispenser nozzle still inserted into the car's petrol tank.
3 The petrol cap has a ratchet to indicate the correct torque and prevent over-tightening.

Another example is your garden lawnmower; it has a safety bar on the handle that must be pulled back in order to start the engine and to keep it running. When released the engine cuts out immediately. The inability to put your car gearbox into reverse when travelling forward is an example of where mistake proofing is applied in life critical situations. An additive, called mercaptan, is put into odourless household gas to detect potential gas leaks, giving yet another example of creative deployment of mistake proofing.

Mistake proofing classifications
Prevention mistake proofing devices

Prevention mistake proofing devices detect a failure before it happens. There are two approaches for prevention mistake proofing:

1 *The control method*: this stops the process immediately just before a mistake or error is made.

2 *The warning method*: this signals the occurrence of a deviation or trend of deviations through an escalating series of buzzers, lights or other warning devices. However, unlike the control method, the warning method does not shut down the process.

Detection mistake proofing devices

Defects are captured early preventing them from escalating to the customer. The rule of 1:10:100 applies here. If we capture a non-conformance at the point of occurrence the cost is 1 unit, it escalates to 10 units if it is captured just before reaching the customer and it costs 100 units if a defect makes its way out into the field or into the hands of the customer.

The three categories of detection devices are as follows:

1 *Contact method*: this method captures dimensional or shape non-conformances though devices that make contact with the product and weeds them out. The contact method can also be 'implicit' through the use of sensors such as a photoelectric eye.

2 *Fixed value method*: this is used to monitor the critical operating parameters of a process such as the correct pressure, etc.

3 *Motion step method*: this method is used primarily for sequential tasks to ensure that they are performed in the correct sequence and without the omission of any steps.

Mistake proofing routine ⏐

1 Illustrate the defect (or potential mistake).

2 Determine where the defect occurred.

3 Does standard work exist? If so, is it adequate and followed satisfactorily?

4 Go to the gemba and observe the standard or target against the actual process in real time.

5 Identify and document potential causes, use '5 Why?' analysis or a similar technique such as: problem – first immediate cause – deeper cause of the first immediate cause – deeper cause of the preceding cause, and continue until the core root cause is determined.

6 Pinpoint the mistake proof classification and device to dissolve the defect cause(s).

7 Implement the device and verify the effectiveness of the countermeasure over time.

Poka yoke review

Mistake proofing devices are generally very inexpensive and can be applied across all industries from software development to transactional services. One differentiator with services is that potentially both the provider and the customer need to be considered in the application of mistake proofing. What happens if the customer forgets important paperwork for the transaction, etc.? It takes two for successful service delivery in many instances.

One prospective caveat of mistake proofing is that the root cause of problems can remain without being analysed. This is because you can develop a certain comfort level knowing that the mistake proofing device will detect or remove the non-conformance from the process. This can lead to precious process information being lost and, more importantly, there is a cost to every deviation from target.

Sometimes it is also highly desirable (from a safety perspective) that failure is built into a process, product or service. One example of this is the break point engineered into certain synthetic hurling sticks to prevent excessive force generation.

Mistake proofing is not a standalone technique in the improvement of quality. Like all Lean applications culture is king. Creating a culture where we recognise and welcome the use of mistake proofing calls for an ethos that attacks problems not people. People must be comfortable reporting problems that are candidates for mistake proofing.

Mistake proofing pushes people to be creative and the simplest ideas for devices from the frontline people can indeed be priceless. Remember the Dana $6.00 example earlier! At the end of the day all your organisation has to differentiate its offerings is the genius of your people.

9

Lean methods and tools (part VI)

Introduction

For the concept of flow to work well many of the core Lean methods such as standard work, visual management, quick changeover (hence inventory reduction), takt time and systematic problem solving need to be bedded down.

Flow incorporates much more than the physical mainstay flow of the product or service, although this is normally the primary target for streamlining. There are many other flows that need to be purposely designed so that they support and interact seamlessly with the primary physical flow of your product or service.

Flow in a hospital environment

In a hospital there are many flows that must interact successfully to ensure that a patient gets the best result. For instance the patient must flow to where the specialised treatment rooms and equipment are located. Providers such as doctors and nurses must be available in a timely manner to provide care for the patient. The flow of information such as the patient's care plan and medical records must be readily accessible at this point of care. Oral and intravenous medication must flow to the patient just when they are needed. Supplies such as IV kits and catheters must arrive in the right quantity on time and in the correct type. Equipment such as vital signs monitors and sterile instruments must flow in synchronisation with the patient's needs also. Process engineering needs to coordinate flows behind the scenes. They must ensure that all of the facilities services and equipment are capable and fully functional at the point of use when needed. This is

▶

quite a complex series of tasks to orchestrate many thousands of times daily in hospitals all over the world. Without deliberate design intervention in this complex series of flows the outcome could be avoidable harm to patients and at best sub-standard care and/or extended patient wait times.

The benefits of flow include:

- *Improved quality*: increased velocity of material or information availability leads to shorter consumption periods and defects are detected in almost real time when the root cause trail is still warm.
- *Lead time compression*: smaller batch size and less queue time dramatically reduces lead time.
- *Productivity*: wasted motion is reduced as is double processing.
- *Space*: facility space is freed up due to capacity increases and fewer inventory staging positions.
- *Cost*: reduced fixed costs such as less capital investment in inventory.
- *Morale*: greater employee involvement in correcting process stoppages through systematic problem solving.

Flow is a time-based competitive strategy. The refocusing of attention from cost to time provides organisations with immense competitive advantage. The authoritative work of Stalk and Hout[1] sets out three rules based on research carried out in 1990.

1 The ¼–2–20 rule states that for every quartering of total lead time, there will be a doubling of productivity and a 20% cost reduction. This research also aligns closely to later work carried out by the George Group[2] in 2002. As a rule of thumb, if this in-process waiting time is reduced by 80%, the overhead and quality cost will drop by 20%. This results in increased operating profit of approximately 5%.

2 The 0.05 to 5 rule states that value is actually being added only between 0.05% and 5% of the total time door-to-door in your organisation.

3 The 3/3 rule states that wait time, during which no value is added, is split three ways, each accounting for approximately one-third of the total lead time. The three categories are waiting for completion of batches, waiting for physical and intellectual rework, and waiting for management decisions to send the batch forward.

One might wonder how velocity (less stopping and waiting) and time compression slashes so much 'hidden' cost. If you consider the sequence of events below we can begin to understand the depletion that sluggish processes are siphoning from the bottom line.

In manufacturing every time a part is stopped (placed into storage along the value stream):

■ someone has to assume the job of managing the parts

■ they have to be placed in containers

■ most likely transferred to a predetermined area of the factory

■ then stacked

■ counted, tagged and booked onto the inventory control system

■ then when it is time to use them they have to be un-stacked, de-tagged and booked off the inventory control system

■ then conveyed to another area of the factory to be consumed!

Can you relate the above sequence of events to your own industry?

River and rocks analogy

Taiichi Ohno used the analogy of an organisation being like a river full of rocks (see Figure 9.1). The water level in the river symbolises inventory and the rocks signify waste. When the water level is high, potential rocks or problems can go undetected due to the water cushion. Problems continue to grow underneath the visible water level. The intention of Lean is to constantly lower the water level through each phase of maturity. This then exposes the rocks and induces compulsory problem solving in order to keep the area operational. The rocks must be shattered through root cause analysis to enable smooth fast flow along the value stream, similar to a boat sailing along a fast flowing river with a flat, rock free riverbed.

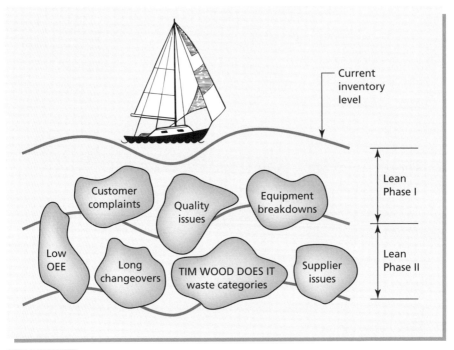

Figure 9.1   River and rocks analogy

Batch size implications for flow

The inevitable consequence of batching work is extended customer lead times. If you consider the implications of batch size in the simplified diagram in Figure 9.2 you can appreciate why this is so. When the batch size per processing lot is 12 units the customer will not receive a finished unit of work until after 36 minutes as it takes 12 minutes for the batch to cycle through each process. Cutting the batch size by 50% (through improvements such as quick changeover) will halve the lead time to 18 minutes. A further 50% reduction will achieve a 75% reduction of the original lead time. This abides by Little's Law which as phrased by Michael George states that Process Lead Time = Number of 'Things' in Progress/Completions per Hour. The ultimate objective would be to get to one piece flow; in this case the lead time would be 3 minutes. Exploiting the batch size economies can achieve an incredible 83% reduction in lead

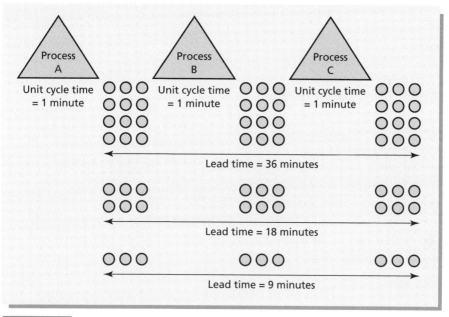

Figure 9.2 Effect of batch size on lead time

time in this instance. Yet the industry norm is exactly the opposite: run as large a batch as possible to achieve economies of scale! The Lean paradigm of economies of flow crushes this widely accepted practice. The principal rationale for running large batches is to amortise the cost of setup time over many units. Toyota broke this paradigm by perfecting quick changeover (see Chapter 7 Section 1). This method allows the setup time, for example of a 2000 ton press, to be reduced from 4 hours to 10 minutes. This allows the batch size to be cut by 96% while maintaining the same production rate. A 96% reduction in batch size will drive a 96% reduction in overall work-in-progress. The overall cycle time of the factory would also be cut by 96% according to Little's Law. Little's Law provides the mathematical foundation for Lean. This practice holds true regardless of whether you are working in a service transactional process or a software development project management function (in this case the batch size would be open incomplete projects).

A concept known as transfer or move batch could also be deployed where it is difficult to reduce batch size due to process constraints.

This is achieved by physically splitting a batch and moving it on to the next process instead of waiting for the completion of the entire batch.

A word on inventory

The traditional view of inventory costs is that they include the capital cost (the cost of capital or the opportunity cost of capital) and holding cost (costs of the store or warehouse, including space occupied, wages, damage, obsolescence (date sensitive) and material handling equipment in the store). Typical figures used by the American Production and Inventory Control Society (APICS) would be a capital cost of 10% per year and a holding cost of 15% per year, leading to an inventory carrying cost of 25% per year. The Lean view goes beyond this as in most cases inventory actually involves far more cost: work-in-progress takes up space on the factory floor (which not only uses space but also prevents compact layouts, which in turn means more material handling and decreased effectiveness of communication, etc.). Most importantly large batches work against the flow metric of EPEI (every product every interval, the ultimate Lean metric) and inflate lead time. The real cost of inventory is more likely to be in the region of 50–80% per annum.[3]

However, take care when cutting inventory as an end goal. Not having inventory in the right place at the right time is often a bigger waste than the cost of having the inventory itself. For instance the cost of stock-outs that result in lost sales and possibly loss of customer loyalty is to be avoided at all costs.

The problem with traditional production scheduling using material requirements planning (MRP)

MRP uses the batch logic of making large runs to get economies of scale. Equipment set-up costs and material handling costs (driven by plant layout and handling procedures) add to the cost of the product or service. By producing more at once, the costs of set-up and handling can be amortised over more quantity (hence the logic that bigger batches reduce costs!). Traditional accounting defines inventory as an asset; the only perceived cost of producing more parts than are needed is the minimal costs of lost interest on money in the bank and storage costs. MRP-induced large batches ensure that any rocks in the river are well disguised through immersion in inventory. MRP also falsely assumes that lead time remains constant even at 100% equipment utilisation levels (see the discussion on balance charts at the end of this chapter). Additionally, quality losses and yield allowances are built into MRP to further hide problems. In short the scheduling system ensures that there is enough inventory everywhere to keep waste and problems hidden.

Preconditions for flow

Seek to level the demand

The starting point for most flow improvement work is to develop a keen understanding of average daily demand in terms of both quantity and mix of work content. The extent of variation present in this data is also a critical consideration. Organisations need to get to the root cause of why the schedule is not level. This could be down to price promotions, excessively long changeovers or the bullwhip effect (swings in customer demand create a bullwhip outcome – a delicate flip of the wrist creates colossal power at the other end of the whip – resulting in over-production upstream and excessive staffing levels to cater for this bogus demand). For example, if a baker is running a price promotion his short-term demand will probably increase. Hence his requirement for more raw materials from his suppliers also increases, which in turn causes his suppliers to order more from their suppliers (and a bit more just in case!) and this continues throughout the supply chain. The demand amplifies at each level and has little correlation with the actual, real, end user demand which remains relatively stable over the longer term.

It is extremely difficult to be continuously responsive to fluctuating demand without enduring mura (unevenness in productivity and quality) and muri (overburden of people and equipment). The attainment of standard work in this environment becomes extremely difficult if not impossible. Muda in all its forms is created when demand is uneven and when resources are overburdened. Most demand, as previously indicated, is in fact relatively stable and predictable at the point of use.

Runner, repeater and stranger

Generally speaking 20% of the work variety in most organisations accounts for 80% of the overall volume (remember the universally applicable 80/20 rule discussed in Chapter 5, Section 1). Indeed it is statistically valid to further predict that 5–7% of a particular type of work that we perform accounts for 50% of the total volume of work variety undertaken. This is a great area to focus on making value flow. Hence it is possible to smooth the great bulk of work entering our organisations. A useful concept to gain an understanding of the demand entering your organisation is runner, repeater and stranger. A runner is work that is very regular; such work normally occurs on a daily basis (most likely being the 5–7% variety mentioned earlier). A repeater is frequently reoccurring work that may take place every other week. A stranger is work that happens less often. It may be seasonal or enter the system every few months or even less often. Separate strategies can be devised to exploit each of these categories of work. For instance it may be economically viable to have dedicated equipment for runner demand to ensure that it is never delayed by the two other categories.

Heijunka

Due to the bullwhip effect even small changes in demand can create chaos throughout your organisation. A concept called heijunka regulates the volume and mix of work produced. It provides daily consistency and certainty to the production schedule so that the Lean system can work in a holistic manner and permit flow. It allows for small batch increments to be released for processing in a levelled fashion throughout the work shift. One of the many counterintuitive advantages of producing in smaller batches is the reduction of risk against changes in customer orders, which happens frequently! Needless to say that producing in large batches all at once is a risky practice.

Heijunka is implemented via a visual scheduling box similar to a 'pigeon box' arrangement. It enables the frontline staff to see what work is queued for completion and the time that it is due to be released. The material handler or runner (see below) removes the kanban cards from the box in their scheduled order to authorise production.

Pitch is the term used to represent a pack out quantity such as a full container or pallet of work. It is preferable that pitch increments are represented by some physical activity happening in your organisation (just like people getting on the train – either they get on or they miss the train). A common way to achieve this is to have the material handler (the train) show up every pitch increment, take away the work completed, and provide the schedule for the next pitch increment. The runner is the pace setter for the entire process and provides the cadence of flow. This has the concealed benefit of improving schedule adherence as problems that affect pitch increment are surfaced every cycle. To create pitch equal to a full box quantity, we multiply takt time by box quantity. Therefore, as a full box or pallet is produced, the material handler comes to take it away.

Runners should be able to understand the value stream demand requirements and communicate abnormalities well through the visual management system. They play an important role in proactive problem solving. Because they continuously monitor the functioning of a line or cell as well as pitch, runners are closely attuned to how well the value stream is fulfilling customer requirements. In traditional organisations, when a problem occurs frontline employees notify the team leader and the problem is addressed *after* it occurs. However, runners are in a unique position to help prevent small problems before they escalate into larger problems that can seriously disrupt the process.[4]

Pacemakers

A pacemaker schedules production at one process (usually but not always at a bottleneck) to pull production into it. All other processes subjugate themselves to the pacemaker process. While local efficiency may be diminished, total system efficiency is instead optimised. A general rule for selection of a pacemaker is that the process must flow after the pacemaker. It is common for the pacemaker to be situated downstream in the value stream. This is because this operation is more in tune with end user demand than processes upstream that can be more susceptible to the effects of potential bullwhip. Again the pacemaker, as the name suggests, sets the pace for the entire value stream similar to the accelerator in your car. This prevents over-production and WIP imbalances between the preceding processes and hence lead time expansion.

Pitch can be visually displayed on a traffic light board at the pacemaker and countermeasures are recorded and implemented for red flag pitch misses. Hence there is real time visibility to schedule attainment and, to reiterate, real time solving of problems before they cause disruption. This is in stark contrast to weekly schedule buckets in which we only know after the fact the percentage schedule attainment. The runner starts and ends his route at the heijunka box (initiating the next round of activity as the heijunka card is issued), which is located adjacent to the pacemaker.

Family identification

Value stream improvement should be categorised by product or service family. These families are identified by a matrix that shows the connection of products (or services) with processes (Figure 9.3). The three rectangular looped products/services would be classified as a product/service family as they are routed through the same series of processes. These are normally classified as one value stream for the creation of flow as they transverse the same series of processes.

Map the value stream

Value stream mapping discussed in Chapter 3 is the methodology for mapping processes end to end and capturing physical, information and people flow in your organisation. To recap, the current state map captures the process as it exists now. Through analysis of the current state the team is able to identify flow interrupters and bottlenecks in the value stream map. When these are cleared the flow of value is enhanced and the speed of the end-to-end lead time increases.

	Process A	Process B	Process C	Process D	Process E	Process F	Process G	Process H
Product/Servive A	X		X	X		X	X	
Product/Servive B	X	X		X			X	X
Product/Servive C		X		X				X
Product/Servive D	X		X	X		X	X	
Product/Servive E	X	X	X	X	X	X		X
Product/Servive F	X				X		X	
Product/Servive G		X		X				
Product/Servive H	X		X			X	X	X
Product/Servive I	X		X	X		X	X	

Figure 9.3 Routing matrix

Takt time

We introduced the concept of takt time in Chapter 3. Takt time establishes the 'beat' of the organisation and this should be in alignment with your customer demand. If demand changes, takt time should also be adjusted to reflect this. Mature Lean organisations often change takt time deliberately to make problems visible through analysis and revision of standard work.

Takt time = net available time per day / customer demand per day

There is a 50-second policy for takt time which states that repetitive operations should not have a cycle time of less than 50 seconds. There are a number of reasons for this. The first reason is productivity – there are always a few seconds lost at the start and end of an operation due to orientation – and common cause variation, etc. If you lose 4 seconds at the start and end of a 25-second cycle, this represents a 16% productivity loss per cycle. However, if the task cycle time is 50 seconds and 4 seconds is lost at the beginning and end of the task, the productivity loss is 8%. Whilst further improvement is obviously required this represents a significant improvement over the shorter cycle time. Quality also improves as cycle time expands as people become customers of their own work. Dependent steps are performed to a higher degree of accuracy as the same person becomes a customer of their own work. Feedback is also instant if quality criteria are violated. Safety, in addition, improves due to diminished risk of repetitive strain injuries. Finally there are also higher levels of job enrichment as people complete more diverse and complete portions of a job from start to finish rather than mindlessly completing a very small element such as drilling a hole in a part.

Identify bottlenecks and variation

The theory of constraints was developed by the late Eli Goldratt (1947–2011). Its central insight is that an hour lost at a bottleneck is an hour lost for the entire value stream (or streams if the bottleneck is a shared resource). A bottleneck is the pinch point or kink in the overall system. A good analogy is a water hose: if there is a kink in the hose the output is governed by the cross-sectional area of that kink. Hence the productivity of the bottleneck determines the productivity for the entire value stream. This has enormous implications for the focus of improvement work. It is the bottleneck that regulates flow, not efficiency of individual resources. Many continuous improvement endeavours are themselves waste if they focus on improving non-bottleneck resources prior to a bottleneck resource.

The theory of constraints uses three primary metrics to measure performance. These are:

1 *Throughput* – the money generated by the system through sales
2 *Inventory* – the money spent to make products or provide services that are anticipated to be sold
3 *Operating expense* – the money the system spends to transform inventory into throughput.

The actual application of the theory of constraints is a five-step process consisting of the following:

1 Identify the system's constraint – the kink in the system.
2 Decide how to exploit the system's constraint: ensure that it is never starved of supply, reduce changeover time, measure OEE, do not process defects, maximise the batch size (only for a bottleneck!) and maximise utilisation of the bottleneck process.
3 Subordinate everything else to ensure that the bottleneck is kept running: policies must support the constraint such as keeping the resource working through breaks, and improve flow to the constraint from non-bottleneck resources through improving changeover in order to reduce batch size at non-bottlenecks.
4 Elevate the system's constraint: break the constraint through speeding it up via process improvements.
5 If, in the prior steps, the constraint has been broken, go back to step 1, identify where the constraint has shifted to in the system and repeat these five steps.

Drum, buffer, rope (DBR) |

The theory of constraints uses a concept called drum, buffer, rope (DBR). The idea of DBR is that the drum is the constraint. It establishes the rhythm for all other processes. The buffer is inventory to shield the drum from being starved of work. The rope is the rate that material is released into the system. This should be in synchronisation with the constraints rate of processing.

Cellular flow

The purpose of cellular layout is to address the root causes of poor flow which include large batch processing, inflated work-in-progress levels or queues, inadequate work balancing, low adherence to 5S, variation in demand and ineffective space utilisation.

Traditionally, equipment is arranged in separate departments where the method of operation is termed 'batch and queue' processing. In a 'batch and queue' arrangement equipment is grouped by similar processing characteristics such as final assembly in manufacturing, the imaging function in hospitals or the check-out facility in a hotel. This disjointing of the flow of value is driven by the flawed assumption of economies of scale (Lean advocates economies of flow) through large batch processing. The end result is the introduction of unnecessary waiting time due to delay in waiting for batch processing to be completed and the transporting of material and information, to name but two of the many unintended consequences of 'batch and queue' mentality.

Cellular layout refers to an operational system in which the equipment is lined up in sequence that permits continuous flow of the production or service fulfilment of your offerings. A common layout for this sequence of working is a U-shaped cell. The direction of flow is normally anti-clockwise to accommodate the 70–90% range of people who are right-handed. The optimum size of a cell is about 5–12 people.

Kanban is often used to pull material from one workstation to the next if true one-piece flow is not yet attainable. Note that in true Lean organisations the primary authorisation to produce is not by a printed schedule from the office; kanban is authorisation to produce to real time demand. The True North aspiration of one piece flow is rarely achieved in reality; hence kanban is the norm rather than the exception in most cells. In essence, flow where you can and pull when you must! The magic of kanban is that it caps work-in-progress and hence enables faster cycle times.

Benefits of cellular operation

These include:

- dramatic increase in lead time as batch sizes are dramatically reduced
- waste elimination in all of the TIM WOOD DOES IT categories
- better quality as issues are surfaced faster – process velocity is faster in comparison with 'batch and queue' processing
- less inventory through the reduction of work-in-progress
- better use of people's capabilities through problem solving and enhanced teamwork
- improved space utilisation is facilitated through the compact layout of equipment and less floor space dedicated to holding large queues of inventory
- equipment can be 'right-sized' (not using over-specified equipment as is common practice in batch and queue layouts where shared resources are the norm: multiple product/service lines are processed through the same equipment)
- flexibility is enhanced as one cross-trained person can potentially run an entire cell (due to close proximity of equipment) as opposed to the need to staff up individual departments fully, even during low demand periods.

The operation balance chart

The operation balance chart (see Figure 9.4) is used to analyse how well an operation is balanced against end user demand or takt time. This is a critical exercise when setting up cellular operations. The example process shown in Figure 9.4 identifies Process 3 as a potential bottleneck in the system. The takt time for the system is

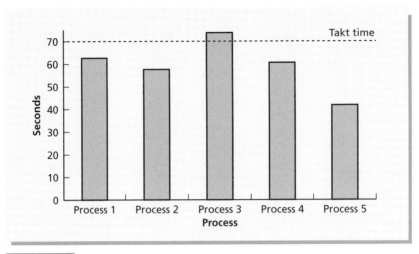

Figure 9.4   Operation balance chart

70 seconds. Even though the process is just a couple of seconds above takt time remedial action is needed to reduce the cycle time at this process step. There are a number of options to do this, the most common being to analyse the process and remove non-value-added work to reduce the cycle time. Another option is to reallocate some of the work elements to other process steps that are below takt time. In reality workstations should be loaded to approximately 75–80% of takt time. When a resource approaches its maximum capacity rating there is an exponential growth in the length of queues due to its inability to absorb the variability of dependent events and natural variation. Anyone who has ever travelled home from work during rush hour traffic has experienced this phenomenon first hand. During quiet periods minor disruptions such as a car stalling at traffic lights for a few seconds have no overall effect on the performance of the network. However, if the network is close to its rated capacity the compounding effect of minor disturbances such as this has a domino effect and traffic jams grow exponentially.

Human implications for flow

As mentioned at the beginning of the chapter the attainment of flow is dependent on many elements of the Lean system being in place to support it. A high degree of equipment reliability is required as disruptions and breakdowns will create havoc in a system where the excess fat has been removed. Excess fat refers to the various classifications of waste such as surplus inventory and extra overhead in the form of free capacity. People need to be developed and competent in Lean practices such as autonomous maintenance and problem solving. Support functions need to be decentralised to each value stream to provide the technical skills to maintain flow and solve process issues in a rapid fashion. It is recommended that support functions like engineering and maintenance are located on the frontlines (a concept known as co-location) rather than in offline office areas to facilitate the requirement for rapid team-based problem solving.

A critical enabling factor in the attainment of flow is to appoint a person who has end-to-end accountability for the delivery of a product or service through flow metrics like lead time and changeover performance. In the pre-Lean environment the organisational structure was composed of departments which were managed by individuals per speciality, such as the engineering manager, but this is no longer the most effective option. Each area looked out for its departments' interests at the expense of achieving end-to-end flow. To compound this individual departments were often measured and rewarded in a fashion that hindered flow. An example of this would be metrics such as utilisation which demand that departments keep their machines and people busy so that the accounting department's overhead absorption figures look positive. One outcome of this behaviour is that over-production is the end result and large batches of production slow down the overall system output. The appointment of a value stream manager who measures the end-to-end performance is an effective antidote to this cycle. Visual management maintenance by frontline people is another behavioural change that smoothes the swift end-to-end progression of the product or service delivery. Visual management tools such as hour-by-hour tracking maintain a steady sense of urgency and hasty response to problems. Entropy is continually at play in all systems, everything degrades without repeated intervention, and visual management enables this intimate focus on the process.

Flow practices review

Many of the benefits of flow are succinct and some are even coun-terintuitive, like slowing down one area in order to speed up the whole. Waste removal is just one-third of the potential savings that Lean can deliver; unevenness in demand and overburden are often forgotten! Heijunka is fundamental to eliminating these through its regulatory effect. Also very important is levelling out the demand on your people, equipment and suppliers. Heijunka prevents the bullwhip phenomenon in upstream processes and the supply chain via smooth, steady demand patterns. Quality problems can easily be found and corrected in a flow environment as the root cause trail is warmer than in batch and queue systems. Less facility space is needed, and tracking of inventory is greatly reduced if not elimi-nated. Almost by default equipment performance is also enforced at a high performance level to support a high velocity organisation. Flow is challenging and demands that people must be developed and grow to support it through high-priority problem solving and the resultant teamwork that this demands.

This chapter concludes Part II which covers the core methods and tools of Lean. The intention of Chapters 4 to 9 is to provide a working knowledge of the core Lean methods and tools that your organisa-tion will require approximately 80% of the time throughout its Lean journey. There are other methods and tools covered in other 'meth-ods' focused books that you can learn about if and when required.

The order of using the various methods is determined by the par-ticular issues or opportunities that your organisation is facing. In the words of Dr Deming, 'need must drive change', so remember to tailor techniques to your organisation's specific requirements.

Leading the Lean transformation

Part 3 covers the Lean culture, sustaining the gains from both technical aspects and people characteristics, and also discusses the generic roadmap to Lean transformation.

10

Developing the Lean culture

Introduction

This chapter discusses the Cathedral model that is deployed to cultivate the development of a Lean culture. The model is a systematic framework for deploying the social behaviours that are required to bring the Lean culture to life.

A parable |

Two bricklayers were working side by side. When asked, 'What are you doing?' the first bricklayer replied, 'I'm laying bricks.' The second bricklayer when asked the same question responded, 'I'm building a Cathedral.'

This parable provides a powerful moral to management about the fortitude of employees driven by purpose and vision. Many leaders understand that the second bricklayer 'sees the big picture' but they miss the emotional significance, that the bricklayer's work has a deeper meaning to him.

We are all building our own Cathedrals one brick at a time. To build a culture of sustained excellence you must understand the purpose and fulfilment that your people get from their work and become aware of their personal Cathedrals. This is their reason for getting up in the morning and the meaning they attribute to their work. Frank Devine's Cathedral model discussed below is a systematic framework for creating and sustaining a culture of excellence and mass engagement of the workforce. Without these twin objectives your Lean transformation will not reach anything close to its potential for achieving excellence in business performance.

The Cathedral model

A study by Zenger–Miller of over 800 organisations involved in service improvement programmes concluded that 'The majority of the problems were related to leadership, skills, strategy and people issues, and only a minority were related to the quality of the improvement methods and tools'.[1] The Cathedral model (Figure 10.1) works on the psychological side of Lean transformation and is a powerful example of a practical and simple (but not easy) method that many academic authors[2] have referred to as 'socio-technical organisation design'. It is a framework that rigorously focuses on and then standardises the critical but few leadership social skills of setting expectations, recognition, coaching and constructive feedback. These are all built on and reinforced through a deep

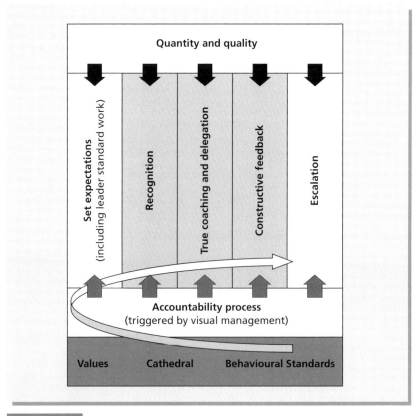

Figure 10.1   Cathedral model

foundation of values and bottom-up Behavioural Standards. The Cathedral model is leveraged to increase the proportion of the workforce exhibiting inner-directed behaviour. Inner-directed behaviour means that you are guided by your own individual beliefs and values rather than external pressures to conform to the status quo. Working at the beliefs and values level of people gets to the root of influencing behavioural change. Employee owned Behaviour Standards (discussed later in this chapter) are the visible manifestation of this work. This in turn leads to higher levels of discretionary effort required to create and then sustain the Lean culture.

The model's foundation

The values, Cathedral concept, and bottom-up Behavioural Standards sit at the foundation of the model because they provide deep meaning, for individuals (Cathedral and individual values) and groups (Behavioural Standards) – see Figure 10.2. It is foundational: if your culture is not bedded down and rock solid further building blocks will descend into disorder through the rigours of time. The point is that many Lean attempts make little lasting change because the methods and tools will provide short-term, initial, quick wins. However, for retention of these gains and further progression, we need to work at the invisible social levels of the organisation. These concealed elements are the values that the organisation stands for, the personal meaning that the work epitomises for individual employees and the daily employee behaviours that drive the actions that deliver results. The values of an organisation refer to the collective standard of behaviour and ethics that the organisation stands for.

The reference to 'Behavioural Standards' in the model is to a process developed by Devine to overcome the problem of values being interpreted differently and thus losing credibility in the eyes of employees. His approach is to develop Behavioural Standards (see Figure 10.2) that are:

▪ measurable or binary (thus not subject to political interpretation)
▪ adaptable to local culture and style (thus not alienating and restrictive such as rules-based systems)

- developed by employees via mass joint decision making processes (not mere 'consultation' or 'negotiation')
- internally self-enforcing and thus more sustainable.

The use of stories (family narratives, etc.) helps people understand the underlying values of a particular situation and reinforces the resolve and spirit that unified Behavioural Standards bring to the table.

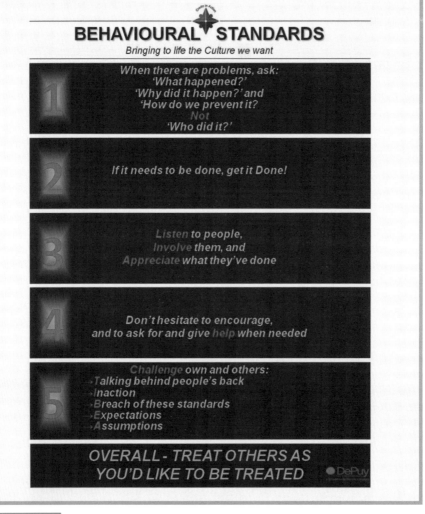

BEHAVIOURAL STANDARDS
Bringing to life the Culture we want

1. When there are problems, ask:
'What happened?'
'Why did it happen?' and
'How do we prevent it?
Not
'Who did it?'

2. If it needs to be done, get it Done!

3. Listen to people,
Involve them, and
Appreciate what they've done

4. Don't hesitate to encourage,
and to ask for and give help when needed

5. Challenge own and others:
Talking behind people's back
Inaction
Breach of these standards
Expectations
Assumptions

OVERALL - TREAT OTHERS AS
YOU'D LIKE TO BE TREATED   ● DePuy

Figure 10.2   Behavioural Standards example

Source: DePuy Cork, Ireland. Reprinted with permission.

Table 10.1 outlines the limitations of using only values in your organisation and the enrichment that Behavioural Standards contribute to the cultural transformation.

Table 10.1 Comparison of Behavioural Standards and values

Issue	Values	Behavioural Standards	Comments
Measurability	Very difficult and prone to interpretation	By definition. Non-compliance is immediately visible due to the way they are created to ensure measurability	A key reason why Behavioural Standards were created
Explicitly challenges what needs to be stopped in the current culture	Focus is on the positive, hence some of the 'harder' issues can be insufficiently addressed	Explicitly addresses these 'hard' issues	Leading by example is not enough – we need to challenge breaches of the Behavioural Standards
Delivers accountability	Very difficult due to interpretation issues above	By definition	A key reason why Behavioural Standards were created
Facilitates 'political'/non-value-added discussion	Yes due to interpretation issues above	Prevents this due to measurability or binary nature	A key reason why Behavioural Standards were created
Encourages focus on behaviour rather than result	Yes	Yes, even more so!	The right behaviours deliver the right results! Focus on the source of the results

Source: Reproduced with permission from Accelerated Improvement Facilitators Training Programme

The Cathedral component in the model foundation sits at the level of the individual. This is the personal meaning and motivation that are attributed to the work and the organisation by individual employees. Remarkable employees are driven by something deeper and more personal than just the desire to do a good job – they are driven by their sense of 'Cathedral' or meaning. To foster the intrinsic motivation and discretionary efforts of your employees begin by asking the question, 'What do each of us see as our own personal Cathedral for our job and the organisation that we work for?' Obviously this will vary from individual to individual but a few collective themes usually emerge. Examples include providing for our families over the long term, sustaining the competitiveness of our company so as to keep local jobs, to 'save lives' rather than 'to push people on trolleys', and 'I clean (hospital) rooms to prevent infections and hence I contribute to preserving life'. In summary, the purpose of the individual Cathedral aspect is about making work meaningful and helping employees to connect with the deeper purpose and contribution to society of their daily work.

Accountability process

The accountability process is the means of ensuring that the focus on process leads to actions for improvement. It is driven from comparing actual performance against expected performance. This is tracked in real time using the various visual management tools discussed in Section 2 of Chapter 4. Achievements as well as deviations from target are tracked by the people operating the process and the reasons for achieved and missed targets are recorded and used to drive higher quantity of recognition as well as to instigate problem solving to close the gaps. In Devine's approach it is crucial to drive recognition not just problem solving. Leader standard work is the cement that keeps the Lean system together (this is discussed in detail in Chapter 11). It helps to create the structure and discipline necessary to ensure that daily problem solving is practised to close these gaps and continually raise the workplace standards. Leader standard work specifies what routines, recognition and coaching are to be widely practised to support the Lean culture. It also makes clear what we should not be doing, hence freeing up time for improvement work and people development. The accountability process appears at the foundational level in the Cathedral model because the repeated comparison between 'what was expected' and 'what happened' triggers a high quantity (see the top of the Cathedral model) and quality of conversations between the leader and employees.

Daily operation reviews are a central aspect of a Lean culture. These take the form of short, focused, stand-up meetings or huddles at the gemba. A synopsis of the previous shift's performance is conducted and actions from the visual controls are reviewed for completion and effectiveness. This is the primary mechanism of driving accountability and longer-term actions are tracked using further visual tracking tools such as the accountability board (see Figure 11.1). The psychology of the visual controls is that it enforces the discipline to follow through on interruptions to the daily workflow at the stage when the root cause footprint is reasonably intact and hence they can be solved relatively quickly. This helps to shift the 100% focus on hitting the daily output numbers to a twin focus of making the output as well as on making improvements. This is in contrast to traditional work cultures: things that went wrong on the previous shift are frequently dropped, and hence the reoccurrence of problems is commonplace. Indeed visual mechanisms may be even more important in workplaces such as offices and engineering design companies where most of the work is invisible. Making the 'invisible visible' through visual tracking of projects, etc. builds disciplined implementation and speed of execution. A further benefit of enforced discipline is that it helps to change habits, which in turn leads to culture change.

A further accountability practice is the gemba walk (see the single point lesson on how to conduct a gemba walk in Figure 7.11). The purpose of the gemba walk is to see the value stream by crossing functional departments on the walk, to grasp the current situation, and ask why things are as they currently are. You also demonstrate respect to those doing the work through involving them in the walk and the resultant improvement actions. The accountability aspects of the walk include checking for adherence to standard work, A3 problem-solving activity and status, 5S maintenance, the status of metrics and the improvements that they are driving. Devine's 'managing on green' concept is a key component of the gemba walk and it challenges 'managing by exception' (what Devine calls 'managing on red'). It results in leaders constantly showing interest in, and recognising (thus driving up the quantity of recognition – see the top of the Cathedral model), what is going well in problem prevention before focusing on the 'reds'. This means that there is a positive side to accountability. We need to recognise and appreciate employees for all the things that are going right. It is easy to forget that when things are going well it is almost certainly because someone has done something well and this should be recognised. Positive reinforcement of good behaviours that resulted in the attainment of green metrics will help to hard wire these behaviours into the new culture.

Set expectations

The first pillar of the Cathedral model is concerned with setting and making expectations explicit. The wise old saying, 'You get what you expect' is a powerful business concept. The rationale of setting expectations is to define the behaviours and actions that are required to sustain the gains and build a continuous improvement culture. The most powerful expectations are those that are mutually agreed between management and their teams. Leader standard work (see Chapter 11) is the instrument that is used to accomplish this in a Lean culture. Expectations should be set that are a challenge for the individual to achieve but are also not impractical or unreachable. Challenging people is a form of respect as it stimulates people to grow: they will generally raise their performance in response to a challenge.

The root cause of not meeting expectations in many instances can be attributed to the fact that they were never stated in the first place! Sitting your employees down to say what you expect from them seems so obvious, but we often assume that people know what we expect. The old adage that common sense is not so common is certainly true in this instance.

The Pygmalion, or Rosenthal, effect[4] concludes that the greater the expectation imposed on people, the better they perform. For example, if one group of schoolchildren is continually told that mathematics is difficult and useless, and another group is continually told and shown that mathematics can be fun, is widely used and, like a computer game, is challenging and rewarding – the difference in eventual mathematical ability will be marked.

Recognition

Employee recognition is one of the most powerful forms of feedback that you can provide. Devine outlines a sequence whereby when a leader gives recognition to one of his team the recipient's self-image increases which in turn raises their self-confidence. This places the person in a state of mind where their receptivity to coaching is extremely high, which in turn increases their capacity to absorb advice and learn, therefore leading to increased competence. Application of these new skills on the job to bed down the learning through practical use improves performance. This in turn provides the opportunity to provide further recognition, hence restarting the opportunity for a virtuous chain reaction of recognition. A true win–win engine of improvement begins to grow at an accelerated rate!

According to Alfie Kohn,[5] only intrinsic rewards motivate over the medium and long term. Extrinsic rewards (for example monetary rewards) fade fast, become expected and may often lead to destructive behaviour. Intrinsic motivation is the natural desire that people have to do a good job and make a positive difference. It is the spiritual reward a person gets from making an improvement to their work.[6] Intrinsic motivation is increased when people feel that they have an impact on the work that they perform. This is known as autonomy. As discussed in Chapter 6 intrinsic motivation is the difference between saying 'You couldn't pay me enough to do that', and 'I can't believe I'm getting paid to do this!' The bottom of the Cathedral model addresses the many individual and collective aspects of intrinsic motivation and places these into a system of improvement.

Cash has low-lasting impact value; research (refer to the study in Chapter 6, Section 1) points out that non-cash recognition delivers a 3:1 return on investment over direct cash rewards. Devine usefully distinguishes the effects of intangible recognition, tangible recognition (giving people things) and reward. His approach favours a reduction in emphasis on rewards and tangible recognition towards a focus on very high quality and quantity of intangible recognition within the context of the Cathedral model. The recognition has to be something that employees want, which is different in various areas of the world and also locally within the same work team. Lunch with the boss may be one person's worst nightmare, another's ultimate experience. People are motivated differently. Asking employees, 'How do you like to receive recognition for a job well done?' is thus a sound thing to do. Even if an employee doesn't answer, you acquire loyalty points for taking the time to ask and showing an interest in the person.

For some, plaques belong on the mantelpiece; others would rather use them as firewood! Involving the recogniser and those involved in the design, implementation and measurement of the recognition process improves its effectiveness. If the answer to the 'What do you want?' question is money, the follow-up question 'What would you use it for?' may provide the true motivator.[7]

As long as the intended recognition has meaning to people it can make them do extraordinary things. Think what people will go through to win coveted sporting medals. How can you create that hunger for your company's recognition symbols? Behavioural science validates that reinforced behaviours stick, which helps to explain how cultures develop, hence the power of focused and continual recognition for desired Lean behaviours.

Recognition suffers from a similar fate to improvement work, the mantra that we just don't have time to do this! Not good enough. Time for planning recognition is a key aspect of leader standard work. Devine argues against allocating a time in leader standard work to actually give recognition but rather there should be a period, ideally at the beginning of each day, where the leader plans how they will integrate recognition into the natural flow of the day, thus not adding to their workload. The design intention is that opportunities for giving recognition are built into the daily work. For example, think about the route you took into work this morning, who you met, what behaviours you observed. What opportunities to give recognition to your people were there on your way to your desk during this brief period? We need to leverage where we already walk.

There are a number of considerations to be aware of when designing your recognition strategy. Quality recognition requires the trait of empathy – a desire to care for and help others. Fairness is a further critical component of recognition: if the same few are continually recognised and others are never acknowledged, your recognition endeavours can have the opposite intended effect than you set out to achieve. A perception of 'pets' can develop and this is damaging to effective teamwork. You need to be aware of how we treat our 'go to' people or employees who continually demonstrate discretionary effort. It is all too tempting to reward these people with even more work! If this continues indefinitely these people will either burn out or switch off due to being taken for granted. It can create a culture where poor performance is rewarded through being given less work and responsibilities.

Recognition should also not be just confined to successful outcomes. A required Lean behaviour is taking initiative and experimentation with new methods. These new methods can sometimes 'fail' to achieve the desired outcome. When we learn from these tests it leaves us in a stronger position to design a stronger test of change the next time. This is an opportunity to recognise the positive intent of the employee and their increased knowledge.

In the 'setting expectations' pillar you should establish criteria for what makes a person eligible for recognition. Anyone who meets the criteria is then recognised. Recognition should not however be dished out so 'over-the-top' that it becomes an entitlement. The danger here is that when it is not received it turns into a grievance. The way we deliver employee recognition is key to its effectiveness. Recognition should be specific about the exact behaviour, use straightforward language and state the positive impact of the person's accomplishments.

True coaching and delegation

The intention of true coaching and delegation is to raise the capability of leaders within the organisation to perform technical processes such as problem solving, but more importantly to enhance critical standardised leader behaviours such as recognition, constructive feedback and coaching itself, to the extent where systematic excellence is achieved. Devine explains the Cathedral model approach to coaching as an integration of two streams of intellectual thought, the coaching stream and the problem-solving stream. A brief outline follows. (Note: the most commonly used coaching approach is GROW which is mapped onto the double-diamond in Figure 10.3. GROW does not integrate coaching and problem solving but is widely understood, especially in English-speaking countries.)

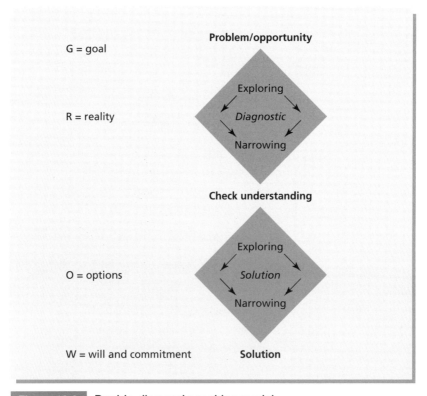

Figure 10.3 Double-diamond coaching model

Socrates was a Greek philosopher famous for his skill in developing himself and others through the use of probing open-ended questions. True coaching aims to achieve the best possible outcome and systematically avoids influencing except when the other person cannot make progress. You achieve results through questions and dialogue instead of orders, through active listening and support rather than controlling. You are encouraging a process of self-discovery. By really listening, you suspend judgement. While you actively listen, you are giving full attention to what the other person is saying and feeling. True coaching increases employees' motivation to take initiative and to accept accountability. Hence the workload for the person coaching is reduced as they delegate work through tapping into the latent capacity for improvement that resides in their people. If a coaching session is blocked, it may be acceptable to seed the process by switching to the command role and suggesting an example of a solution. It is important however to remember that telling is our natural default style and we must try to resist this urge in coaching sessions.

Devine's work has many parallels with the Toyota concept of kata. The kata concept is covered in detail in the excellent book by Mike Rother called *Toyota Kata: Managing People for Improvement, Adaptiveness, and Superior Results*. Kata translates loosely as developing routines or daily behaviour patterns – routines for making improvements and also routines for how to coach people to make improvements. These routines are similar to the Behavioural Standards described in the Cathedral model. The objective of both is to standardise the critical behaviours and build new habits that are required for a true learning organisation to take hold.

The continuous raising of problems makes the thresholds of our knowledge apparent. This requires that a combination of coaching and problem solving is called for. Both models use the scientific approach to coaching people. Devine's double-diamond (see Figure 10.3) coaching model merges the HR stream of coaching with the problem-solving structure of A3 PDSA cycles. Rother also illustrates how Toyota uses succinct rapid coaching cycles of 15 minutes or less to deploy the improvement kata of asking the five questions posed in Table 10.2.

Table 10.2 Comparison of Toyota kata and the Cathedral model

Kata coaching cycle for improvement	*The Cathedral model*
1. What is the target condition?	Accountability process guides the conversations arising from visual management and leader standard work
2. What is the actual condition now?	Visual management (target versus actual) and first diamond (diagnostic) of double-diamond coaching
3. What obstacles are now preventing you from reaching the target condition?	First diamond emphasis on diagnosis and driving out assumptions and logical errors
4. What is your next step (start of next PDSA cycle)?	Emphasis on immediate application of outcomes of the accountability process in the Cathedral model
5. When can we go and see what we have learned from taking that step?	Standard daily start of shift reflection on 'Where can I develop and strengthen the culture, where can I see opportunities to coach and give recognition, and reinforce the Behavioural Standards naturally today?' Leverage where we walk (go see) on a daily basis and constant comparison of visual management actual v. target

Both approaches place emphasis on the quality and quantity of conversations. The intention is not to hold 'event' type coaching, instead it is incorporated into the normal daily work via 'little and often' sessions that are indistinguishable from the daily work. Both approaches are light touch (assume good intentions), hard on the process and framed to develop people's skills through the problem-solving and coaching processes.

Both kata and the Cathedral model recommend cost–benefit analysis for cost reduction only, not for decisions that will be required to move through obstacles on the way to the target condition. The approach is to use cost–benefit analysis but in a way that helps us reach the target condition, i.e. if the analysis reveals that a countermeasure is too costly, the next step is to determine how it can be done less expensively.

In essence both mindsets bring to life the invisible deeper thinking and counterintuitive mindsets that are so often the missing link in Lean transformations.

Constructive feedback

Constructive feedback is used when someone's performance (or some aspect of their behaviour) is below the line of what is acceptable. It requires some upfront planning. Constructive feedback is not negative feedback; it is focused on the process and closing the divergence between expected and actual performance. Employees will react better to constructive feedback from you (it is specifically not criticism, the focus is on the situation) only after you have what Devine calls 'earned the right' through previously having taken the time to recognise and coach the person and focused on their development – you do not just come down on them at the first sign of a mistake.

(Note: accountability via visual controls triggers constructive feedback, when there is a gap in expected versus actual results. However, there is also a motivational flip side to accountability through 'managing on green'; if people do meet and exceed their targets recognition is given.)

Escalation

Escalation is used in the event of a serious breach of conduct or if constructive feedback has failed to deliver results. Escalation can be formal or informal. An example of informal escalation is when we take an issue, jointly, to a different place (for example to a higher level to get it resolved).

Quantity and quality

The quantity and quality of deployment of the Cathedral model are paramount. The quantity facet denotes that the model elements are not standalone: it is a system. If we set expectations and do not provide recognition for excellent performance, it is highly probable that performance will degrade over time as employees perceive that they are being taken for granted. Similarly when employees do not know what is expected of them it is difficult to provide constructive feedback.

The quality component implies that we must deploy all the elements of the model in a world class manner. Systematic excellence is required; this means that each element must be developed and practised using first-rate standards.

Keeping in line with systems thinking, we note that both quantity and quality interact. There is no point in delivering the elements of the model in an exceptional way if we do not do it often enough. Likewise there is no point in developing expectations for a 'select few' when we are striving to develop a culture where everyone is a vital cog in a well oiled Lean machine. You have to keep practising the basics over and over to become excellent at anything in life, be that passing a ball in sport or recognising the achievements of your employees.

Review

Disciplined application of the Cathedral model is the catalyst to transform organisational culture to one of sustained operational excellence. The foundational elements of organisational values, employees' personal Cathedrals and Behavioural Standards provide the fortification for a high-performance culture. The model also standardises critical leadership behaviours such as clarifying expectations, recognition, coaching, constructive feedback and escalation. These drive accountability for excellent performance into the fabric of the organisation. A key output of long-term use of the Cathedral model is heightened employee self-esteem. This is really important in an improvement culture that needs motivated and confident people taking daily initiative to improve their work.

Employee inclusion in local improvement and decision making changes their beliefs and attitudes in a positive manner towards management and the organisation. It builds genuine trust. Think about how many things we take for granted every day that depend upon a system of trust. Whatever you do on the tools and methods side of Lean will be undermined by the individual's self-esteem unless you take it into consideration. The countermeasure to this is deployment of the Cathedral model to develop the culture that fosters excellence.

The Cathedral model works as a system and hence it cannot function effectively in isolation (by practising sections in a standalone manner). The application of the model as a whole is greater than the sum of its parts. As an example, just using the recognition and coaching pillars of the model will not deliver the full potential of cultural enrichment possible or even the full potential of recognition or coaching, to sustain the Lean transformation.

Acknowledgement

This chapter is based on the work of Frank Devine. Frank developed the Cathedral model based on a synopsis of the best management practices. He specialises in accelerating the pace of culture change and the engagement of employees on the Lean transformation journey. He is also a visiting lecturer at Cardiff University where he specialises in the 'getting buy-in' aspects of Lean on the MSc in Lean Operations curriculum. He can be contacted at: **accelerated-imp@aol.com** or see **www.acceleratedimprovement.co.uk** for case study examples of the results of applying the Cathedral model combined with mass employee engagement.

11

The technical side of sustaining Lean

Introduction

The potential competitive advantage between a Lean and a pre-Lean organisation are not a 10% difference but can be a 100–1000% advantage in quality, cost, lead time and people development.[1]

It is common to double the performance of True North metrics each time (generally up to five passes of value stream mapping and kaizen activity) processes are re-studied.

You may well have heard people saying that Lean is just common sense: the perception that Lean is easy is one of the major root causes of failing to achieve the level of results referenced above. It is relatively straightforward to initially apply the physical tools but implementing the Lean management system in parallel and sustaining the gains is another matter altogether.

To enable continuous improvement you need to build a system that is designed to highlight problems. An example of this is andon (see the Glossary) or 'pulling the cord' to stop the line policy whenever a deviation from the standard condition or abnormality is detected by the frontline employee. This ensures that quality problems and other issues are highlighted immediately when problems are small and have not caused disruption.

Systems thinking

A system is a collection of interdependent elements that works in an interactive manner. None of the elements acting alone can do what the system does. Each sector of your organisation should be evaluated only in terms of how well it furthers the system's purpose. In your organisation individual departments can affect the way other areas function. We have become accustomed to managing our organisation by improving its separate silos (engineering, marketing, operations, logistics, customer service, etc.). The common result of this thinking is to make scatter gun improvements that do not improve the end-to-end system performance and hence the reason why many uninformed Lean efforts fail to translate to bottom-line results.

Worse still, improving discrete departments in isolation (without the end-to-end system lens) can have the unintended consequence of making the overall system performance poorer. For example, a raw materials saving (good for procurement department metrics) might lead to higher costs in final assembly due to the longer cycle time to process the material on a shared bottleneck resource (an hour lost at a bottleneck is an hour lost for the entire plant). Hence the overall system cost gets worse! Viewing your organisation as a system will help to prevent this deficiency in joined up thinking. Multiple departments must interact in a seamless fashion (just like the plumbing system in your house) to deliver customer value, hence the fallacy of working to maximise the performance of individual departments in a segregated manner. Each department should be evaluated (using value stream mapping) in terms of how well it furthers the organisation's overall purpose. The Lean aim is to synchronise all departments to work in a simultaneous and collaborative manner that will continuously improve the overall system's performance.

Lean management itself is also a system. The sustained success of Lean will depend on the integration of the philosophy, methods, people and processes, not the performance of individual elements. This appreciation will aid in making decisions about both the design of the Lean system and improvements to it.

Hoshin kanri strategy deployment

The hoshin strategy process described in Chapter 2 facilitates the systematic and methodical deployment of Lean, which in turn boosts the prospect of long-term sustainability. Hoshin in essence will help you take a systematic long-term view of the direction your organisation is heading. It then works backwards to the vital, few, short-term, 'must-do, can't fail' objectives for the current year. These objectives should be in alignment with the longer-term strategic direction. The projects and people you need to deliver these objectives are identified on the x-matrix (see Figure 2.4), along with the metrics to track their progress. Monthly strategy deployment reviews will help keep the business focused on monthly improvement leaps, as opposed to the maintenance focus of most monthly board meetings. The aim of the monthly review process and the continual adjustment process is to embed Lean thinking as the new management system that spans all the activities within your organisation.

Lean daily management system

The daily management system is a series of methods and practices which aims to build a sustained culture of problem solving and improvement. It consists of five interconnected elements.

1. Visual management centre (VMC)

This is the central communication area for your local work teams. The work group members manually update sheets on dry wipe boards (on an hourly basis) with key performance process metrics, schedules, improvement actions, cross-shift issues, etc. The consequence of actively maintaining and responding to the VMC information is progressive elimination of recurring and frustrating problems. The visuals provide the process focus, discipline and accountability that embed Lean into the daily work culture. This prevents the common practice in business where you wait until the end of the day (often the month end!) to discover how the process is working. Frequent and small increment measures of process performance are best to detect problems at the point of cause. The visuals provide systemic motivation for improvement through transparent peer accountability and connecting people to results.

A visual display known as the accountability board (see Figure 11.1) is a very useful trigger to build productive tension in your organisation so that assigned actions are completed. An example of the value of the accountability board is when the driver of a particular A3 problem-solving sheet (see Chapter 5, Section 1) places an action from the document under the assigned owner on the accountability board and in the due date column. The board is then reviewed at the daily meeting shift huddles. When used in this way the board becomes the centralised area where all the improvement actions are collated together.

Name	1	2	3	4	5	6	7	8	9	10	11	12	13	14	15	16	17	18	19	20	21	22	23	24	25	26	27	28	29	30	31
Joe			■		■			■			■				■					■				■		■					
Tom	■	■			■			■		■			■		■		■														
Patricia	■			■		■								■							■		■						■		
Ned																															
Alan			■		■									■			■				■		■	■				■			
Paddy		■						■			■						■						■								
Mick			■						■					■				■				■			■			■			

Figure 11.1 Accountability board

Another useful board is the Kamishibai board (see Figure 11.2). Kamishibai means sequence of events. This board contains cards that detail the critical tasks that must be carried out during each shift to ensure a successful day. The cards are colour coded, red on the front and green on the back. When the tasks are completed the cards are turned to the green side so that there is an instant visual reminder of the completion status of critical tasks.

Further details of the various visual management tracking methods can be reviewed in Chapter 4, Section 2.

The VMC is a move from managing the organisation based on financial metrics (lagging metrics of past performance) to the creation of a

Blue Team Shift	Deviation Tracking	Brown Team Shift	Deviation Tracking
Task A		Task A	start up meeting overrun
Task B		Task B	
Task C		Task C	
Task D		Task D	
Task E		Task E	
Task F		Task F	
Task G	unplanned breakdown	Task G	
Task H		Task H	
Task I		Task I	
Task J		Task J	
Task K		Task K	
Task L	fire drill	Task L	
Task M		Task M	
Task N		Task N	

Figure 11.2 Kamishibai board

system that enables processes to be managed in real time (the drivers of financial performance). Process-based work group metrics such as number of problems solved, 5S audit percentage score, overall equipment effectiveness, changeover time, ideas/employee and waste walk compliance, all drive process excellence, which in turn drives the end of month result metrics.

2. Start-up meetings

These are daily stand-up meetings in front of the VMC generally lasting less than 15 minutes. The purpose of the stand-up is to review the previous shift's performance and to communicate information about the current day's priorities. A response plan is often formulated to address problems that have carried over from the previous day.

3. Daily waste walks

The purpose of a waste walk is to:

- break down barriers between departments through improved communication and collaboration

- look for waste across the organisation and coach people to see concealed waste
- assist management to keep in touch with the frontlines and provide visible support in solving problems and to turn opinions into facts through 'go see'
- facilitate the development of a problem-solving culture
- drive action items and A3s to the accountability board in the VMC
- develop people's skills and build relationships and trust so the frontline people will reveal problems in the presence of management, hence improving communication (Lean is about attacking problems not people!)
- provide process confirmation (check what was committed to be done is done)
- nurture the building of a high-performance improvement culture.

Waste walks should be completed at all levels in the organisation from the top right through to the frontline supervisors. You can track waste walk compliance using simple 'hotel style' checklists as shown in Figure 11.3. This subtle checklist will speak volumes as to who is really behind Lean in your organisation and who is merely paying lip service to it.

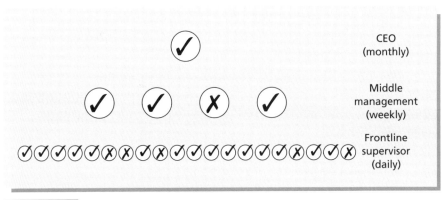

Figure 11.3   Waste walk metric check sheet

4. Idea management system

Visual idea boards are a great mechanism for you to gather ideas about improvements from the frontlines. Most employees have lots of ideas and are willing to share them, but often lack a channel to share them. What would be the impact on your organisation if your supervisors devoted 15–30 minutes every day to improvement tasks? The idea management system provides the conduit to make this a reality. The process of setting up the idea management system for your organisation is discussed in detail in Chapter 6, Section 1.

5. Leader standard work

This locks down the critical tasks that must be completed to both sustain Lean and also drive future continuous improvement. It makes expectations explicit for what actions and behaviours are required. It is best practice if you develop leader standard work in a collaborative manner with your people at all levels, from the CEO through to your frontline team members. It builds discipline, which is one of the key behaviours required to make the Lean system prosper.

Leader standard work (see Figure 11.4) provides a structure and routine that will help your supervisors shift from a sole emphasis on making the numbers to a twin and equally important emphasis on making improvement *plus* making the numbers *every day*. In summary, leader standard work develops a routine not just for doing the work, but also for continually improving the work.

The five elements work together as a system to bring the Lean culture to life. Holistically they drive everyday improvement and nurture the sustaining of these gains. The teams' VMC is the dashboard that indicates how the area is performing and this drives improvement actions at the daily stand-up meetings. Waste walks keep everyone in touch with the area where customer value is created and creates a tempo to implement the assigned improvements from the daily stand-up meetings. The idea management system

Leader Standard Work   Name: Area C Supervisor   Date: 1-Mar-2012

Daily			Issues / Interruptions / Follow Ups	Weekly		
Time	**Task**			**Day**	**Time**	**Task**
09:00	Daily Start of Shift Meeting at VMC			Mon	09:30	A3 Problem Solving Review
09:30					12:00	Yogoten (improvement spread) Conf. Call
10:00	Daily Waste Walk				16:00	121 Coaching
10:30	Frontline Idea Implemetation Support					
11:00	Frontline Idea Implemetation Support			Tue	09:30	Cathedral Model
11:30	Update VMC Tracking Sheets				16:00	121 Coaching
12:00					16:30	Metrics Review Meeting
12:30	Check email					
13:00	Lunch			Wed	09:30	Lean Project
13:30	Standard Work Review				16:00	121 Coaching
14:00					16:30	5S Audit
14:30						
15:00	Review Labour Plan			Thur	09:30	Strategy Review
15:30	A3 Problem Solving					
16:00				Fri	16:00	Stand Back & Next Week Planning
16:30						
17:00	Check email / Next Day Planning					
17:30						
18:00						

Quarterly				Monthly		
Time	**Task**			**Day**	**Time**	**Task**
4 Hours	Networking			Week 1	2 Hours	Hoshin Review Meeting Preparation
4 Hours	Forecasting			Week 1	2 Hours	Hoshin Review Meeting
1 Day	Team Off-Sites			Week 2	2 Hours	Staff Communication
3 Days	Supplier Development			Week 2	4 Hours	Before and After Photos
4 Hours	Town Hall Meeting			Week 3	4 Hours	Training Other
				Week 2	4 Hours	Leadership Development
				Week 3	10 Hours	Monthly 121 with Group Leader
				Week 2	8 Hours	Kaizen Activity
				Week 1	1 Day	
				Week 4	2 Days	Kaizen Activity
				Week 1	4 Hours	HR Topics

Figure 11.4 Leader standard work example

provides the mechanism for employees to take engaged ownership for local decision making in their areas through the daily implementation of small ideas that are instigated from the VMC. Finally, leader standard work provides the structure and time to ensure that all the Lean methods are maintained and the actions are addressed in a manner that engages and develops the frontline team.

Sustaining Lean through problem solving

One of the biggest success or failure points for long-term Lean success is management's attitude towards problems. If the attitude and message from management is, 'Don't come to me with problems, just solutions', much of the potential of Lean is lost. People will conceal problems for fear of reprisal. Dr Lucian Leape, a professor at the Harvard School of Public Health, said that, 'the single greatest impediment to error prevention is that we punish people for making mistakes'.[2] In many industries problems are only reported when they can no longer be concealed. This is a huge lost opportunity as root cause analysis and problem solving deliver a tremendous return on investment both in terms of cost savings and employee development. To capitalise on this unlikely leverage point you must change your attitude towards problems. Think about what would happen if you thanked your people for reporting problems!

When you embrace problems they become the starting point for the next round of improvement. For this to transpire our processes need to be designed to bring any deviation to the surface immediately (see the Lean management system discussed earlier in this chapter). Once people report problems and begin the systematic problem-solving process it is imperative to work through all the nine steps of the process (see Chapter 5, Section 1). The majority of organisations work through the first few steps and then fail to perform due diligence on the remaining steps. They simply find another problem to solve or indeed put a sticking plaster over the problem and consequently the cycle of problem reoccurrence and fire-fighting continues. One of the challenges of sustainability is to develop the discipline and review structure to steer problems through all the nine steps of the process. To further the complexity of real life, certain problems are never solved for ever; conditions of processes can change causing factors to interact that can deem one time counter-measures invalid. The antidote to this as a Lean thinker is to ensure that the process will make this evident (through the various visual controls) so that the next round of refinement can begin.

If we focus on developing human problem-solving skills rather than cost savings, the savings will come as a natural outcome. There will be thousands of problems to solve in your Lean transformation – again this is a positive thing. To sustain this flurry of activity we need to dedicate problem-solving resources and a plan to support problem solving throughout the organisation. This supervisor in a Lean environment is the person who picks up the problems at the various visual control points (see the Lean management system at the beginning of this chapter) and daily team stand-ups, and facilitates the resolution of this with their team members.

Training within industry (TWI)

TWI is a long-established effective training programme. It first achieved widespread prominence during World War II when hundreds of thousands of people needed to be trained fast and effectively to support the manufacture of equipment to meet the demands of the war effort.

Going back to basics is one catalyst for sustaining Lean; TWI is about doing the basics exceptionally well. TWI consists of three programmes that cover three core jobs of supervisors:

1 how to instruct employees on how to perform a particular job correctly, efficiently and safely (job instruction programme)

2 how to improve the work methods (job methods programme) through problem identification and improvement skills

3 how to deal effectively with people (job relations programme) through effective communication and motivating people.

Standard work (see Chapter 5, Section 2) is a foundation element for sustaining Lean as it compels us to examine and improve current work methods. However, the creation of standard work is not enough. This knowledge needs to be transferred from explicit procedural knowledge in the standards to tacit knowledge in employees' minds. Job instruction is the programme that accomplishes this. Job instruction uses a combination of telling, showing, listening, trying out and doing to embed the important steps and key points of carrying out a task. Engaging the multiple senses of the trainee really enhances the quality of the training and its long-term retention. Regular support check-ins and feedback further close the learning loop. Standard work is about doing the basics, and Lean is all about doing the basics outstandingly well over a sustained period. The TWI methodology supplements this practice through job instruction and additionally teaches people to question existing standards for improvement opportunities through the job methods programme. And to complete the trilogy, the job relations training programme trains supervisors on how to lead people in a participative manner and develop teamwork to maximise the effectiveness of both job instruction and job methods. For a more detailed dive into the power of TWI that is beyond the scope of this text, please refer to the further reading section for this chapter.

Metrics

The things that get measured get improved. Measurement generally improves performance.[3] Sustaining Lean in my experience is unattainable without changing your current performance measurement system to track the new behaviours and actions that will drive improvement. Transformational Lean *end-to-end* metrics drive accountability for both meeting output targets and improving the system. End-to-end is a key distinction of Lean metrics, meaning that the whole process is measured from start to finish (including the hidden white spaces between processes, such as time dwells and inventory stashes). The reason for this is that customers experience processes from the start to the finish, not as individual departments. Accountability does not mean that the metrics should be used for dominating and judging people. Their purpose in the Lean culture is to increase actionable feedback that improves process understanding and hence prompts ongoing learning and improvement. The intention of the metrics and increased transparency needs to be communicated clearly to your people to dispel fear and to build consensus. Analogies to other areas in life can be powerful here. In sport both players and fans love measurement: without statistics on player performance or the scoreboard, etc. the competitive edge and thrill factor is greatly reduced. The measurement system also needs to be aligned across functions with True North metrics (see Chapter 1).

You need metrics to both maintain the system and improve the system. True North is guided by the desire for perfection in quality, cost, delivery and employee engagement. As discussed in Chapter 1 the selection of metrics should consider a blend of process, balancing and result metrics. In fact the number of process metrics (leading indicators that drive the results) should as a rule of thumb outnumber result metrics by a factor of four. You need to deeply understand your business (refer to hoshin kanri and value stream mapping in Chapters 2 and 3), and gain a clear grasp of what drives the creation of value and what destroys it, to ensure that we are measuring the right things. This can be a humbling practice and egos need to be set aside for the greater good. Metrics must also be modified as they are deployed throughout the organisation to make them relevant at each level.

Review

The technical aspects for sustaining Lean cover linking the transformation journey to the strategy of the business. Hoshin kanri builds this linkage and evolves Lean into *the* management system that will deliver the strategy. Lean is not a bolt on; to work it needs to encompass all the functions that are performed in the organisation. Lean is a radical departure from the traditional directive approach to managing your business and the new participative style requires strong leadership. The deployment of methods and tools is necessary but not sufficient. It needs to be supported by a parallel deployment of the Lean daily management system, as without this any initial routine will just not take root and become the new, established routine. In any Lean conversion there is a strong demand for a robust, people centric, training system – the time tested TWI programmes meet this need. Finally, you will need to think about how you will know how you are doing in the new Lean paradigm. The old ways of measuring will no longer cut it. Lean metrics are required and as with all things Lean they are very different from the classical business school approaches to performance measurement.

12

The people side of sustaining Lean

Introduction

If you do not appreciate the people aspects of sustaining Lean your organisation's transformation will be disappointing at best. Lean is high-maintenance activity; it takes more or less the same effort to keep the improvements in place as it does to put them into operation at the outset. While the practices, tools and principles are visible, the management thinking and routines to sustain Lean are invisible. If we keep managing in the same way as we did in the pre-Lean environment the improvement gains will not stick, much less evolve into everyday improvement. Lean cannot be effectively applied in a piecemeal fashion. Your organisation will not be effective through the application of the methods and tools in isolation because the philosophy, methods and human side of Lean are tightly integrated and dependent on each other. The system must be rolled out in a holistic manner.

Using Lean as a means to reduce people is usually a fatal blow to sustained improvement. People will not improve themselves out of a job. And, as we have already seen, people reduction is not a goal of Lean. Growth (both business and people) and waste elimination are the objectives of Lean and it goes without saying that people are not waste.

You probably appreciate by now that over 95% of what we do is non-value-added or waste through your customers' eyes. This means that there are far greater possible gains in cutting cost through waste elimination than in cutting cost through people reduction. There are, however, circumstances where organisations are employing excessive numbers of staff, often through years of mismanagement. This situation violates the 'respect for people' pillar as people are not utilising their talents fully and hence eventually become disengaged in the workplace. This situation should be proactively managed through redeployment to growth areas. If this is not an option, lay-offs can be a last resort option. This should be done in a supportive fashion, where the company makes every effort to help with new career opportunities for those affected. If a company has large cash reserves, it is the best long-term option if people are trained and developed for a period whilst new business opportunities are explored. However, job losses due to improvements are not acceptable business practices in a true Lean transformation. This is not only from a moral viewpoint; it makes business sense to use freed up resources from improvement to make even further process improvements.

Leadership

> *'To lead people, walk beside them ... As for the best leaders, the people do not notice their existence. The next best, the people honour and praise. The next, the people fear; and the next, the people hate ... When the best leader's work is done the people say, "We did it ourselves!"'*
>
> Lao Tsu *(founder of philosophical Taoism)*

Most managers are trained to manage (maintain the status quo), not lead; to lead is taking your organisation in a new direction. It is the leader's job to sell and lead by example the new way of Lean thinking and culture, every day. Gary Convis, the former GM of Toyota in Kentucky, uses the description 'to lead the organisation as if you have no power' to describe the leadership style at Toyota. In other words, oversee the organisation not through the power of decree, but through example, coaching and assisting employees to achieve their objectives.

The highest form of leadership you can develop for sustained Lean success is known as servant leadership. This is the genuine sentiment that you want to serve first and foremost. The phrase 'servant leadership' was coined by Robert K. Greenleaf in *The Servant as Leader*.[1] Qualities that a servant leader exhibits are a passion for developing people, taking the long-term view, being process focused and having patience and humility. Servant leaders are more concerned about serving others than they are about their own achievements or rewards. Treat others as you would want to be treated is the True North ideal here. Additional qualities include treating others with respect, listening emphatically, appreciating people, holding people accountable (a manifestation of respect – their work is important) and being truthful. This is not a soft or fluffy concept; the business case is echoed in the sentiment that if we take care of our people they will take care of us. When Sam Walton opened his first Wal-Mart store in Arkansas in 1962, he said: 'If you want to ruin your business, just treat your employees bad because they will take it out on your customer.' How would you as a Lean leader describe your own attributes in comparison with the ones listed in this paragraph?

The message here is that sustained organisational change starts with individual change. The best Lean organisations that I have worked with begin this process at the boardroom level, one person at a time, and it then flows downwards to the leaders throughout the organisation.

If individual change is required what needs to be changed? You need to demonstrate both in words and by your actions that you believe that people development and process improvement go hand in hand. Consequently, this requires the transition from an authoritarian style of leadership of commanding your people on what to do, to a philosophy of developing people through coaching. This is a major shift in the way most businesses are run. Leading people with process goals and not financial directives creates higher levels of engagement, and if we get the process right the financials will take care of themselves. To do this requires high-touch leadership and spending time on the frontlines coaching and developing problem solvers on a daily basis to improve the current standards. Chapter 10 showed how you could take the journey towards changing the culture of your organisation.

In a Lean environment the worst problems are concealed problems. Hence the new role of management is to both facilitate the design of the organisation so that problems are raised when they are in their infancy and to ensure that people are empowered and supported to address these problems. Therefore a vital part of sustaining Lean is building a culture that practises problem solving and process improvement every day. The top performing Lean organisations make no distinction between the routine daily work and improvement problem solving. The continuous and everyday focus on problem solving builds deep improvement capability. The result is the growth of talented Lean thinkers at the frontline, work team level, to the point where making improvements becomes an unconscious competence. The Lean daily management system (discussed in Chapter 11) is the physical mechanism for creating the Lean culture. However, even more important is the continuous nurturing of invisible aspects through the Cathedral model (discussed in Chapter 10).

Engaging people in Lean

Look after the basics

A good way of engaging people in the Lean journey is to find out what niggles and frustrations they have with their current work. Solving these at the outset is a sign of genuine commitment to the transformation journey. If the fundamentals that enable people to do their best at work are not in place your company will be on the back foot straightaway. So you need to address these first. This includes ensuring that everyone is trained and qualified to do their jobs and they know what is expected of them, they have the correct equipment and tools to perform their jobs and they get regular feedback on their performance.

Management integrity is crucial for sustaining Lean – we must do as we say and treat everyone with equal fairness. Solving people's 'hassle factors' sends out the message that Lean can help people to make their work easier.

Many Lean journeys today take a discontinuous approach to improvement rather than a continuous one. There are stop-start improvement blitzes every few weeks or months. This is not a true application of the Lean philosophy. To realise the full potential of Lean we need to practise on a daily basis, just like top class athletes do. The reason for this is to keep sharp and to develop the thinking and observation skills to be continually spotting waste. Discontinuous improvement will only keep you at your current level of performance due to the eroding effect of entropy and other interacting factors. As a manager you must cultivate your people to develop the sensitivity to see problems and to be alert to waste every day, and feel comfortable in raising them via their local visual management centre.

Hierarchy of needs

Maslow's hierarchy of needs was a model developed by Abraham Maslow in 1943. He listed five needs to describe the ladder of human motivations. In order to achieve the next level the lower needs in the ladder must be satisfied before those higher needs become motivators. To fully engage the hearts and minds of your people you need to satisfy all the levels of this model, and you should think about how your organisation is currently satisfying these needs.

The five needs that are relevant to Lean transformation are:

1 *Physiological*: these are the needs required for survival such as air, food and water. Lean improves the probability that an organisation will survive and prosper in the long term, hence providing stable employment that in turn will provide good wages for people to purchase the essentials of life such as food and water.

2 *Safety*: these are the needs necessary for a sense of security such as health, employment and a good home. Lean provides a people centric and safe work environment in terms of a physically safe work environment according to this need. It also provides a psychologically safe environment where people's ideas and opinions are welcomed and acted upon in a timely manner.

3 *Social*: these are the needs vital to a feeling of belongingness such as friendship, intimacy and family. Teamwork, trust and

collaborative relationships are cornerstones in realising business improvement in a Lean system.

4 *Esteem*: these are the needs crucial to feeling respected, confident and appreciated for your achievements. The 'respect for people' pillar (discussed in Chapter 1) is a precondition for long-term prosperity through the application of Lean. This manifests itself in respect for people's talents and the continual development of these for the benefit of the employee and the growth of the company.

5 *Self-actualisation*: these are needs related to intellectual growth and fulfilling an employee's true potential. Challenge is a key theme in Lean, and people rise to a challenge when it is framed as 'their' challenge. Challenging people in a constructive way to achieve stretch objectives nurtures their growth and the fulfilment of their potential. The triumph of achievement and the spiritual sense of accomplishment that accompany progress through performance improvement increase the desire to continue the journey of achieving further success.

If you keep Maslow's five needs in mind it will help you design a successful Lean roadmap from a people engagement side. This is crucial as nothing will happen without engaged and involved employees!

Job enrichment

Job enrichment is a further way of motivating employees on the Lean journey. It provides them with the opportunity to maximise the full range of their talents. It was developed by the American psychologist Frederick Herzberg in the 1950s. Job enrichment aims to redesign jobs to make them more intrinsically rewarding. This means that they appeal to the person's sense of self-worth. Characteristics that will help you build enrichment into jobs are:

▪ *Skill variety*: increasing the number of tasks that your employees are competent to perform builds skills and mastery, and increased motivation as boredom is alleviated.

▪ *Task identity*: the degree to which employees perceive how their job affects the overall delivery of a product or service. A job has a high task identity if your employees do it from the beginning to end with a timely and visible outcome.

■ *Task significance*: the degree to which the job has a substantial purpose and meaningful impact on the lives of other people, whether these people are in the immediate organisation or in society. A job has high task significance if people benefit greatly from results of the work. A non-cynical environment is required for this element to be sincere. A clear connection between one's work and the organisation's visions nurtures task significance.

■ *Autonomy*: this is employee empowerment to intervene in process disruptions, etc. and requires trust in people's self-management and the removal of fear of being punished for honest mistakes. Trust is a manifestation of respect for people, and is required to break down barriers between departments which are an essential requirement for the Lean principle of flow – value flows *through* departments.

■ *Feedback*: access to information and collaborative input from peers regarding the quality of your work is another form of job enrichment. Training and coaching should be provided to address identified performance gaps. Recognition for a person's success is another potent form of feedback. Celebrations of milestones that mark progress and facilitate employee interaction with the end users of their work builds pride and also fosters intrinsic motivation.

'Recognition is the free fuel that drives your business.'

Lee Cockerell (former Executive Vice President of Walt Disney World Operations)

We all engage when we feel valued for the work we do and when our opinions are listened to. Our frontline people in general know far more about our processes than we do as they are operating them every day. Do we ever ask, 'What do you think?', 'How would you make this better?' or 'What is the one thing we could do better?' It is surprising even today how often this is neglected and many workers still feel like second class citizens as a result of their treatment by directive management attitudes.

Ideal state mapping

Another major source of motivation for improvement is comparing actual performance to ideal (see the ideal state value stream map in Chapter 3). Acknowledge how much waste exists in all the work your organisation does every day (remember the 95% non-value-added aspect of pre-Lean processes). And yes, this is true regardless of the industry sector you work in. Lean works in all sectors, as Table 12.1 illustrates. We all perform generic processes at work – the common denominator is people doing work.

Table 12.1 All work is a process

Manufacturing	*Services*
Strategic planning	Strategic planning
People development	People development
Design new products	Design new services
Process orders	Process applications
Purchase materials	Purchase supplies
Manufacture products	Provide services
Payroll	Payroll
Demand management and logistics	Demand management and logistics (most)
Accounts receivable	Accounts receivable
Accounts payable	Accounts payable
Recruit people	Recruit people

Involving management in mapping key value streams builds a compelling motivation to improve performance. This is one of the main reasons why management must actively participate in Lean activity, as without practising Lean themselves managers will not fully understand the potential for improvement.

Self-efficacy

Self-efficacy is a further motivational factor to leverage for sustaining Lean. Self-efficacy is a person's confidence in their capability to carry out an assignment. Without confidence in our own ability, we cannot perform to our potential. The central premise of Lean is to harness the full potential of your entire workforce. Previous performance experiences are the most significant source of acknowledgement that affects the development of self-efficacy. To build self-efficacy in a Lean environment we must build up people's confidence and ability through continuous participation in problem solving and the implementation of small improvement ideas. Small is beautiful and bite sized improvements have a higher probability of success, hence bolstering self-efficacy. If and when 'failures' are encountered they must be treated as positive experiments (the connotation that a test of change can either pass or fail) and learning opportunities. They must not be treated as occasions to assign blame. This behaviour motivates people to continue to engage in problem solving. The resultant increase in capabilities that the problem-solving process develops furthers self-efficacy which in turn translates into a virtuous cycle of greater participation in improvement. A true win–win situation arises!

Oh, if only we had the luxury of time for improvement work!

> *'You will never find time for anything. If you want time you must make it.'*
>
> Charles Buxton (philanthropist and politician)

One of the most common reasons I hear when improvement activity stops is 'there is so much going on, we're too busy to allocate time for improvement work'. The predominant culture in most of our organisations is one of fire-fighting – implementing temporary fixes to problems. In addition we are predominately working around or patching up problems without addressing their underlying causes.

Appreciate common and special cause variation

Common cause variation is a normal effect arising from factors interacting in your processes. For example, the time for your pizza delivery to arrive on a Friday night is a natural consequence of interacting factors such as customer demand (walk-in, phone call and internet), the number of employees working, pizza variations mix, and the expertise of those handling the order. The important thing to bear in mind about common cause is that it is a natural outcome of every process. A process with only common cause variation is considered to be stable and its outcomes are predictable. The pizza manager can use Lean to improve the performance of individual (bottleneck process first!) processes through methods such as standard work. This will improve the overall capability of the business and reduce the range and impact of common cause variation on the performance of the business.

Special cause variation, on the other hand, is variation in performance that can be attributed to an unusual factor or number of factors impacting on a process. It develops from some unusual event or incident (usually one of the 6Ms discussed in the cause and effect diagram, see Figure 5.1). For example the time it takes the pizza delivery man to deliver the pizza may be significantly affected by heavy traffic caused by a concert in the area or his car breaking down on his way to your house. The run chart also discussed in Chapter 5 (see Figure 5.5) is used to identify the early signs of a special cause entering a process and it enables us to react before the customer sees the effects.

Unfortunately it is common practice to observe organisations reacting to special cause variation, as in the example above, in unstable processes and believing that they are working on improving the capability of the process. A markedly more effective approach is to work on improving the capability of the process so as to minimise the probability of special cause(s) affecting your business. When stability increases, a virtuous circle transpires: people spend less time fire-fighting the chaos from processes and have more time to spend on further improving stability. This in turn generates even more time for proactive improvement work. Hence the more kaizen we can perform the more time we will have for kaizen in the long run and hence the potential for incessant increases in performance.

> *'If you don't have time to do it right, when will you have time to do it over?'*
>
> *John Wooden (basketball player and coach)*

Leverage the facts

Value stream mapping demonstrated that pre-Lean organisations spend 95% of their customer fulfilment time doing tasks that increase cost and do not deliver value that the end customer is willing to pay for! Under those circumstances, why would anyone spend all of their time on their regular job? When this realisation becomes accepted and engrained across the organisation, the excuse that there is no time for improvement simply becomes insupportable. Hence improvement work and kaizen activity should be mandated as an expected part of everyone's job description. It should not be treated as a nice to do discretionary activity when spare time becomes available.

A powerful analogy to help people realise that we can make time for Lean is to connect with people's outside passions such as their hobbies or sporting activities. We seem to be able to creatively make time for these dedicated pastimes in our lives despite many competing activities. Try to draw out ideas from your people about how we can treat Lean as a passionate pursuit and what resultant actions will allow us to make time available.

Leader standard work releases time for improvement

Leader standard work makes time for improvement by systematically asking people to examine their current workload and to make decisions about what current non-value-adding activities they should stop doing. Ask, what can be delegated straight away and in future through training and developing other employees to take on the tasks that, in turn, nurture that person's growth through up-skilling.

'Patching up' a problem every day is hugely wasteful (this is like weeding the garden and leaving the roots intact) when compared with a countermeasure that tackles the root cause(s). Hence, the seemingly wasteful practice that some Lean organisations adopt of deliberately providing extra capacity in the work week to allow for kaizen activity is vital to sustaining the gains.

Stephen Covey talked about four spaces in relation to effective use of our time. Many tasks are urgent, the temptation to do them now is strong, but are they important? The four spaces are as follows:

1 Important – Urgent: make the numbers (customer fulfilment tasks) and pressing issues. **(Do these now, they pay the bills!)**

2 Not Important – Urgent: such as interruptions, many meetings (many meetings are enormous time wasters, track these for a week in your diary and you will be amazed at how much time they swallow up!). **(Manage these by cutting them short, rejecting them and avoiding requests when working on high priorities.)**

3 Not Important – Not Urgent: such as leisurely surfing the web and time wasting. **(Avoid these!)**

4 Important – Not Urgent: such as proactive Lean improvement work and development of others and yourself. **(Plan in *non-negotiable* time to do this work after category 1 items are completed.)**

The last space often seems a nice to do, but this is where we need to spend more time as this is the important work that assures the organisation's future. Conscious awareness of these categories will help to ensure that you dedicate time for Lean.

The capability trap

In their seminal paper Nelson Repenning and John Sterman[2] set out a compelling case for overcoming the dilemma of failures in process improvement endeavours. They provide the example whereby increasing the work week by 20% through overtime might increase output by 20%, however only for the duration of this overtime. In contrast, improvement in process capability will boost the output generated by every subsequent week that you work.

They state:

'While it often yields the more permanent gain, time spent on improvement does not immediately improve performance. It takes time to uncover the root causes of process problems and then to discover, test, and implement solutions, and the resulting change in

process capability (to become evident) … As the performance gap falls, workers have even more time to devote to improvement, creating a virtuous cycle of improved capability and increasing attention to improvement … Shortcuts are tempting because there is often a substantial delay between cutting corners and the consequent decline in capability (due to a "grace period" where the gradual decline in capability is not immediately noticeable).'

The authors explain that a common mistake that management make in light of the delay in performance improvement is to conclude that the particular improvement method is not working and it is abandoned. To overcome this requires the awareness that there is a 'worse-before-better' dynamic at play.

80/20 Pareto rule

The 80/20 rule (see Chapter 5, Section 1) is another powerful focusing principle in the quest to make time available for process improvement. Identify the 20% of activities that are delivering 80% of the effectiveness in your 'routine work' and transition the remainder of your time to the 'non-routine' activity of process improvement.

'Besides the noble art of getting things done, there is the noble art of leaving things undone. The wisdom of life consists in the elimination of non-essentials.'

Lin Yutang (writer and inventor)

The Lean drive for perfection does not allow time for a breather. Consistency and initiative keep the Lean flywheel turning. When business gets frantic, that is when we most need Lean, because it is at these demanding times that Lean can provide the greatest benefit. Every big problem you now face that is making your day crazy was once a small problem. This is a powerful statement for you and your organisation to reflect on: what big problems do you have now that started out like grains of sand? The Lean system is designed to surface these small deviations at the point of cause, hence greatly increasing the likelihood of stamping them out in their infancy.

'There is a time in the life of every problem when it is big enough to see, yet small enough to solve.'

Mike Leavitt (US politician)

Communication

The way that Lean is framed in your business will have a major impact on how the transformation process is perceived. Will we lose our jobs as a result of improvement or will we be saddled with more work? A communication plan is an essential element of Lean transformation. If you do this well you'll alleviate employee concerns regarding the fear of the unknown.

Communicate the positive personal and business impacts to people. These include safer work areas, job security, higher levels of involvement in running local work areas, less frustrating wasteful work, and business growth due to shorter lead times, higher quality and lower costs.

Communication stops the rumour mill in its tracks. In most organisations there are tremendous communication deficits. After three days of hearing a message we recall only approximately 10% of the message. Hence a common rule of thumb is to 'overdo' the communication that you think is adequate by a factor of ten. To maximise the effectiveness of your communication it needs to be delivered in various ways such as group meetings, one to one coaching sessions, in print, via websites, and through the organisation's visual management centres.

Middle management

Middle management, and typically supervisors, are arguably the group with most to lose and the least to gain from Lean. They are pulled from all sides, for example they have to keep their team engaged and also deliver the expectations of the senior management team. They are essential to success as they are the critical link between the frontlines and management. In the short term this 'loss' factor is really felt, as there will be additional work requirements (problem solving and people development), however over the longer term efficiency and productivity gains combined with reduction in mistakes and defects will be of colossal benefit to them. You need to ensure that your middle management have the full support of the top management team.

A propensity for risk taking

'People who don't take risks generally make about two big mistakes a year. People who do take risks generally make about two big mistakes a year.'

Peter Drucker (writer and management consultant)

The creation of an environment where it is acceptable to fail is a further building block for sustaining Lean. Progress always involves a certain level of controlled risk taking. Playing it safe could turn out to be the highest risk strategy of all if your organisation goes out of business! Risk taking can be fostered when the leader recognises that efforts made for the right reasons *will* sometimes fail. A supportive response to these failures sends the message that risk taking in the pursuit of commendable goals can become a positive learning experience, will be tolerated, and indeed encouraged.

A rising tide should lift all boats

To support the 'respect for people' pillar, the benefits of Lean should not be confined to just increasing shareholder value. All stakeholders in the process should share in the benefits. Gainsharing ensures that improvement work benefits everyone. Gainsharing is a system in which an organisation seeks higher levels of performance through the involvement and participation of its people. As operational performance gets better, employees share financially in the savings. Gainsharing measures are typically based on True North metrics (people growth, cost, quality and delivery) which are more controllable by frontline employees rather than the macro, corporate wide, practice of profit sharing. Dividends are self-funded and calculated on savings generated through the Lean transformation.

Review

It is important to state that sustaining the momentum is one of the great challenges of all management and business practices; this is not confined to the Lean transformation. Application of the Lean methods and tools is necessary but not sufficient to realise the full potential of Lean to deliver sustained operational excellence. You must go further, and address the people side of Lean. The journey to transforming your organisation is all about leadership. Engaging everyone in the practice of everyday improvement is certainly a major shift for most organisations, and to sustain the Lean transformation you need to crack this challenge. Leaders have to develop effective tactics both to release time for improvement and also to weave improvement work into the daily routine work so that they become the inseparable way that the business is run. To make a leap of faith from the comfort of the status quo, employees need vivid and compelling communication throughout the journey. The frontline supervisor is of critical importance in making Lean endure. In reality Lean is two steps forward and one step back; mistakes and problems are good and need to be embraced. The positive bottom-line impact of Lean should be distributed so that all stakeholders benefit. Lean leaders recognise that they need to measure differently than in the pre-Lean environment to develop the new habits and behaviours that are required to sustain and continuously improve performance. Finally, to achieve true Lean means not just sustaining what we have improved, but also continuing to make more and more improvements along the staircase towards True North.

13

Putting it all together: the Lean roadmap to transformation

The objective of this chapter is to synthesise the book into a generic roadmap for organisational transformation. Some steps are referenced back to earlier chapters in the book and other concepts are introduced or repeated to reinforce their value.

Introduction

While every business embarking on the Lean journey will have different challenges based on its particular set of circumstances, there are several established key steps that can help you reduce resistance, spread the learning, and build the type of commitment and engagement necessary for Lean to thrive. That said, there is no single prescription for Lean transformation. The journey must be planned and initiated based on your own organisation's unique needs, cultural maturity, opportunities and pressing issues. For example, if your company is about to go under, the bleeding of cash must be stopped first. In this instance the Lean roadmap would be very much focused on rapid cost reduction and aggressive application of methods such as kaizen events (see Chapter 6). The building of a Lean culture in this instance would come after the bleeding has stopped and the threat of extinction has been averted. However, to build sustainable transformation for the long term there are many elements that need to be fused together. Hence it is useful to provide a generic roadmap that can be used as the initial map for you to design and plan your journey towards the True North concepts of perfection in quality, cost, delivery and employee engagement.

GENERIC ROADMAP

It is good practice to structure the Lean journey as a macro level PDSA cycle with multiple smaller PDSA cycles within this larger cycle. The large-scale cycle has the following components:

- *Plan*: includes the roadmap and diagnostic methods such as hoshin kanri, the Lean assessment, and value stream mapping.
- *Do*: is making the improvements through practice of the methods and tools.
- *Study*: is the creation of a learning organisation, one example is the application of the Lean daily management system.
- *Adjust*: is spreading successful changes, building sustainability, and identifying the next layer of improvement opportunity.

A generic Lean roadmap is shown in Figure 13.1.

1. Understand value through the eyes of your customers

An essential starting point for your Lean journey is to gain a deep appreciation of the value that your products or services deliver to your customers. We can be the leanest organisation in our business sector and still not survive if our customers do not derive value from our offerings. Customers buy outcomes, not products or services. We must know who our customer is and they can be either internal (the next person to receive the result of our work) or external (the end user). The Kano model shown in Figure 13.2 is really useful to initiate a dialogue and increase your understanding of what your customer defines as value.

The model was developed by Dr Kano in Japan while he was researching customer requirements for the airline industry. As illustrated in Figure 13.2, the horizontal axis represents the level of fulfilment regarding a given customer want. This ranges from not

(Plan) Diagnostic	(Do) Deploy	(Study) Sustainability	(Adjust) Expansion
Understand value through the eyes of your customer	Pilot Lean model area and spread plan	Lean daily management system	Further model areas
Articulate the business case for transformation	Build the Lean knowledge	Lean culture enrichment (the Cathedral model)	End-to-end value streams
Lean assessment	Methods and tools	Hansei	Lean development*
Value stream mapping			Supply chain*
Build leadership commitment and expectations setting			Accounting for Lean*
Hoshin kanri strategy deployment			Hansei
Management of change			
← 0–3 months →	← 1–6 months →	← 2–3 months →	← 3 months and forever →

Figure 13.1 Generic Lean roadmap

*Detailed coverage of Lean development, supply chain and accounting for Lean are beyond the scope of this book. A brief overview of each is provided in the glossary and further reading sources are identified in this chapter's references where you can learn more.

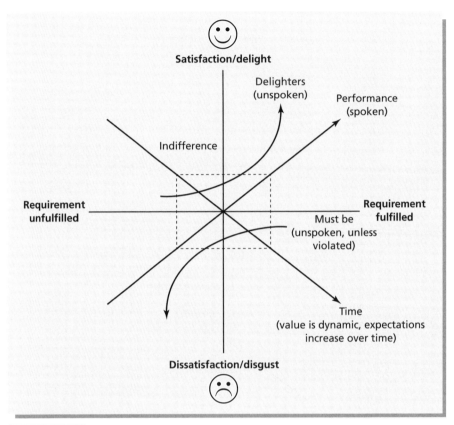

Figure 13.2   Kano model

Source: adapted from Dr Noriaki Kano,[1] reproduced with permission of the Asian Productivity Organisation

fulfilled at all on the left side to complete fulfilment on the right side. The vertical axis represents the level of customer satisfaction ranging from complete dissatisfaction at the bottom to complete delight at the top. There is an area around the centre of the model where the customer is insensitive; it is depicted in the figure as a neutral zone of indifference.

Must be needs are a given and an example would be a clean hotel room. These needs are normally unspoken and their presence will not provide increased satisfaction, however their absence will result in extreme dissatisfaction. *Performance* needs are normally spoken and the motto is, 'More is better'. One example would be internet access in your hotel room. *Delighters* are normally unspoken and provide an unexpected positive experience or excitement for your customer. An example of a *Delighter* in a hotel room would be free, cooled champagne in a sterling silver ice bucket and hand-made chocolates in your room on arrival. It is important to recognise that value is dynamic; it changes over time. What was once a *Delighter*, might now be a *Performance* need, and some time in the future may well become a *Must be* need. Perhaps in many parts of the world free internet access in your hotel room has descended down the ranks from being a *Delighter* five years ago towards being a *Must be* unspoken need today.

You should grasp how your current product or service fits against the Kano model and what the opportunities to differentiate your business from the competition are. This will highlight if you are providing what customers value – and some more! This exercise can turbo charge the results of Lean transformation from both a cost saving perspective and enhanced revenue generation.

2. Articulate the business case for Lean transformation

It is useful to use both push and pull messages to convey the business case for change. A push message articulates the risk and concerns of continuing to operate as we currently do. A pull message paints a picture of the opportunities and benefits that will be realised through the adoption of Lean.

Management understanding and belief that Lean will directly address core business problems is fundamental. Without this there is no business case for Lean and with no business case there is no compelling reason to change. The business case creates the 'Why?' for transformation. Crafting the business case at the True North metrics of quality, people growth and engagement, delivery and cost helps to frame the opportunity. Some example questions for developing the 'What do we want to achieve from Lean transformation?' include:

▪ Can we gain 10% market share by achieving half the industry average of customer complaints? (*Quality*)

- Can we increase employee engagement to the level that our employee turnover costs are half those of our nearest competitor? (*Engagement*)
- Can we increase revenue by halving our lead time? (*Delivery*)
- Can we decrease costs by 20% through eliminating waste and exploiting the capacity that is released through this waste elimination? (*Cost*)

An important factor to consider is that you must ensure that improvements realised through Lean translate to the bottom line financials. Otherwise we have claimed savings that are illusory. You have to take advantage of the improvements, ranging from improved employee capability to released capacity from waste elimination. To translate the improvements to the bottom line requires further work. This can take many forms including growing the business or developing the capability to do more with the same resources of people, space and equipment. The business case for Lean can and should alter over time as industry conditions change. For example, if you have released capacity in the system, a natural follow-on step might be to transform your business development and new product/ service processes to make them more effective at winning new business to exploit these capacity savings.

3. Lean assessment

(See the template in the Appendix.)

A Lean assessment is a series of Lean criteria that identifies areas of opportunity for improving the performance of your business. The outcome should be a gap analysis of the current condition of the organisation versus the desired ideals of True North. This will then serve as key data for the hoshin kanri strategy deployment workshop. The Lean assessment should not be a one-off exercise; frequent assessments (every six months is common) help to track progress and indeed slippage, providing input into where focus is needed.

Your leadership team must also gain an appreciation for organisational readiness for Lean transformation and the current capability and skills of your frontline people. A further powerful diagnostic tool to gauge both the appetite for change and probability of success is a management change readiness assessment shown in Table 13.1. (Note: RAG is the acronym for red, amber or green status.) Red and amber items are prioritised under the 'Difficulty to mitigate' heading and then actions are taken to alleviate these factors.

Table 13.1 Lean readiness assessment

Readiness factor	Readiness status (RAG)	Difficulty to mitigate	Actions to mitigate
Leadership commitment			
Appetite for increased performance transparency and less hierarchy			
Vision of desired future			
Business case for Lean is defined			
Understand the time and resource commitment			
Lean knowledge and understanding of potential for performance improvement			
Accountability for change is defined			
Capability for developing Lean at the work group level			
High levels of mutual trust between management and frontline staff			
Information is shared openly			

Readiness factor	Readiness status (RAG)	Difficulty to mitigate	Actions to mitigate
Competing initiatives are identified and Lean is seen as the philosophy to accelerate and leverage these through the Lean management system			
Baggage from past 'programme of the month' initiatives or previous failed attempt(s) to introduce Lean exists			

4. Value stream mapping

Value stream mapping (VSM) is a visual method of showing both the physical and information flows in an end-to-end system or sub-system. The VSM shows on one page or zone an 'x-ray' of the business that diagnoses waste and process obstacles at a glance to the trained eye. See Chapter 3 for the value stream methodology and discussion on:

- current state (as is baseline including capacity and demand analysis)
- ideal state (True North vision to release attachment to the status quo and build tension for change)
- future state (realistic medium-term target).

Value stream mapping will provide guidance as to what are the highest leverage points in the system and where would be a good place to start the initial Lean pilot (discussed later in this chapter).

As the Lean transformation matures and expands beyond the initial pilot model areas, management needs to consider how to restructure the organisation by key value streams as identified by the product/service matrix (discussed in Chapter 3) and to have one person accountable for the total end-to-end flow of value. This is an extensive departure from the traditional practice of structuring organisations by department or centres of expertise. The organisation by value stream is in alignment with customer needs (customers flow horizontally) through your organisation. The traditional practice of the vertical organisation arrangement by department (pull out your business management hierarchy tree – it flows downwards and your customers flow across!) impedes the flow of value to customers.

5. Build leadership commitment and set expectations

'Why should we care about Lean?' Engaging and building alignment through a shared understanding and vision for the Lean journey is the basis for successful transformation. The senior leadership team needs to be deeply committed and singing from the same hymn sheet in order to lead by example. The paragraph below is a great analogy to show your management team the power of alignment:

> *'Aligned geese will fly thousands of miles in a perfect V formation – and therein lies the secret: as each bird moves its great wings, it creates an uplift for the bird following. Formation flying is 70% more efficient than flying alone. At a distance, the flock appears to be guided by a single leader. The lead bird does in fact guide the formation, winging smoothly and confidently through the oncoming elements. If the lead bird tires, however, it rotates back into formation and another bird moves quickly to the point position. Leadership is willingly shared, and each bird knows exactly where the entire group is headed.'*
>
> *Anon.*

Initiative fatigue is another potential blockage to securing management commitment. Is the prevailing perception in your organisation that Lean will go out as quickly as it came in? How is Lean different? Lean differentiates from other improvement approaches in that it takes a holistic stakeholder approach to transformation. Simultaneous and congruent improvement in quality, employee engagement, delivery and cost is possible. Demonstrating these multi-faceted benefits and the positive business case helps to convince management how high the bar can be raised. This helps to dissolve the occasional unfounded belief that Lean is an expense and not an investment.

> *'The greatest danger for most of us is not that our aim is too high and we miss it, but that it is too low and we reach it.'*
>
> Michelangelo

It is also effective to build tension for a better way by defining the ideal state versus the current state and then working backwards to a realistic, medium-term, future state vision. It is common to witness management sitting in a fool's paradise thinking everything is great but the ideal state vision often provides a major jolt to this attitude. The management team need to have a firm grasp of current reality and a frank distaste of being there. Hence it is advantageous to have the diagnostic work completed prior to selling Lean to the senior leadership to take the leap to Lean management (better still if it does not need to be sold, i.e. the CEO drives the change agenda). In essence Lean needs to evolve into a non-negotiable moral obligation to continuously improve the business for the gain of all stakeholders.

A further beneficial tactic during this phase is to invite a CEO from an organisation that has successfully transformed its business through Lean to speak to your management team. This in the author's experience invariably leads to a study tour of this exemplar organisation. Book study clubs are another very popular concept used for engaging leadership. For example, a certain chapter of a book is read between meetings and at the next get-together team members discuss the issues raised and take away concepts and lessons to test in their areas.

The Lean change agent must not mince their words regarding the degree of change that is required. A deep commitment to both cultural and technical change is necessary. The Lean methods are relatively straightforward and actually uplifting to roll out. However, keeping the new practices and behaviours in place and continuously improving is an entirely different challenge. This is when the human side of change or cultural adjustment is central.

The management of change is discussed later in this chapter.

The transition to Lean management means managing in a very different manner than your organisation currently does. This requires a paradigm shift in how managers currently run their businesses. At the simplest level, a paradigm in business is the collective way of thinking that we have as a group. Management must deliver a top-down directive that Lean is the new way of running the business. Lean is as much about transforming thinking as it is about transforming processes. Table 13.2 lists attitudes that are engrained in many pre-Lean organisations on the left-hand side. To accomplish transformation requires that managers' attitudes should transition towards the new paradigm on the right-hand side of the table.

Table 13.2 Paradigm shifts

Old paradigm	New paradigm
Knowledge is power	Involvement of all employees and visual transparency of information and metrics is power
Command and control – management makes all the decisions and knows best how to run the business	Lead as if you have no power – by example and open-ended questions. You can't lead if you can't teach, and you can't teach if you aren't willing to learn. Build trust through deploying decision making down to the level where the work is performed
Power and prestige are important	Influencing skills and coaching are important: true power is continuous learning and this begins with humility
Manage from the office	Get out of the office and manage from the gemba to stay in touch and support people in a collaborative manner
Keep employees busy at all times	Produce only what is needed to the rhythm of the end user demand
Avoid mistakes	Welcome problems and learn from mistakes through testing controlled experiments

Linking the Lean transformation to the delivery of the business strategy helps to convince the senior management team that Lean is not a superficial bolt-on of tools that are nice to try when you get some spare time. Lean is a complete management system for transforming the performance of the business, but it is not a magic bullet solution. When the planning and buy-in phases are completed it boils down to hard work and commitment to a new way of thinking and working. Managers must perform some soul searching to decide if they are ready for this commitment. They must also be willing to let go of hierarchy and having the majority of control for decision making, and be comfortable with increased levels of performance transparency.

One of the most powerful tactics to turn sceptics into believers is to get them directly involved through participation in kaizen events in the early days of your Lean transformation. Lean is learned by doing and the power of its philosophy is only fully experienced during these intensive, accelerated, improvement events.

> *'Man's mind, once stretched by a new idea, never regains its original dimensions.'*
>
> Oliver Wendell Holmes (US author and physician)

The development of a succinct elevator pitch[2] on the benefits that Lean will bring to frontline employees, addressing factors such as improved job satisfaction, increased involvement and skills development, higher levels of trust, improved communication and a safer workplace, will serve leaders well for engaging people.

Finally, and far from least, please revisit the Lean daily management system described in Chapter 11. This is designed to facilitate leadership engagement and commitment on an ongoing basis.

A powerful exercise to perform with your entire senior management team at the early stages of the Lean transformation is to spend a few hours together (not as a formal hoshin kanri workshop but to gain accelerated consensus for the new direction) and write your operating philosophy and vision of where you collectively need to go on a flip chart. Then your entire team works to reach consensus on what the business stands for and how you are all going to deploy Lean to deliver this. End of story – the commitment is made!

6. Hoshin kanri strategy deployment

(Refer to Chapter 2 for a detailed discussion of this strategy deployment process.)

It is difficult to create a new culture if you do not know the results you need to achieve, so the first step is to define your desired future. This is where the hoshin kanri strategy deployment process provides clarity and facilitates alignment with your preferred future.

Hoshin kanri also addresses other prerequisites for enabling the success of Lean, it facilitates the building of alignment and consensus with the new direction at all levels of the organisation, it further moulds the business case for Lean, both for the near and medium term, and finally identifies how success will be measured and who is accountable. The eight steps discussed in detail in Chapter 2 are:

1 Reflection on the previous year's performance
2 Review of the organisation's vision, mission and values
3 Objectives for the forthcoming year
4 Alignment building and action plans
5 X-matrix development
6 Implementation
7 Monthly evaluation
8 Annual evaluation.

7. Management of the change plan

'It is not necessary to change. Survival is not mandatory.'

W. Edwards Deming

John Kotter[3] identifies eight change implementation prerequisites; they are highly applicable to Lean transformation.

1. Creating a sense of urgency

Fear of change is genuine and usually unspoken. A compelling driver for change is often required. This could range from the loss of your main customer to the onset of a recession that threatens the business's very survival. Leadership can create this sense of urgency by building the external story for change in advance of Lean transformation. This story would address such questions as:

- Why do we need to change?
- Why have we chosen Lean over other improvement philosophies?
- What will the transformation look like?
- What will each person's role be in this transformation?

The true challenge is to overcome apathy and the wait and see attitude. You need to engage people's hearts and minds, working on both the rational and emotional sides of the human psyche. A strong change story will place emphasis on the benefits that Lean can bring to all stakeholders – employees, customers, suppliers and the wider community – as well as to the business and its shareholders.

Focusing on what is wrong provokes blame and resistance. A more beneficial angle to take is to focus on the positive emotional benefits of the proposed change. Leadership communication should place emphasis on the positive changes that the transformation will bring to all stakeholders such as improved employee engagement as a result of more involvement in decision making and enhanced job security. People do not necessarily dislike change, they do not like *to be* changed, so involving them throughout the change process is a fruitful tactic. A good change management technique for addressing the concerns and highlighting the benefits of the change programme in your organisation is a stakeholder analysis. A stakeholder analysis (shown in Table 13.3) identifies the various stakeholders and what the change will mean for each of them along with the benefits and disadvantages. An action plan is then developed to address the concerns and augment the benefits. It is a great exercise to work through with the core Lean team to understand potential risks before widespread rollout of the communication process.

Table 13.3 Stakeholder blank document

Stakeholder	What will change for this stakeholder group during the journey?	What will this stakeholder group view as a benefit of the Lean journey?	What will this stakeholder group view negatively?	How can we mitigate these concerns?
Employees				
Customers				
Suppliers				
Community				
Organisation				
Shareholders				

2. Creating a change guiding coalition

A Lean promotion office (LPO) is commonly established to guide the Lean transformation. This group should be comprised of well respected people who have strong credibility and are trusted within the organisation. The team should have strong leadership capabilities and be represented by all stakeholders. This team's key purpose will be to coordinate the Lean transformation and to navigate the inevitable challenges and roadblocks along the journey.

The role of the LPO includes:

■ leadership alignment to True North metrics
■ annual and monthly hoshin kanri adjustment reviews
■ resource requirements for improvement (including workforce development and training)
■ linkage between senior management and the frontline

- encouraging management to participate directly in improvement events as this is the richest form of learning (operational leaders should be driving education and execution of improvements in their areas)
- facilitating cultural transformation
- continuous communication
- prioritising improvement activities
- overseeing the Lean budget for training and other low-cost investments for 5S deployment, etc.
- monitoring progress and general reporting.

3. Developing a vision of the required company future state and a strategy to achieve it

An effective vision describes a clear picture of what the organisation will look like after a period of Lean transformation and it appeals to all stakeholders. It should be concise so as to provide guidance for daily decision making towards attainment of the vision, and adaptable to potential changes in the marketplace.

In the Lean rollout the hoshin kanri strategy deployment process described in Chapter 2 accomplishes this step.

4. Communicating the vision and strategy to the entire workforce (communication to *all* levels)

Many organisations under-communicate by a factor of 10 during change. People generally forget approximately 90% of what they hear after three days. Hence it advisable to err on the side of over-communication! People need to be immersed in the new direction that the business is moving towards. This should happen continuously and in multiple communication media such as one-to-one coaching dialogues with supervisions, emails, visual management storyboards and newsletters. The highest form of communication is leaders behaving and acting in a manner that is consistent with the aspired vision.

> *'What you do speaks so loudly that I cannot hear what you say.'*
>
> Ralph Waldo Emerson (essayist, lecturer and poet)

5. Empowering people and removing barriers

Leadership must remove obstacles that impede improvement and release time and resources for Lean application. The frontline supervisors are accountable to senior management and must deliver the business objectives without alienating frontline staff who ultimately deliver customer value. These supervisors are fundamental to developing frontline people, leading the transformation and sustaining the gains. They require strong and continuous support from management to achieve the dual objective of delivering on customers' requirements and releasing time for their frontline teams to drive continuous improvement. Metrics can be adapted or created to monitor this dual objective and also to capture how well supervisors are developing their people. Lean metrics are discussed in Chapters 1 and 11.

The target condition for a Lean supervisor is to spend their time in the following proportions: make the numbers 1/3, coaching 1/3, and improvement work 1/3.

A day in the life of ...

... a typical Lean supervisor includes the following activities:

- facilitate the routine 'make the numbers' meetings
- lead by example using the Lean principles as guidance
- monthly employee one-to-one meetings and continuous application of the Cathedral model
- teach standard work to team members and update training records and visual display of these
- audit compliance to standard work and visual management
- coach people in systematic problem solving
- lead kaizen activities and roll out the Lean methods and tools as required
- nurture teamwork between departments
- skills assessment and cross training
- safety improvement
- daily and monthly reporting
- general administration: attendance and staffing issues, and coordination of countermeasures from identified deviations from target.

The people who most strongly resist Lean often tend to be the most experienced and respected employees and they generally do so with good intentions. The past success of the organisation was achieved by doing things a certain way, so changing how things are done jeopardises everything in their minds. We need to address this challenge through constructive feedback that addresses why the change is required and makes it clear that their support and changed behaviours and actions are critical to success. If people cannot buy in – and there are always a minority (a general rule of thumb is 3–4% of the organisation) – then they need to think about whether they should find another place to work. This is the hard reality but the factual side of conversion from a culture that no longer satisfies current and future business needs. The old adage 'If you can't change the person, change the person' applies to these passive resistors. People will be given the information, coaching and time to make the leap, but some will be unwilling to jump on board. An analogy from the horticultural domain, 'A few goats can very quickly undo the work of many gardeners', explains why this tactic of removing active resistors is both necessary and in alignment with the 'respect for people' pillar. Not addressing this small minority can derail the entire journey and threaten the survival of the organisation and therefore the livelihoods of the majority who are willing to make the leap of faith.

6. Generating short-term wins

Early scores on the board through the attainment of quick visible wins is a great way to build momentum and get the flywheel of improvement turning. This provides the added advantage of positive feedback which helps to improve morale and also converts sceptics or those sitting on the fence into believers. The central challenge for leadership during this early phase, and indeed further afield, is to run the daily routine business of satisfying customers and then in parallel work on improving the business system. The wisdom of the capability trap discussed in Chapter 11 provides both motivation and guidance to overcome this challenge.

7. Consolidating gains and producing more change

Entropy (discussed in Chapter 5) is waiting in the long grass to pull down our improvement accomplishments at all times. The best countermeasure to entropy and sustainability challenges is to continue the process of neverending improvement and spreading of the changes to other value streams. Growing the problem-solving muscle in the organisation also helps to consolidate the gains and offset the eroding effect of entropy.

8. Anchoring new approaches in the culture

Lean practices need time and nurturing to take root, and it takes as much effort to keep them in place as it does to put them in place initially. This requires that leaders are developed within each work group who are capable of keeping the Lean culture going through their leader standard work, monitoring of the visual controls to drive accountability and the daily discipline required for success. Management produces order and consistency, leadership produces change and movement, and both are needed to sustain Lean.

8. Pilot the Lean model area and spread plan

Pilot areas are a deliberate approach to deploy Lean as an initial controlled test of change to prove the concept. They provide a focused and controlled playing field for experimenting and learning about Lean. This strategy of deployment is known as an inch-wide, mile-deep approach to change. Once the concept is proven the success and new skill capabilities can be leveraged and spread to other areas of the business organically. The tactic is to go narrow and deeply into a defined area (or a particular value stream) and intensively apply the Lean methods and the Cathedral model to build a showcase area, both technically and culturally. The pilot area can be kaizen event based (see Chapter 6) to accelerate the pace of change. The pilot area must be given active support from all support functions to nurture success and then be allowed the time to take root as the new way of working.

Additional benefits of a model area pilot approach to transformation include the following:

▪ It begins the Lean journey!

▪ It provides the physical evidence that Lean works and gives other areas of the business a 'go see' model.

▪ Immediate results and return on investment are achieved. If your organisation is not yet fully committed to Lean, it is extremely important to achieve some early wins to build momentum.

▪ It demonstrates how high the bar can be raised.

▪ Participants use the Lean learning model of 'learn, apply and reflect' to build internal improvement capability fast and to accelerate learning from the experience.

▪ It sways non-believers and helps to create wider organisational buy-in.

The selection of the pilot area is dependent on a number of factors:

▪ There is a compelling business need for change in the area.

▪ The area is a bottleneck as identified by value stream mapping (see Chapter 3).

▪ The area already has a high performance culture and strong leadership and is ripe for kaizen; the probability of success is high.

When you have achieved momentum, bedded down and are sustaining the changes, expand your scope to the entire value stream or other value streams as well as to support functions such as the office, design function, supply chain, etc. over time.

If the business is under intense pressure you can have numerous pilots in different areas at the same time. They may be at different levels of maturity, but they should all be steadily improving and learning from one another. You can also develop a redeployment plan for employees who have become available owing to productivity improvements in one pilot that moves them into another pilot area to help with its improvements.

The early proof point applications of Lean are primarily event based such as 5S rollouts and kaizen events to build knowledge. They are normally facilitated by an external improvement adviser. The focus is on fixing processes and demonstrating results. As the pilots widen and grow to include the end-to-end value streams they should be owned and led in large part by the area management. It is best practice if one manager is accountable for end-to-end flow in the value stream.

9. Build the Lean knowledge

Lean has evolved into a comprehensive management system; however various elements of the journey are counterintuitive. Hence the engagement of an experienced, external, Lean improvement adviser can be truly helpful in accelerating the journey and delivering real bottom line results faster.

Criteria for selecting a good improvement adviser

▪ Excellent people skills and the adviser's chemistry suits the organisation's current culture.

▪ A good influencer to get people to willingly change.

▪ Not agenda driven but customer and process focused.

▪ Strong business acumen – understands the financials and what it takes to exploit improvements to the bottom line.

▪ Solid expertise in Lean management and systems thinking, and a proven transformation track record with a generic but flexible roadmap to transformation.

▪ Appreciation of the purpose of the process rather than improving activity (e.g. improve the billing process or cash collection: payment is the purpose?).

▪ Is capable of adapting the transformation to your industry domain-specific needs.

▪ Ability to tackle cultural change and strong competency in change management and behavioural change.

▪ Robust facilitation and conflict resolution skills.

▪ Coaches rather than performs the improvements to build local ownership; develops internal capability and self-proficiency.

▪ Provides continuity of support after 'events' to nurture sustainability for a defined period.

---

10. Lean culture

A twin approach to cultural change accelerates the pace of improvement. The classic question of what comes first, the chicken or the
egg, comes to mind. Does performance excellence drive a high-
performance culture through the immersion in a workplace that
demands compliance to high standards in behaviour and hence
action? Or do we create excellent performance through culture
change at the outset? There are varying viewpoints on which is the
best approach, culture change first and Lean methods second, or *vice
versa*? Both tactics have merit; hence the recommendation is to work
on both in tandem. A good tactic to use in your organisation is to
create an inch-wide, mile-deep Lean pilot showcase area (refer back
to point 8 above) and also apply the Cathedral model (see Chapter
10) in this area. Leader standard work which is integrated into the
Cathedral model is behavioural based and this is a potent tool for
effecting cultural change and igniting people's intrinsic motivation.
It facilitates the refocusing of employee actions from performing a
single function to the dual role of making the numbers and continuously improving. Add the Cathedral pillars of recognition, coaching
and constructive feedback and you have a potent alloy for accelerating the transition to a Lean culture.

In a Lean culture all employees have an aligned and vivid understanding of the organisation's purpose and the objectives it is
working towards on the journey towards True North. People are comfortable at challenging the status quo and highlighting problems.
Problems are not seen as embarrassing. Knowledge is shared openly
through cascaded visual management systems and through multiple communication channels. Respect for people is evident in all the
organisation's undertakings, even at the expense of short-term business goals. Management appreciates that people are the engine of
improvement and not a cost to be minimised. Hence people development is given equal priority to process improvement. In essence,
a Lean culture transpires when people use disciplined thought and
apply disciplined action using the structure of PDSA cycles.

The soft side of business transformation is the hard element.
Changing people's behaviour is a challenging but requisite step

for Lean to take hold. This is often overlooked during Lean transformation and explains why the cultural aspect should be a
critical consideration. The objective of developing a Lean culture
is to enable people to think and subsequently act in a way that
achieves superior results. The culture is centred on mentoring, facilitating, teaching and learning how to solve problems without delay,
so they are not passed along to the next customer. Businesses need
to decide what they need to stop doing (old limiting behaviours)
and what they need to start doing (new empowering Behavioural
Standards; see Figure 10.2 for details about Behavioural Standards).
Successfully deployed, Behavioural Standards bring to life the Lean
culture through new actions that are in alignment with the Lean
philosophy. Your actions are always producing results – but they
may not be the results you want!

Culture diagnostic questions

Questions to access and grasp the current state of your organisational culture
include:

1 How would you describe the organisation's purpose based on its current priorities?

2 To what extent does the mission of the organisation really inspire and
   guide behaviour?

3 What department(s) has the most influence?

4 What seems to be management's most important consideration in general?

5 How does decision making normally happen?

6 What do employees care most about?

7 Do employees deeply understand what their customers value?

8 How do you currently execute important initiatives?

9 What do you currently measure?

10 How is success measured?

11 How are problems perceived?

12 Do employees hide problems through fear or embarrassment?

13 Is the typical reaction to problems to find someone to blame?

14 Is identifying problems damaging to career progression?

15 Is Lean seen as a means to up-skilling and career advancement, or
   the opposite?

16 Is there an environment of trust between management and employees, and between departments?

17 How do we solve problems?

18 Do the same problems keep recurring again and again?

19 Is controlled risk taking encouraged?

20 What happens when employees' undertakings fail?

21 How do we communicate with one another?

22 Are employees comfortable with challenging management and highlighting breaches of acceptable conduct or Behavioural Standards?

23 What is the approach to conflict when it arises?

24 What criteria do we have for hiring new employees?

25 How do people generally get promoted?

26 How does one acquire influence and reputation?

27 Do employees demonstrate teamwork and a spirit of collaboration?

28 How do people act if they disagree with one another?

29 What behaviours get recognised?

30 What behaviours generate constructive feedback?

31 Do people follow through on commitments?

32 How are new ideas received?

To expose behavioural gaps that leadership needs to address you should compare the answers to the questions in the box against:

■ the five Lean guiding principles of purpose, system, flow, people and perfection, discussed in Chapter 1

■ the behaviours bullet points in the next box (and your own organisation's Behavioural Standards developed through the Cathedral model in Chapter 10).

Pervasive in the creation of a Lean culture is the formation of a strong problem-solving system for making improvements and developing people. Problem solving is supported through stand-ardised work (see Chapter 5). When people cannot adhere to the standard, problems will naturally be exposed through tightly linked Lean processes. This in turn demands that we must respond imme-diately to these issues or the process will cause chaos. The resolution of these problems is led by the actual team performing the work.

Behavioural changes

At a high level the behavioural changes required for a Lean culture need to shift from:

▪ a results only focus: achieve the results by whatever means possible

▪ silo-based thinking: concerned with islands of excellence or improving departments in isolation and without consideration of the overall system's aim

▪ command and control: telling people what to do

▪ distrustful: intolerant of failures and blaming people when things go wrong

▪ a hierarchical focus: experts solve problems

towards:

▪ a process focus: appreciation that excellent processes are the means to great results

▪ systems thinking: the interaction and dependency of people, structures and processes

▪ leader teaches: go see the actual situation and develop and mentor teams in problem solving

▪ reflection and humility: the nurturing of a learning organisation through the use of PDSA cycles and controlled risk taking (and view failures as learning experiences)

▪ collaboration: everybody is involved in problem solving and improvement.

The emphasis is placed firmly on solving problems at the root cause level, not just patching up the symptoms. This requires that people work through all stages of the systematic problem-solving process using multiple cycles of PDSA as required. Studying and adjusting, not just planning and doing, is a major facet of Lean cultural change. We are relatively competent at planning and doing tasks, but in general we are woefully inept at confirming our actions and drawing conclusions from them (studying and adjusting).

Sustained application of PDSA embeds new thinking patterns in employees and helps to build the Lean culture through its engrained philosophy of:

▪ truly question every process, bringing problems to the surface and carefully defining them, not just at the level of their symptoms

- understand the root cause(s)
- develop countermeasures that are viewed as interim until tested under a wide range of conditions and over a defined period of time
- plan the test of change on a small scale (or larger scale if the degree of belief is very strong that the change will be successful and the people in the area are receptive to the proposed change)
- closely monitor and study what is going on in the test
- learn from what happened and turn the lessons into the next PDSA cycle.

PDSA enables users to understand the complex interdependency of systems through structured testing and uncovering of the potential unintended consequences of changes. An example of an unintended consequence would be a purchasing agent sourcing a lower cost glove but during use the gloves were splitting and causing contamination to the company's food products leading to increased levels of discarded items. Hence overall system cost was actually increased. Disciplined use of structured PDSA cycles would have greatly increased the probability of predicting this inadvertent effect.

Employees learn new technical and soft skills through real time, on-the-job training in the form of problem solving. Good Lean leaders create the environment for problem solving through continuous communication that problems occur because the system allows them to occur, not because people intentionally cause them. It is also emphasised that every problem is a learning opportunity and a productive concept, not a distraction from the 'real' work. When employees become comfortable with this paradigm and are not blamed when problems occur, a virtuous cycle of improvement begins to develop. Tapping into the problem-solving brainpower that your employees might otherwise keep to themselves drives performance excellence. A common side benefit is that when people start working on improvements, they have less to disapprove of and morale, by and large, improves.

11. Sustaining Lean

The work group are the only employees continually at the process. Hence the best sustaining system is a robust problem surfacing system. This requires that the capability is built within the work team to solve problems at the root cause(s) level on a daily basis. Chapters 11 and 12 provide an overview of this and numerous other practices for sustaining the gains.

12. Hansei

The Japanese term hansei translates as reflection and fits into both the *study* and *adjust* stages of PDSA. It is a form of constructive criticism and fosters the deep thinking required for Lean transformation.

> *'Few people think more than two or three times a year. I've made an international reputation for myself by thinking once or twice a week.'*
>
> George Bernard Shaw (author and playwright)

The concept is about capturing and utilising lessons learned through reflecting on performance and initiating new ways to improve at all levels. Organisations often make the same mistakes repeatedly. A true learning organisation captures errors, determines their root cause(s) and puts in place effective countermeasures.

Hansei questions

Characteristic hansei questions include:

- What went well?
- What helped it to go well?
- What could we have done better?
- What hindered us from doing this better?
- What have we learned to enable a better performance next time?

Even when things go well hansei should be performed in order to look for ways to perform even better and, equally important, to understand what conditions existed that enabled success. In mature Lean organisations hansei is commonly performed daily at the individual employee level to reflect on the day's performance and opportunities for improvement to do the job even better tomorrow. For hansei to take root the organisation must value and support it, release time for it, and measure it to ensure it is engrained into the daily work culture.

Review

Lean appears easy on the surface: 'Sure, it's just common sense', you will commonly hear. However, if Lean were that easy, sustaining it would be a given and every company would be tremendously successful! This chapter details a generic roadmap to Lean transformation. The starting point is to understand what it is that your customers see as the value that your product or service delivers. Then the business case for Lean needs to be widely articulated to build a compelling reason for change. Detailed process diagnosis in the form of a Lean assessment and value stream mapping diagnose what we need to do differently to deliver the business case for Lean. Managers must be willing to change how they currently manage and be out there leading the transformation daily. Lean delivers the best results when it is integrated into the organisation to the degree that it is leveraged to deliver the business's strategic objectives. Changing habits in your personal life is challenging; changing numerous people's habits in an organisation is an even greater challenge. Hence a robust and continuous process for managing change needs to be diligently worked through. When the groundwork has being completed, it is time for action.

A pilot approach to deploying Lean is the author's recommended approach. This will provide you with the philosophy for your company and foster learning through doing. In tandem with the technical changes, a Lean culture can be nurtured in this focus area to evolve Lean into a sustaining daily practice. You will experience surprises and mistakes along the way and that is fine as long as you learn from them and keep going. The hope for your business is that Lean will evolve into the management system that delivers your strategy and that the Lean mindset is woven into the collective thinking of your organisation.

Glossary

(Of terms not discussed in detail within the book)

Andon   This is a visual control device frequently combined with an audible alarm that employees on the frontlines can activate to signal the occurrence of an issue or problem. Its purpose is to expose and communicate problems as soon as they occur and to kick start improvement work to solve the issues when they are still minor.

Bottleneck   The slowest operation in any process. Improving this should be the basis for prioritising improvement work. Time lost at the bottleneck is time lost for that entire value stream.

Continuous improvement   This is an attitude where people recognise that there is always room for improvement in the current state of any system. Implementing incremental improvement ideas on an everyday basis is the manifestation of this way of life.

Customer experience   Customer experience is the sum perception of all occasions a customer interacts with a provider of products or services, over the period of their relationship, be that a one-off or reoccurring association.

Failure demand   Failure demand describes the demand on the resources of an organisation caused by the errors created by the organisation in the first instance. This historically is a large segment of the demand that enters organisations and is a high leverage point for the focus of improvement work. The opposite of this is value demand, which is concerned with providing customers with the right service they want first time around.

Gemba   This is a Japanese term that refers to where the actual work is performed. Lean refers to gemba as being the place where value is added to a product or service. You are encouraged to conduct gemba or waste walks between management and the frontlines. This fosters relationship building and hence awareness of waste (also commonly called muda) and improvement countermeasures. Waste walks should always be performed in a collaborative manner and not be used to point the finger or play the blame game.

Inventory   The hard cash and materials invested in by an organisation in order to fulfil customer requirements. This is almost always an excellent initial cost saving opportunity. Inventory should be viewed as money on a pallet! This includes all forms of inventory, be that raw materials, work-in-progress, supplies or consumables and finished goods.

Lean accounting   This practice consists of two streams. One stream is application of Lean methods to your organisation's accounting and measurement processes. This eliminates waste, frees up capacity, and reduces mistakes similar to when Lean is applied to your other mainstay processes.

The second stream is to adapt the accounting processes so they reflect improvement and provide simple and timely information that is suitable for decision making in congruence with Lean transformation. Accounting for Lean does not require traditional accounting practices to run the frontline processes. (However, you are still required to comply with GAAP and tax reporting requirements.)

Traditional management accounting uses methods like standard costing, activity based costing, variance reporting, cost-plus pricing and complex financial reports. For example, traditional labour efficiency and overhead absorption metrics motivate batching of work and high inventory levels. Keeping people busy building inventory (even if there are no sales) makes traditional accounting measures look good. If we reduce inventory through Lean and synchronise the rate of employees' work in certain departments (i.e. sometimes slow down the pace of operations) to produce to the rate of customer demand, some traditional accounting metrics get worse.

Hence Lean organisations need to have a clearer understanding of the real costs associated with their value streams for decision making purposes. Standard costing is flawed in some aspects as it misses important factors such as the profit contribution of certain product/services and their impact on bottleneck resources (even worse for shared resources). An hour lost at a bottleneck is an hour lost for that entire business line. Lean accounting tracks value stream cost and the benefits of improvement by supplementing traditional accounting with real time (not monthly like customary accounting practices) process metrics of performance. These are primarily maintained at the gemba by the frontline workers.

Lean development   The objective of Lean development is to deeply understand customer needs (both spoken and unspoken) and the problems that your product or service is solving. Unspoken needs are teased out through Lean organisations' innovation processes to deliver differentiated products and services. Lean development delivers new products/services/software fast (generally twice as fast as traditional development processes) via removal of development waste, and high levels of transparency through visual management and built-in quality practices. Lean development vigorously challenges (through the use of value engineering, quality functional deployment, 3P and other Lean methods)[1] existing designs where generally 70% of costs are locked in at this design stage. It provides alternatives that improve cost, maximise value, ease fulfilment of the product/service, and support the 'green' economy from 'cradle to landfill'. In essence, Lean development merges two streams of best practice, design excellence and delivery excellence of the design.

Lean supply chain   This practice is concerned with streamlining the supply chain, delivering product/services faster to the end customer, with minimum waste. A Lean supply chain is a great enabler for any organisation that strives for excellence because often the greatest proportion of cost for business is on purchased supplies. The Lean supply chain seeks to maximise end-to-end flow from raw material to customer receipt. It requires cooperation among many businesses and systems thinking is required to maximise the end-to-end delivery of the product or service.

Process   A process is a sequence of tasks that cooperatively brings about a distinct purpose. Most pre-Lean processes are ripe for improvement work. All value is created as the result of a process.

Process capability   Cpk is the measure of process capability; it tracks how close a process is running to target with minimum variation. The industry standard to satisfy customers is that your Cpk index should be running above 1.33. A process can be running with low variation and still be off the target or conversely a process may be running at the target but the variation in performance can be high. Cpk tracks the performance in terms of meeting the target with low variation.

Process mapping   A process map lists every step that is involved in the fulfilment of a product or service. There are special symbols to indicate 'operation', 'delay', 'move', 'storage' and 'inspect'. It helps to identify waste. Process mapping is also powerful for standardising processes after improvement. The mapping should be done at the gemba, not in an office (if you are not mapping an office process). Once the map is complete the individual steps can be brainstormed into those that add value, those that are pure waste and should be eliminated as soon as possible, and those which are value-added enabling (needed to support the process in the short term). It is a great tool for generating ideas about alternative solutions to achieve the purpose of the process. An enhancement to the basic map is a person–equipment map which highlights what the person is doing during the equipment cycle time and helps to uncover wasteful time gaps. A good analogy to obtain input for this type of chart is to ask if you would sit and watch your washing machine clean your clothes for the full cycle!

Spaghetti diagram   A spaghetti diagram is a waste diagnostic tool to trace the motion of people carrying out their jobs or the route that a product or service takes during fulfilment. A person's movement is tracked on a layout drawing of the area. In pre-Lean workplaces the movement generally reflects a bowl of spaghetti – the lines tracking the motion are normally tangled and crossed over each other. The diagram is used to examine current layouts and the waste of motion that poor layouts induce forever. Improved layouts and location of machines and equipment can be accomplished through the application of this simple tool. Often merged with the use of pedometers (the participant's consent should be sought beforehand) to track the movement of an employee over a shift. Management often underestimate the cost of people motion. Historical studies from the author's experience reveal, for example, that a nurse walks 4–5 miles per shift due to poor ward layouts and searching for equipment and supplies. This is the equivalent of about 90 minutes' walking per shift away from the patient's bedside. Consider the cost of this per hospital in terms of wasted hours and inferior patient outcomes. (There is a direct correlation between the percentage of nurse time at the bedside and improved outcomes.)

Stakeholder   A stakeholder is a person or group of people who are affected by a process or project improvement, either directly or indirectly.

System   A system is a collection of interdependent components that works interactively to deliver customer value. None of the elements, acting alone, can do what the system does. There are three types of systems, namely mechanical, organic and socio-technical. The parts of a mechanical system, like a car, can be designed to work together to further the system's purpose: transportation. The organs of organic systems, like the human body, are genetically designed to further the purpose of living. A business organisation is a socio-technical system with some parts that can be designed, such as technology, roles and processes, and other elements that must be led, namely people.

True North   The organisation's ultimate aim, there are four True North goals:

1 Employee growth – Frank Devine of Accelerated Improvement Ltd. defines True North as '100% discretionary effort by 100% of your employees, 100% of the time'.

2 Quality – the concept of striving for zero defects.

3 Delivery – fastest lead time through the quest for one-piece flow processing.

4 Cost – the journey towards 100% core value-adding steps.

Variation   This is the great enemy of Lean. Variation in time and demand is found in every process from supply chain demand amplification to dimensional variation. Learn to distinguish between common and special cause variation and treat them appropriately.

Work-in-progress   This is the amount of unfinished work that is awaiting completion. Lean aims to reduce work-in-progress (WIP) so as to reduce costs, increase quality (through faster feedback) and, more significantly, reduce lead time. (WIP inflates lead time proportionally, i.e. reducing WIP by 50% provides a corresponding improvement in lead time.) In manufacturing, WIP is product parts or sub-assemblies, in service industries it is primarily time or open projects.

Yokoten   The concept of yokoten is concerned with sharing improvements and learning. It is practised when teams and departments share how they overcame problems with solutions, with the aim of motivating other teams to learn from these solutions and adapt them for use in their own areas.

References and further reading

Chapter 1

[1] Ohno, T. (2009), *Workplace Management*, Gemba Press

[2] Moen, R. and Norman, C. (2010), 'Circling Back', *Quality Progress*, November edition

[3] Krafcik, J. (1988), 'Triumph of the Lean Production System', *Sloan Management Review*, Vol. 30, Issue 1

[4] Womack, J., Jones, D. and Roos, D. (1991), *The Machine that Changed the World: The Story of Lean Production,* Harper Perennial.

[5] Womack, J. and Jones, D. (1996), *Lean Thinking: Banish Waste and Create Wealth in Your Corporation*, Free Press

[6] Taylor, F. (1997), *The Principles of Scientific Management*, Dover Publications

[7] Hounshell, D.A. (1984), *From the American System to Mass Production, 1800–1932: The Development of Manufacturing Technology in the United States*, Johns Hopkins University Press

[8] Krenn, M. (2011), 'From Scientific Management to Homemaking: Lillian M. Gilbreth's Contributions to the Development of Management Thought', *Management & Organisational History*, Vol. 6, Issue 2

[9] Ford, H. (1989), *Today and Tomorrow – Special Edition of Ford's 1926 Classic*, Productivity Press

[10] Toyota Motor Corporation (2001), 'The Toyota Way 2001', internal document, Toyota City, Japan, April

[11] Liker, J. and Ogden, T. (2011), *Toyota Under Fire: Lessons for Turning Crisis into Opportunity*, McGraw-Hill

[12] Brophy, A. and Bicheno, J. (2010), *Innovative Lean: A Guide to Releasing the Untapped Gold in Your Organisation to Engage Employees, Drive Out Waste, and Create Prosperity*, PICSIE Books

[13] Bicheno, J. and Holweg, M. (2008), *The Lean Toolbox*, PICSIE Books

Chapter 2

[1] Akao, Y. (2004), *Hoshin Kanri: Policy Deployment for Successful TQM*, Productivity Press

[2] A SWOT analysis is a strategic planning method used to assess the strengths, weaknesses, opportunities and threats influencing an organisation or specific project. Strengths: traits that set the organisation apart. Weaknesses: elements that put the organisation at a disadvantage. Opportunities: outside factors that can improve performance. Threats: outside factors that exacerbate performance

[3] Kaplan, R. and Norton, D. (2004), *Strategy Maps: Converting Intangible Assets into Tangible Outcomes,* Harvard Business Press

[4] Langley, G., Norman, C., Moen, R., Nolan, K., Nolan, T., Provost, L. (2009), *The Improvement Guide*, Jossey-Bass

[5] OEE metric: see Figure 7.8 of this book for additional detail

[6] Fukuda, R. (1997), *Building Organizational Fitness: Management Methodology for Transformation and Strategic Advantage (Corporate Leadership)*, Productivity Press

[7] Ibid.

Chapter 3

[1] Stalk, G. and Hout, T. (1990), *Competing Against Time: How Time-based Competition is Reshaping Global Markets*, Free Press

Further reading

Rother, M. and Shook, J. (1999), *Learning to See: Value Stream Mapping to Add Value and Eliminate MUDA*, Lean Enterprise Institute

Duggan, K. (2002), *Creating Mixed Model Value Streams: Practical Lean Techniques for Building to Demand*, Productivity Press

Chapter 4

[1] Maltz, M. (1994), *Psycho-Cybernetics*, Simon & Schuster

[2] Marx, D. (2001), 'Patient Safety and the "Just Culture": A Primer for Health Care Executives'

www.mers-tm.net/support/Marx_Primer.pdf (accessed January 2012)

[3] Special thanks to Ciaran Cuddy of Klasmann-Deilmann Ireland Ltd. for suggesting to move the day by the hour board into a week by the hour board during our work together at the gemba

Chapter 5

[1] Ford, H. (1989), *Today and Tomorrow – Special Edition of Ford's 1926 Classic*, Productivity Press

[2] Deming, W.E. (2000), *Out of the Crisis*, The MIT Press

[3] Perrow, C. (1967), 'A Framework for the Comparative Analysis of Organisations', *American Sociological Review,* Vol. 32

[4] Baldwin, J. (2010), *Fifty Famous People*, Kessinger Publishing, LLC

[5] Dinero, D. (2005), *Training Within Industry: The Foundation of Lean*, Productivity Press

[6] Marriott, J.W. (1998), *The Spirit to Serve: Marriott's Way*, HarperBusiness

Further reading on A3 problem solving and coaching

Shook, J. (2008), *Managing to Learn: Using the A3 Management Process*, Lean Enterprises Institution Inc.

Rother, M. (2009), *Toyota Kata: Managing People for Improvement, Adaptiveness, and Superior Results*, McGraw-Hill Professional

Chapter 6

[1] Robinson, A. and Schroeder, D. (2004), *Ideas Are Free, How the Idea Revolution Is Liberating People and Transforming Organisations*, BK Koehler

[2] Kohn, A. (1999), *Punished by Rewards: The Trouble with Gold Stars, Incentive Plans, A's, Praise, and Other Bribes*, Mariner Books

[3] Brophy, A. and Bicheno, J. (2010), *Innovative Lean: A Guide to Releasing the Untapped Gold in Your Organisation to Engage Employees, Drive Out Waste, and Create Prosperity*, PICSIE Books

Further reading on idea management systems

For a detailed analysis with multiple real-life best-in-class case studies and a detailed roadmap to implementing an IMS see:

Brophy, A. and Bicheno, J. (2010), *Innovative Lean: A Guide to Releasing the Untapped Gold in Your Organisation to Engage Employees, Drive Out Waste, and Create Prosperity*, PICSIE Books

Graban, M. and Swartz, J.E. (2012), *Healthcare Kaizen: Engaging Front-Line Staff in Sustainable Continuous Improvements*, Productivity Press

Imai, M. (1986), *Kaizen: The Key to Japan's Competitive Success*, McGraw-Hill/Irwin

Further reading on kaizen events

Hamel, M. (2009), *Kaizen Event Fieldbook: Foundation, Framework, and Standard Work for Effective Events*, Society of Manufacturing Engineers

Chapter 7

[1] Shingo, S. and Dillon, A. [translator] (1985), *A Revolution in Manufacturing – The SMED System*, Productivity Press

[2] Ford, H. (1989), *Today and Tomorrow – Special Edition of Ford's 1926 Classic*, Productivity Press

[3] Hoffer Gittell, J. (2005), *The Southwest Airlines Way*, McGraw-Hill

[4] See note 1

[5] Heinrich, H.W. (1941), *Industrial Accident Prevention, A Scientific Approach*, McGraw-Hill Book Company, Inc., 2nd edition

Further reading on TPM

Bicheno, J. (2008), *The New Lean Toolbox*, PICSIE Books

Willmott, P. (2005), *Total Productive Maintenance: Delivering Benchmark Levels of Business Excellence through TPM*, WCS International Ltd.

Chapter 8

[1] Whited, H.M. (1997), '*Poka-yoke varieties*', The power of mistake proofing forum, 6 August, Moline, IL

Further reading on kanban

Bicheno, J. (2008), *The New Lean Toolbox*, PICSIE Books

Gross, J. and McInnis, K. (2003), *Kanban Made Simple*, Amacom

Further reading on poka yoke

For a definite guide to mistake proofing in healthcare where it is so needed read:

Grout, J. (2007), *Mistake-Proofing the Design of Health Care Processes*, AHRQ Publication No. 07-0020

And also for other areas:

Hinckley, M. (2001), *Make No Mistake*, Productivity Press

Marx, D. (2001), *Patient Safety and the 'Just Culture': A Primer for Health Care Executives*, www.mers-tm.net/support/Marx_Primer.pdf (accessed January 2012)

Shingo, S. (1986), *Zero Quality Control: Source Inspection and the Poka Yoke System*, Productivity Press

Chapter 9

[1] Stalk, G. and Hout, T. (1990), *Competing Against Time: How Time-based Competition is Reshaping Global Markets*, Free Press

[2] George, M.L. (2002), *Lean Six Sigma: Combining Six Sigma Quality with Lean Production Speed*, McGraw-Hill

[3] Bicheno, J. (2004), *The New Lean Toolbox*, PICSIE Books

[4] Tapping, D., Luyster, T. and Shuker, T. (2002), *Value Stream Management*, Productivity Press

Further reading on flow practices

Duggan, K. (2002), *Creating Mixed Model Value Streams: Practical Lean Techniques for Building to Demand*, Productivity Press

Glenday, I. (2008), *Breaking Through to Flow*, Lean Enterprise Academy Ltd.

Vatalargo, J. and Taylor, R. (2005), *Implementing a Mixed Model Kanban System*, Productivity Press

Chapter 10

[1] Clemmer, J. (1992), *Firing on All Cylinders: The Service/Quality System for High-Powered Corporate Performance*, The Clemmer Group

[2] William Pasmore, James Taylor, David Felten and Enid Mumford for example

[3] Twomey, B. (2011), 'Beneath the Waterline – A Study of the Effect of Applying Leader Standard Work to the Social Aspects of a Manufacturing System on the Performance of the System', Cardiff University, MSc in Lean Operations Dissertation

[4] Rosenthal, R. and Jacobson, L. (2003), *Pygmalion in the Classroom*, Crown House Publishing

[5] Kohn, A. (1999), *Punished by Rewards: The Trouble with Gold Stars, Incentive Plans, A's, Praise, and Other Bribes*, Mariner Books

[6] Robinson, A. and Schroeder, D. (2004), *Ideas Are Free, How the Idea Revolution Is Liberating People and Transforming Organisations*, BK Koehler

[7] Schwarz, J. (2007), *The A to Z of Idea Management for Organizational Improvement and Innovation*, Total Quality Systems Software

Chapter 11

[1] See Figure 3.5 and the discussion in Chapter 3's case study for why this is possible. Note that this case study, although fictional, is typical of the author's experience of the findings from value stream mapping

[2] Testimony, United States Congress, House Committee on Veterans' Affairs, Dr Lucian L. Leape, MD, 12 October 1997

[3] Kaplan, R. (1992), 'The Balanced Scorecard – Measures that Drive Performance', *Harvard Business Review*, January–February

Further reading

Dinero, D. (2005), *Training Within Industry: The Foundation of Lean*, Productivity Press

Spitzer, D. (2007), *Transforming Performance Measurement: Rethinking the Way We Measure and Drive Organizational Success*, Amacom

Chapter 12

[1] Greenleaf, R.K. (1991), *The Servant as Leader*, Robert K. Greenleaf Center

[2] Repenning, N. and Sterman, J. (2001), 'Nobody Ever Gets the Credit for Fixing Problems that Never Happened: Creating and sustaining process improvement', *California Management Review*, Vol. 43, No. 4

Chapter 13

[1] Kano, N. (1996), *Guide to TQM in Service Industries*, Asian Productivity Organization

[2] A Lean elevator pitch is a brief description of what Lean is and why it matters. It is concise and can be delivered in the time it would take to move between two floors in a lift. Done well and internalised by your leadership team an elevator pitch will help to communicate a consistent and concise message to your people during impromptu interactions. A good elevator pitch should connect people at both the logical and emotional levels and portray the benefits of Lean and what differentiates it as a philosophy for people development and process improvement. Lastly it is good to include a hook or invitation for the message recipient to become involved in the journey towards excellence and the benefits that this will bring for them

[3] Kotter, J. (1996), *Leading Change*, Harvard Business School Press

Further reading

Maskell, B. (2011), *Practical Lean Accounting: A Proven System for Measuring and Managing the Lean Enterprise*, Productivity Press

Morgan, J. and Liker, J. (2006), *The Toyota Product Development System: Integrating People, Process and Technology*, Productivity Press

Taylor, D. and Brunt, D. (2000), *Manufacturing Operations and Supply Chain Management: The LEAN Approach*, Cengage Learning EMEA

Glossary

1. Bicheno, J. and Holweg, M. (2008), *The Lean Toolbox*, PICSIE Books

Appendix: Lean assessment

Lean management system element	Instructions: Score – the criteria are cumulative, e.g. to score 4 you also need to satisfy criteria 0–3. This is not a 100% scientific audit: you may have higher level ratings in some areas without the foundation of lower building blocks. The real value is the dialogue this creates and an action plan.					
	Level 0	**Level 1**	**Level 2**	**Level 3**	**Level 4**	**Level 5**
Business case for Lean (Chapter 1)	Management are unaware of Lean	Management firmly believes in Lean and the business potential	The business case for Lean is explored by senior management	The business case for Lean is outlined by management and linked to the delivery of the organisation's strategy	The business case for Lean is linked to the True North ideals of perfection in quality, people growth, delivery and cost	The business case for Lean is understood by *all* employees and they can articulate succinctly how Lean is delivering the objectives
Lean principles (1) Purpose (2) Systems Thinking (3) Flow (4) People (5) Perfection (Chapter 1)	There is no awareness of the Lean principles in the organisation	Management firmly believes in the value of the Lean principles	The Lean principles are understood at all levels	Employees are led by purpose (understand why) rather than being assigned tasks and know the overall impact of their work	The Lean principles collectively represent the mass thinking patterns of the organisation	The Lean principles guide every decision and action performed daily by *all* employees
Continuous improvement (Chapter 1)	There is no evidence of continuous improvement, all efforts are spent on doing the daily routine activities and fire-fighting	There are occasional improvement projects active in the business	Time is scheduled to practise 'event' type improvement bursts on urgent business issues	Event type improvement is systematic and aims to continually break bottlenecks in the business	Incremental improvement is practised daily in 'exemplar' areas of the business	Continuous incremental improvement is practised daily by *all* employees and there are weekly systematic breakthrough events
Respect for people (Chapter 1)	Employees are viewed as a cost to be minimised and kept busy at all times	People's time is wasted doing >50% non-value-adding or wasted work. Mura and muri are also rampant in the business	People are laid off when improvements increase productivity	People are doing the jobs that they are qualified to do – there is strong skill–task alignment	Frontline employees are involved in daily decisions and are given the time and support to participate in the removal of muda, muri and mura	Respect for people guides all business activities and extends to customers, employees, suppliers, shareholders and the community

Lean operating system (Chapter 1)	There is no Lean operating system	The Lean operating system has been developed but is no more than wallpaper	The Lean operating system is embedded into certain exemplar areas of the business	Some elements of the Lean operating system are spreading to various areas of the business in a piecemeal fashion	One end-to-end value stream has the Lean operating system embedded into the way people work	The Lean operating system is embedded organisation wide and is the way we work around here
Understanding of customer value (Chapter 1)	There is no systematic metric that captures customer value	Customer satisfaction is measured on 'spoken' kano model needs only	There is a deep appreciation and plan to address customers' unspoken 'basic' needs and unspoken 'Delighter' needs	Customer focused metrics are in existence, e.g. number of complaints, wait time, lead time, on time delivery, customer experience survey, etc.	We have performed an ethnographic study of our customers (studied them using our offerings in the field)	Customer satisfaction is measured on 'spoken' and 'unspoken' kano model needs
Hoshin kanri strategy development (Chapter 2	There is no long-term strategic plan for the business and coordination of improvement activities across the business is ad hoc	The company strategy is developed but not clearly understood throughout the organisation	The company understands the critical strategic priorities and there are plans and metrics in place to address the gaps	The process of 'catchball' and consensus building is fully in evidence during the annual strategic development process	The link between the strategy and the daily work is clear and actionable through the Lean daily management system	All employees can articulate the long- and near-term strategic objectives and the daily priorities are in alignment with these goals

Lean assessment (part I)

Lean management system element	Instructions: Score – the criteria are cumulative, e.g. to score 4 you also need to satisfy criteria 0–3. This is not a 100% scientific audit: you may have higher level ratings in some areas without the foundation of lower building blocks. The real value is the dialogue this creates and an action plan.					
	Level 0	**Level 1**	**Level 2**	**Level 3**	**Level 4**	**Level 5**
Value stream mapping (Chapter 3)	There are no product or service families value stream mapped	The value streams are mapped for most families, however there is no action plan for improvement being deployed	The value streams are mapped by the management team only for most product families and action plans have kicked off	The value streams are mapped in a collaborative manner with the frontline staff and with support process. Action plans are delivered	All product/service families are mapped to the level of current, ideal and future state. Future state actions plans are active	The future state value streams are frequently transitioning to current state maps and the improvement cycle is being repeated persistently
5S workplace organisation (Chapter 4)	5S is not used	5S audit score is 10% or greater over a three-month period	5S audit score is 25% or greater over a three-month period	5S audit score is 50% or greater over a three-month period	5S audit score is 75% or greater over a three-month period	5S audit score is 95% or greater over a three-month period
Visual management (Chapter 4)	Visual management is not in evidence	Performance metrics and targets are tracked on the frontlines	Performance metrics and targets are tracked on the frontlines and used to drive daily resolution of problems	Visual controls clearly highlight abnormal conditions at a glance in the workplace	All processes have visual mistake proofing devices for the top potential failure modes	All the information for workplace decision making such as standards and status storyboards is available at a glance and is up to date
A3 problem solving (Chapter 5)	Fire-fighting is the normal reaction when problems occur	Employees are trained in systematic problem solving	Problems are viewed positively. Employees are comfortable to raise all abnormalities and are supported to fix them	Problems are solved to root cause(s) level via systematically working through all nine steps of the A3 process using PDSA cycles	Problem solving is the primary mechanism used to develop people	The A3 process has evolved to be the way that people cognitively think about problems even in the absence of the A3 sheet itself

Standard work (Chapter 5)	Every employee performs their work in their own preferred way	Standards are developed by specialists from the office and just posted in the workplace	Standards are developed for all repeatable processes in collaboration with the people doing the work	Standards are developed for all repeatable processes with the people doing the work: train against the standards using TWI	Standards are used to drive kaizen when they cannot be adhered to	Standards are frequently changed and improved as a result of kaizen and employee engagement in improvement
Idea management system (Chapter 6)	There is no system in place for capturing employee ideas	Suggestion boxes are located around the business and are opened every few months	Visual idea boards are widely deployed across the business and ideas are posted for management to address	Visual idea boards are deployed across the business and small ideas are implemented by the idea originator with their supervisor's coaching	Ideas are shared and leveraged at all levels and between departments. The quality of ideas is improving as people's skills improve	All employees are implementing two small ideas per month
Kaizen events (Chapter 6)	Kaizen events are not practised	Kaizen events are run a few times a year in a scatter gun approach, the improvements do not stick and the areas regress	Kaizen events are run a few times a year in a scatter gun approach and the gains are still locked in after three months	Kaizen events are used to accelerate the development of a focused showcase exemplar Lean area to create a 'go see' model	Kaizen events are used to extend the model area to an entire value stream model line	A Lean promotion office is staffed up from employees released from kaizen productivity improvements and they are organised and facilitated yet further

Lean assessment (part II)

Instructions: Score – the criteria are cumulative, e.g. to score 4 you also need to satisfy criteria 0–3.
This is not a 100% scientific audit: you may have higher level ratings in some areas without the foundation of lower building blocks.
The real value is the dialogue this creates and an action plan.

Lean management system element	Level 0	Level 1	Level 2	Level 3	Level 4	Level 5
Quick changeover (Chapter 7)	Quick changeover is not practised	Quick changeover is piloted in the model area	Quick changeover is deployed on value stream bottleneck processes	Changeover is reduced by 50% for all key processes	Quick changeover of greater than 75% improvement is exploited to avoid additional capacity expense and to win new business	Management leverage quick changeover to perform even more changeovers hence increasing flexibility and reducing lead time
Total productive maintenance (Chapter 7)	Total productive maintenance is not practised. The operating philosophy is break–fix	Maintenance is scheduled and proactive	Frontline employees perform autonomous maintenance	OEE is measured on all bottleneck resources	There has been zero downtime due to equipment breakdowns in the last six months	New equipment is specified and purchased to support TPM integration
Flow (Chapter 9)	The value stream value-added ratio is less than 1%	The value stream value-added ratio is greater than 5%	The value stream value-added ratio is greater than 10%	The value stream value-added ratio is greater than 15%	The value stream value-added ratio is greater than 20%	The value stream value-added ratio is greater than 25%
Kanban (Chapter 8)	The waste of overproduction is rampant in the business	Kanban is used to control the stock of supplies and reduce stock management time	Spoilage or obsolescence is reduced to zero for the last six months	The operation becomes self-scheduling as workers now control flow	Kanban audits continually challenge excessive inventory in the system	Lead time is best in class in the industry due to the regulation of overproduction
Poka yoke (Chapter 8)	Mistake proofing devices are not used to lock out the potential of mistakes becoming defects	Mistake proofing devices are applied to every process in the Lean exemplar model area	Detection mistake proofing devices (contact, fixed value and motion step) are applied (if possible) to the top 20% of failure modes	Prevention mistake proof devices (control and warning) are applied (if possible) to the top 20% of failure modes	A3 problem-solving countermeasures design out the potential of identified root cause(s) using mistake proofing devices	Abnormal conditions prevented from becoming a defect through mistake proofing are tracked and root cause(s) is understood

Lean culture (Chapter 10)	Management are unaware of the Cathedral model	Behavioural Standards are developed in a collaborative manner that is congruent with the creation of a Lean culture	Visual management on the frontlines makes performance transparent	Visual management on the frontlines makes performance transparent. Either recognition, coaching or constructive feedback is practised	Leader standard work is deployed at all levels of the organisation and compliance is visually managed	Intrinsic motivation is fostered through the relentless rate of improvements and people growth. Gainsharing increases income
Lean management system (Chapter 11)	Lean management system is not in operation in the area	A visual management centre is operational at the work team level, is fully up to date and driving daily improvement	Daily stand-up meetings are held at the visual management centre in each value stream to review the previous shift and issues	Waste walks are conducted in a tiered manner from the CEO to supervisor level at a set frequency. Waste walk compliance is tracked visually	Idea activity is developing people to the point where structured problem solving is now the default collective thinking on the frontlines	Behavioural changes are being driven through leader standard work which is deployed in a tiered manner
Lean leadership (Chapter 11)	The default management style is command and control	Leaders spend greater than one-third of their time at the gemba coaching and leading improvement	Leaders use this time at the frontlines to develop people through the practice of systematic problem solving	Leaders participate regularly in hands-on kaizen activity	Leaders 'lead as if they have no power' through coaching their peers in a participative style and asking Socratic style questions	Leaders deploy the Cathedral model during their work day. There is no distinction between the daily routine work and the Cathedral model

Lean assessment (part III)

Lean management system element	Instructions: Score – the criteria are cumulative, e.g. to score 4 you also need to satisfy criteria 0–3. This is not a 100% scientific audit: you may have higher level ratings in some areas without the foundation of lower building blocks. The real value is the dialogue this creates and an action plan.					
	Level 0	Level 1	Level 2	Level 3	Level 4	Level 5
Resources (Chapter 11)	There is no time made available to perform improvement work	Time is released for improvement events periodically by management	The capability trap is understood – not improving provides a 'grace' period and improvement deteriorates performance for a period	A virtuous circle is in evidence where problem solving is freeing up time for more problem solving and hence process capability is improving	People are released to the Lean promotion office as a result of kaizen productivity gains to drive even further improvements	Capacity is exploited: the organisation is able to take in new business with the same existing resources to grow revenue
Employee engagement (Chapter 12)	Employee engagement is not measured	Employee engagement ratio of <15%	Employee engagement ratio of <30%	Employee engagement ratio of <45%	Employee engagement ratio of <60%	Employee engagement ratio of >75%
Communication (Chapter 12)	There is no formal channel for organisational communication	Communication is sporadic at best and information is viewed as a management privilege as there are low levels of trust	There are formal communication sessions and 'coffee talks' are delivered on a monthly basis	There are multiple communication channels on a continuous basis such as 'coffee talks', via website, email, print and other media	Visual management is evolved to the level that communication for all factors of organisational activity is updated live in real time	Weekly one-to-one mentoring and coaching sessions are cascaded from the boardroom to the frontlines for all employees
Lean metrics (Chapter 11)	There are no metrics in place to measure process or results	There are result metrics in place for cost only	There are result metrics in place for people development, quality, delivery and lead time	There are process and result metrics in place for people development, quality, delivery, lead time and cost	True North metrics are measured throughout the organisation and are driving daily improvement	The organisation has transitioned fully to Lean accounting metrics at the gemba, per value stream, and daily continuous improvement is pervasive

People development (Chapter 12)	When problems occur the first reaction is to look for someone to blame. Management manage from the office and do not coach people	Culture is measured through an annual cultural audit, but there is little action taken to address weak elements	Culture is measured through an annual cultural audit, there is an action plan to address weak elements	Problems are widely raised without fear of retribution and root cause analysis is rapidly initiated at the work team level by supervisors	Cross training and job rotation are a living practice throughout the organisation	Promotion from within is a widespread practice and the primary characteristic for promotion is a track record of Lean leadership
Supervisor development (Chapter 12)	Supervisors are pulled from all sides and their day consists of turf battles and firefighting to make the numbers	The supervisors receive strong support from senior management; their day is a dual focus of make the numbers and improve every day	Supervisors are immersed in the Lean philosophy and methods through deep practice and they appreciate the purpose behind the methods	Standardisation has being applied to all the processes in a collaborative way between the supervisor and their team	Supervisors are proficient problem solvers and are capable of coaching their team. Their daily routines are enabled via Leader standard work	The supervisor picks up all problems in their area and frames problem solving to develop their team using training within industry (TWI)
Management of change (Chapter 13)	There is no process in place to manage change throughout the Lean transformation	A compelling business need is articulated that has created a strong sense of urgency for change	There is a Lean promotion office established with a vision for change and has strong influential leadership within the office	The vision for change is pervasive throughout the organisation and roadblocks to the attainment of the vision are systematically removed	Early visible wins are realised to build momentum as the Lean deployment is spread across the organisation	The organisation's structure is amended to reflect value stream management and Lean behaviours receive formal recognition
Exemplar Lean model area (Chapter 13)	Lean is applied in a superficial manner across the organisation and has no 'sticking' effect – the gains regress quickly	The model area is successful in a non-strategic area and is sustained but there is little bottom line impact	There is a successful strategic exemplar area, however senior leadership have not been sold, hence no foundation for spreading Lean	Management are fully sold on the exemplar model area and it is viewed as a strategic priority	There is a spread plan for the exemplar area to be rolled out to the end-to-end value stream, with full management support	The exemplar value stream is used as the 'go see' model to deploy Lean throughout the organisation

Lean assessment (part IV)

Index